SUDDEN INFLUENCE

How Spontaneous Events
Shape Our Lives

Michael A. Rousell

Foreword by Robert Sylwester

PRAEGER

Westpo

Library of Congress Cataloging-in-Publication Data

Rousell, Michael A., 1953–
 Sudden influence : how spontaneous events shape our lives /
Michael A. Rousell.
  p. cm.
 Includes bibliographical references and index.
 ISBN 978–0–275–99321–4 (alk. paper)
 1. Life change events. 2. Self-esteem. I. Title.
 BF637.L53R68 2007
 155.9'2—dc22   2007000070

British Library Cataloguing in Publication Data is available.

Library of Congress Catalog Card Number: 2007000070
ISBN-10: 0–275–99321–3
ISBN-13: 978–0–275–99321–4

First published in 2007

Praeger Publishers, 88 Post Road West, Westport, CT 06881
An imprint of Greenwood Publishing Group, Inc.
www.praeger.com

Printed in the United States of America

The paper used in this book complies with the
Permanent Paper Standard issued by the National
Information Standards Organization (Z39.48–1984).

10 9 8 7 6 5 4 3 2 1

To Laura

4UIM

Contents

Foreword

This book focuses on the profound impact that unexpected events can have on our beliefs and behavior. Mike Rousell was already fascinated by the phenomena when I became his graduate advisor about 20 years ago. His doctoral dissertation, which focused on an intriguing element of the issue, shifted his initial informal interest into a scholarly exploration of the underlying theoretical and research base. We maintained contact over the years through periodic visits and email exchanges, so I knew that he had continued to study the phenomenon.

When I thus set out to read the book manuscript that you're about to read, I knew that his initial interest, doctoral studies, and career trajectory had matured his understanding. What I didn't know was how well he had put it all together into a very interesting, informative, and useful book—something that you'll also soon discover.

We're a social species, very dependent on each other in complex symbiotic relationships. For example, mechanics fix the cars of doctors who heal the maladies of farmers who grow the food that mechanics eat. We trust the capabilities and judgment of others many times a day. Most such events simply enhance the normal flow of life, and have no lasting psychological effect.

Sudden Influence explores events that can unexpectedly and seriously affect our view of ourselves. Such spontaneous events often occur with no prior thought of their long-range psychological effects. Indeed, we're often surprised to discover later how an off-hand comment or intervention we made had a major positive or negative effect on the life of another person. I recently had dinner with a former much-respected colleague whom I hadn't seen in decades. During our conversation, I recalled some advice he had given me early in my career that profoundly and positively changed the way I viewed my work as a university professor. My friend had absolutely no recollection of the conversation—and even suggested that I may have misinterpreted whatever advice he gave.

I suspect that you have similar stories to tell, and Dr Rousell's book is replete with such anecdotes, and with useful explanations of how such spontaneous events can have a major effect on our cognitive processes and subsequent sense of self. More important, the book suggests how we can best respond when such unexpected events occur, and how we can positively use the phenomenon to enhance our interactions with others.

Robert Sylwester
Emeritus Professor of Education
University of Oregon

Preface

The human genome project and functional magnetic resonance imaging (fMRI) technology provides us with unprecedented amounts of fascinating information about ourselves. Each new discovery enriches our understanding of the biological part of the human species. We even have the technology to clone a human being. At times, our knowledge about the human species seems boundless. So why do our lives still seem so mysterious?

In spite of immense genetic knowledge, the latest technological instruments, and innovative cognitive theories, we still can't predict a person's self-esteem and outlook on life. The reason it has remained a mystery for so long is three-pronged. Until recently, we were unable to foretell which formative events would take place in people's lives, how receptive they would be to their experiences, or how those events would affect their self-esteem and outlook on life. While predicting which events will unfold in our lives remains doubtful, current information on spontaneous change teaches us how to determine receptivity to critical events and then modify these effects on vulnerable psyches.

On the one hand, we are innately suspicious of spontaneous change. Darwin's evolutionary model as a slow stream of incremental and cumulative changes is the paradigm that most of us implicitly use for everything from species mutation to personal skill acquisition. When we've tried to change a bad habit, we found it a tediously long process with lots of obstacles and setbacks. We typically don't see spontaneous change in ourselves, thinking that our own personal growth occurred slowly as we matured, learning consciously from our experiences. We also like to believe we were big players in sculpting our own personality and destiny, making deliberate choices as we navigated through our early years.

On the other hand, while skeptical of spontaneous change in ourselves, we act as though our words can produce significant and immediate effects in others. Who among us had not given advice or a carefully worded comment, expecting it to create a significant effect on the lucky recipient of our wisdom and experience? As a school counselor, I've had countless parents call me, asking me to speak to their children, expecting me to "just talk to him" to put him on the path to success. Implicit in each of these parental requests is the expectation that a psychologist has the words and know-how to initiate dramatic and instant change. These parents fondly remember a time when their children listened to their weighty words and did what they were told. Now that their children are older, experimenting with independence, those days are long gone, but many parents still think (hope) that psychologists may hold the key.

Stories of sudden and dramatic transformation engage us. We see spontaneous change in the movies, whereby the central character undergoes some traumatic event, an epiphany occurs, the world takes on a new hue, and the character suddenly changes. In the *Wizard of Oz*, the cowardly lion suddenly finds courage. In the movie, *Star Wars: Return of the Jedi*, Darth Vader suddenly sees the light and becomes a good Jedi knight. *Shrek* turns from grumpy troll to kind and considerate friend.

In the romantic comedy *Shallow Hal*,[1] an emotionally overwhelmed nine-year-old boy named Hal hesitantly approaches his dying father's bedside for a final farewell. The heavily sedated father, a preacher, motions for his son to approach so that he can give him advice for life. "Don't be satisfied with routine poon tang. Find yourself a classic beauty, with a perfect can, and good totties. That will put you in good stead with the lord. Hot, young tail is what it's all about." The father gasps his last breath and the son, Hal, promises to make his father proud. As a grown man, his friends think he's a wonderful guy with one shortcoming: absurd shallowness with female beauty. Later, trapped in a stuck elevator with Personal Transformation Guru Anthony Robbins, Hal confronts his shallowness with women. Robbins offers an intervention. Using a spontaneous hypnotic trance, Robbins gives Hal the suggestion, "From this moment on, whenever you meet someone in the future you'll see their inner beauty." Hal then falls in love with a sweet, thoughtful young woman who he finds stunningly attractive. All his friends see her as physically unattractive. The story ends when he realizes that inner goodness trumps superficial beauty. Sudden and dramatic changes make for good storytelling because they are part of the human experience.

The first task of *Sudden Influence* is to convince you of this simple fact: spontaneous and momentous change is a crucial part of human existence. We all undergo profound and sudden changes, but few of us recognize it as such, until now. The second task is to teach you how to recognize and manage these profound events.

Acknowledgments

This book contains brilliant ideas, discoveries, and theories by eminent scientists, psychologists, and physicians. I synthesized their efforts within my conceptual framework to produce the book you are about to read. To all of them, I offer my utmost regards for their hard work, creativity, and influence.

Special thanks to Dr. Robert Sylwester, my doctoral advisor and mentor for the last two decades. His consistent encouragement, dedication to scholarly work, and tireless efforts continue to amaze me. Professor Geoffrey Mills also deserves special mention. His interest in my field and faithfulness in my ability to produce this book helped keep me on track.

This book took an inordinately long time to move from conception to print. Literary consultant Elizabeth Lyon stayed with me through countless rewrites. Her skills in editing played an instrumental role in this work. She frequently referred to me as a poster boy for perseverance. Elizabeth also introduced me to my agent, Jeffery McGraw of The August Agency. His tireless work, support, and further editing are the reasons my book finally made it to Praeger Publishers. Thanks also to Debbie Carvalko from Praeger who encouraged and nurtured me through the publishing process. Clement, at New Generation Imaging, looked after the final, tedious, details.

On a personal note, my wife and children indulged me and allowed me to spend thousands of hours on research and writing. I tried not to cheat them from the important things in life. That said, I could have cleaned, painted, mended, and cooked more often. I love you and appreciate your patience and support.

My life is blessed with strong women. Thanks to my mother Vera who loved me unconditionally, my spouse Laura to whom I owe everything, my daughters Leanne and Kary who inspire me, my mother-in-law Della who continues to teach me how life should be lived, and my granddaughters Paige, Lauren, Kaitlin, and Nathalie who bring me laughter and joy every day.

Former New York Mayor Rudolph Giuliani always attended the funeral of a city worker killed on the job. In late August 2001, he attended the funeral of a rookie firefighter killed in a blaze. He approached the grieving mother to convey his condolences and was amazed by her composure. In his words, ". . . she was speaking calmly, drawing her words from a reservoir of courage that was unimaginable to me." When he asked where she found her strength, she replied, "When terrible things happen, I try to concentrate on the good parts of life and celebrate them even more than I had before." He didn't know it then, but these words would become his guiding light two weeks later when he faced the World Trade Center attack.

Reflecting back on the early moments of 9-11, he recalls hurrying up the street to the press conference. Confused and shocked by the horrific events, he didn't know what to say to the citizens of New York, only that they needed leadership. "I suddenly remembered what Mrs. Gorumba (the firefighter's mother) had told me: On any given day, we may experience both the best and worst of life, and it is important—crucial, in fact—to embrace the beautiful even as we shoulder the terrible." Rather than focusing on the horror, he highlighted the heroism and courage of the citizens, when they needed it most. His reaction on that day illustrates how Mrs. Gorumba's words, at her son's funeral, made a spontaneous impression that profoundly changed how he experienced the world. He didn't change his view consciously; it changed instantly at the funeral and emerged automatically later, in the appropriate context.[1]

Why are some events so influential while others hold no sway? *Sudden Influence: How Spontaneous Events Shape Our Lives* answers this question by presenting a new perspective: Spontaneous Influence Events (SIEs).

During emotionally intense events, our suggestibility to new perceptions soars. At this time, events may spontaneously produce an indelible impression, dramatically changing how we experience ourselves and the world we live in. I termed these events *spontaneous* because of their inadvertent nature, *influence* because of their powerful effect, and *events* because they occur during significant incidents.

One of the oldest questions in the world is, "Why are we the way we are?" The answer to that question determines our choice of spouse, where we live, level of happiness, parenting style, career choice, success; in other words, everything. Although this fundamental question of identity is never entirely answered, the concept of SIEs provides a corner piece in the puzzle.

This book supplies insights into spontaneous change. Understanding spontaneous change brings greater awareness to some of the most profound and perplexing moments from our past, many of which passed unceremoniously. Understanding spontaneous change can help uncover why we are the way we are, and aid us in sculpting who we want to become.

The last decade witnessed a continuous cascade of popularized reports portraying critical moments in people's lives that radically changed their mindsets. The best-selling *Chicken Soup for the Soul*[2] collection fills the bookstores. Oprah Winfrey's popular "Angel Network"[3] celebrates ordinary people who unwittingly inspire greatness in others. These stories resonate in all of us because we share similar experiences.

This past decade also yielded an unparalleled explosion of scientific knowledge in emotions and neurobiology. New scientific equipment and innovative methods have unmasked previously mysterious processes. This flood of neurobiological information gives us a clearer understanding of cognitive processes, how they work, and what they produce.

Only now is the scientific yield full enough to write *Sudden Influence: How Spontaneous Events Shape Our Lives*. Science now speaks with authority about the perplexing question of spontaneous personal change—those unexpected events that fundamentally and instantly change how people experience themselves and their worlds.

Spontaneous change has always been a serendipitous event, initiated during a burst of emotion, often ignored as quickly as it erupted. We now have the scientific wherewithal to map this process and describe the results. Those who subscribe to the narrow view that change is slow and incremental will find themselves challenged. Those who have *consciously* experienced spontaneous change will now be able to understand why and how. I emphasize *consciously* because all of us undergo spontaneous changes throughout our lives, but few of us become aware of the process. Conscious awareness typically eludes us for the most part because profound and spontaneous change happens at an emotional level; emotions then guide subsequent behavior unconsciously through urges.

OUTLOOK AND SELF-IMAGE

How we experience the world (outlook) and how we experience ourselves (self-image) make us who we are and drive our behavior. This first anecdote illustrates a sudden and dramatic conversion of a person's outlook on the world.

A middle-aged woman sat in a clinic's sitting room waiting to be fitted for a prosthesis to replace the leg she lost in an accident. Although considerable time had passed since the accident and she had adjusted well, she continued to feel emotionally devastated by her loss. The woman watched as a young boy with a patch over his eye played with some toys. The thought of losing an eye at such a tender age made her own plight seem minor by comparison. She struck up a casual conversation and eventually asked what happened to his eye. He replied, "Oh nothing. I'm a pirate." The word "pirate" transformed her immediately and changed her entire outlook. She vividly imagined the romantic thrill of sailing the high seas in search of adventure. Sometime later, the little boy asked what happened to her leg. She replied proudly, "I'm a pirate too."[4]

This second anecdote illustrates a sudden and dramatic conversion of a self-image. Sonya recalls a momentous event from her youth. As a young girl, she felt tormented by her prominent height, slim appearance, and dentured teeth. She spent most of her school day hunched over, masking her height, and defending herself from the verbal barbs hurled her way by her classmates. Her teacher, overhearing one of the insults, intervened after a student called the young girl "Beanpole." The teacher described Sonya as an ideal model type, statuesque and elegant, suggesting that she should consider that exotic field of employment. Hearing her teacher, she then stood proudly, displaying her full height. "Yes," she thought, "statuesque indeed. Maybe I could be a model."[5]

It may be frightening to think that some inadvertent comment or critical incident can shape a life profoundly, for good or ill, toward hope or despair. Movement in either direction is equally as powerful and just as common. The person's *perception* of the meaning of the event (not the event itself) is the determining factor that charts the course.

This text contains many anecdotes by adults who credit their lifelong positive outlooks, peaceful bliss, or immense success to a singular moment of spontaneous influence in their childhoods. These stories lift our hearts. Sadly though, I also share anecdotes of devastating moments that produced debilitating mindsets and destructive patterns. Whether positive or negative, SIEs change us at our core level, through our emotions.

GUIDED BY IMPULSES

Emotions drive our behavior, and impulses are the instruments our emotions use to steer us. Spontaneous change produces dramatic effects on our impulses. The result: our personal compass needle shifts and we move in a different direction.

Our genetic heritage endows each of us with the ability to survive by learning from our environment. Emotional eruptions, those moments of intensely arousing responses, act like neurological floodlights. They grab our attention, telling us that something important is happening in the environment and that we should look closely. But emotional eruptions only brighten the picture. They do not specify what lessons are best learned. To a large degree, emotional arousal is general in nature.[6] At these times, an enlightened guide, one who understands spontaneous influence, can construct a positive lesson. An inept guide may initiate emotional devastation.

Consider the two examples that follow. In the first example, a negative event initiates a negative result. A woman, although armed with good intentions, accidentally triggers a considerably destructive mindset in her niece. Remember that an emotional event itself only initiates a readiness for influence. The perception of the event determines the result. The second example is also initiated by a negative event, but note how a positive perspective from an emotional guide during a negative event can initiate an empowering mindset.

Example one: A young girl sits anxiously at the dinner table, playing with her food, awaiting news of her father's health. The girl's aunt gently informs the child that her father just passed away. The child freezes in shock. The aunt tries to help and says, "Your father was sick and he died. Eat up now, so you don't get sick." Thirty years later, the young girl, now an obese adult and frustrated with boundless failed attempts at weight loss, turns to a psychologist for help. During therapy, she spontaneously regresses and recalls the critical episode with her aunt. Together with the psychologist, they uncover her unconscious impulse: "Eat and you won't die."[7]

Example two: A young boy witnesses an automobile accident and is enlisted to assist by an adult present at the scene. Near nausea, the young boy follows the instructions stoically. The adult commends the boy's poise and gentle manner. Fifteen years later, while training in emergency para-medicine, the boy from that event recalls how this earlier incident shaped his life. The adult's encouraging comments highlighted his personal strengths and nudged him toward a fulfilling career. From that time forward, he took an interest in emergency aid and caring for others. "It just seemed so natural to enter this field."[8]

As adults, we can inform ourselves about spontaneous influence and learn to spin positive mindsets from negative events. This book addresses this considerable and rewarding task. We can become our own enlightened guide. Children aren't so lucky. Children will definitely benefit from a SIE-wise guide who can productively elicit positive effects during impressionable emotional eruptions. If no guide is present during the event, or soon thereafter, the result may be either positive or negative, depending on how it is interpreted by the child. Negative events tend to produce negative tones and mindsets. It takes an exceptionally strong will, not entirely common in children, to spin a positive mindset from a negative event.

NEITHER NATURE NOR NURTURE

Why is it that one average child works hard to excel at school while another average child gives up easily? Don't look to the parents. Some parents are hard working and encouraging but have unmotivated, under-achieving children. Some parents provide little constructive support or emotional nourishment, yet their children may show admirable ambition and industry. Some discouraged children grow up in affluence, while some highly motivated children grow up in relative poverty. Every scenario is represented. While debates about nature versus nurture dominate our intellectual landscape, we often miss the most critical factors that shape our destiny. When we examine humans collectively as a species, biological dispositions and environmental factors are *generally* correct and are relatively accurate at predicting large-scale trends. However, when we look at individual differences, it is SIEs that shape each of us: how we experience ourselves and how we perceive the world.

IT'S ALL ABOUT PERCEPTION

Our genetic endowment gives us our basic equipment and the environment does the tuning.[9] Some of this tuning comes through socialization by parents, teachers, family, and peers. *Sudden Impact* is not about the gradual shaping and forming of our personality; rather, it focuses on those moments of sudden and dramatically momentous change. In *The Blank Slate*,[10] Pinker speculates that the greatest environmental influence may be unique experiences. But why do some compelling events go unheeded while other unremarkable events make such a profound impact?

The answer lies in the receptiveness of the recipient, *not* in the persuasiveness of the event or the message. A mundane event to you might emotionally jar someone else into a mental state of soaring suggestibility, thereby setting the groundwork for a SIE. The opposite is also true. Some event that hits you with an emotional hammer might seem inconspicuous to someone else. Consider the following unremarkable event experienced by acclaimed playwright Wendy Wasserstein. She considers this a turning point in her profession.[11]

Wasserstein recalls a time early in her career when she was walking with a friend who was the artistic director of a local theater. The friend suggested to her that he would love to stage her show if she would rewrite it. She waffled with self-doubt, undecided about taking the offer. Her friend stunned her with the next comment. "You have the chance to redo this play and be taken seriously, and in my opinion, the way to be taken seriously is to take yourself seriously. If I were you, I'd take the chance at the rewrite—because I, for one, take you seriously." Until then, Wasserstein always feared not being taken seriously. Twenty years later, she finds herself on the verge of tears when she remembers that moment. In her words, "When a friend turns to you and says, 'I take you seriously,' it guides the rest of your life."

Those words created a SIE for Wendy, but they may not have for you or me. Why? First, the topic was emotionally loaded for her because of her fear of not being respected. Second, she was currently experiencing a moment of substantial self-doubt. Third, the message was delivered by a trusted friend in a position of authority.

Do you ever wonder why some people with immense personal resources and vast opportunity seem stuck and disheartened? On the other hand, do you know those who've led difficult lives with a myriad of obstacles yet seem resilient and successful? The framework of spontaneous influence sheds new light on our personal development, helping us uncover why we are the way we are.

The following section describes a personal conversion I experienced many years ago. To many observers, it looked like a mundane event, but it changed my life dramatically, although slowly. My heightened receptiveness at that time created a brief window of spontaneous influence whereupon an unremarkable statement changed me forever.

SEEDS OF CHANGE

A small acorn, planted firmly in rich soil, yields a mighty oak. When you have an idea in your head, in many cases a suggestion planted during elevated suggestibility, you instinctively gravitate toward events and circumstances that enhance the fulfillment of that idea. You often proceed without any conscious awareness; doing it naturally because it feels *right*. The feeling *right* comes from an unconscious urge to fulfill some embedded suggestion. The following story describes a SIE I experienced myself during my senior year of high school.

No one except my parents expected me to add up to anything, but that meant little to me because parents are supposed to think like that. Besides, I gave them every reason to lose faith. I caused trouble at school from the day I started. Several factors eventually changed my direction in life, but the seed for growth came in a health class from a teacher I had only briefly known.

I hated school and I couldn't wait to be free of it. Only one month remained in my public education. On this fateful day, a young teacher was covering a class for his colleague. Rather than teach a lesson, the instructor decided to talk about future goals and careers. For some reason, he addressed me directly. I just dismissed him like I did most teachers, but he insisted. Something snapped in me and my emotional floodgates opened. He looked at me in shock as I ranted and raved about the injustices of school and the inhumanity of teachers. I compared school to prison and declared my commitment to righting these wrongs. I pledged to write letters to newspaper editors, talk to magazine columnists, and interview with talk-show hosts. The educational system needed changing, and I planned to be the instrument of that change. Arriving at the end of my tirade I paused, waiting for a predictable dismissive adult response.

I remember what happened next as if it occurred yesterday. He said, "Rousell, if you really want to change the system, you can only do it from the inside. If you mean what you say, you should become a teacher." I looked at him contemptuously and laughed out loud, but inwardly my foundations were crumbling. My emotionally charged response created a vulnerable mental state that bound me to his suggestion. I didn't realize how influential his words would be until many years later when I formulated my thesis of SIEs. In the meantime, I failed my first two years of university in the Faculty of Arts. I never considered teaching as a career until my wife convinced me that it increased my ability to garner employment. Thus began my ordained journey, but I didn't know it at the time.

During my early teaching career, my heart went out to those who struggled the way I had—those at-risk students who hated school. A variety of circumstances over the years eventually landed me in graduate school, taking a degree in counseling. I remained unaware of why I was drawn to working with children, but it felt right. Much later, the pieces started coming together. At 33, I formulated my theory of Spontaneous Influence Events, completing my doctoral dissertation five years later.

The previous example of a critical moment is only one of many I've experienced over the years. SIEs all look rather obvious once you see them, but discovering them requires overcoming some barriers.

BARRIERS TO UNCOVERING SPONTANEOUS INFLUENCE EVENTS

These critical moments wield enormous power. For most of us, these events are the most critical factors in our lives. They shape us and our destinies. Ironically, awareness of our own critical events remains elusive because spontaneous influence occurs instantly and the effects are automatic. Change takes place at an emotional level, usually without any cognitive assessment or evaluation. In the book, *Curious Minds*, developmental psychologist and Pulitzer Prize finalist Judith Rich Harris describes why uncovering formative events can be daunting:

> A mental mechanism that operates below the level of consciousness doesn't leave conspicuous traces of its activities in memory. The reason we don't know why we turned out the way we did is that some of the mental mechanisms responsible for how we turned out didn't keep us informed about what they were doing. We cannot recall what was never encoded in the first place.[12]

Accordingly, most readers will find it extremely challenging to uncover all their significant events. However, once informed, SIE-wise readers acquire the means to avoid these kinds of chance effects in the future.

Can you name all the critical events in your life? Who and what were the biggest influences? Another reason the recognition of spontaneous influence remains challenging is because we are all predisposed to explain events through retroactive analysis. In other words, we impose our current thinking on past events to make sense of them in the present. The following anecdote, while not a SIE, illustrates this point humorously.

One day I walked out of the washroom to find my wife and children laughing heartily on the couch. My wife had just told our daughters to listen at the door, promising that I would whistle shortly before I departed. Apparently I had. I say apparently, because I certainly wasn't aware of it. Having no recollection of whistling, I concluded that they were just having fun with me. Several days later, lost in deep thought in the washroom, I reached for the toilet paper. I heard myself whistle. Shocked, I started to laugh. What was going on? Upon reflection I determined the origin of such odd behavior. During my toilet-training, my mother would often leave me seated on the toilet while she went about her housework. I was to alert her when I finished. I would signal my readiness with a whistle—a behavior that became unconsciously ingrained.

The explanation of the origin of my whistling was accepted readily by my wife and children because it served the purpose of explaining my behavior in a seemingly rational way. I'm not entirely sure of its accuracy. Why? Because of our predisposition to examine our past behavior rationally, we usually look back at events in our lives and recall a more logical development rather than one that may actually have taken place.[13] In reality, we spend most of our lives in the relatively uneventful flow of day-to-day living, punctuated occasionally with provocatively dramatic events that generate unpredictable results.

The rational and deliberate process of persuasion takes place over time. We can arm ourselves against such influence because it is detectable, and we can even dispute it because of its discernible nature. Spontaneous influence differs in that it is sudden, usually unintentional, and frequently takes place outside conscious awareness. We can't dispute or arm ourselves against something we don't acknowledge. Recognizing and managing spontaneous influence when it happens remains slippery because most of us don't know the indicators. The early chapters of *Sudden Influence* teach you how to identify the signposts of spontaneous influence. The later chapters teach you how to manage SIEs when they arise.

RECOGNIZING YOUR OWN SPONTANEOUS INFLUENCE EVENTS

Spontaneous Influence Events are not new. They have always shaped us. We just don't acknowledge them or even comprehend that they exist because we haven't developed a framework to understand them. This book acts as a guide in the discovery process.

As a young man, I went on a recreational fossil hunt in the Badlands of Alberta, a famous dinosaur site in Canada. My friend and I wandered around the barren lands looking for dinosaur bones. After several unsuccessful hours, near giving up, we met a fellow bone-hunter and inquired about his luck. He pointed to the ground beneath us, telling us that the stones we were standing on were actually bones of a rather common species of dinosaur, but that his interest lay in only rare samples. Stunned, we looked down at what we thought were merely common rocks, loosely embedded in the weathered soil. He reached down, grasped one of the loose stones, rolled it around in his fingers as he examined it and said, "This looks like part of a rib from an Edmontosaurus." Now that a clearer idea of what to look for emerged, our hunting improved measurably. After reading this book, your ability to recognize SIEs will also progress noticeably.

When I first discovered the mechanism of spontaneous influence, I began reflecting on my youth, looking back for signs of them in my own life. After more than two decades of researching this field, I still experience those *Aha!* moments when I suddenly recall a critical moment from my past. Being the pioneer of SIEs, you'd think I'd have uncovered all of them from my own past. Absolutely not, and I don't expect to. Spontaneous influence, by its very nature, fits seamlessly into our lives, and unless we know what fabric to examine, discovering all of our own events remains unlikely. Looking back and uncovering some of our critical moments increases our awareness of why we are the way we are. This understanding helps us see how these events continue to operate in our lives. We then begin to see spontaneous influence everywhere, in varying degrees.

Once we recognize SIEs, our ability to notice more of them increases, and eventually we grow adept at *feeling* them as they continue to occur in our lives. This is the natural progression of understanding spontaneous influence: learning what they are and how they work, finding them in our past, seeing them in others, and finally noticing them in the present. Conscious passage through this progression arms us to intervene during actual events.

If you want to find these moments, your childhood provides fertile ground to begin your own search. Once you see the most vivid and dramatic examples there, you'll start to find them in the present. That is one reason why I use mostly childhood examples; they are considerably more demonstrative. Events from your past formed your present mindset. A journey in self-discovery begins with the formative years. Examining conspicuous childhood examples guides you in the process of self-discovery, equips you to recognize events in the present, and prepares you to assist others during their moldable moments.

This book gives us a conceptual grip on a previously intuitive but undescribed experience. While the process of sexual selection and evolution has always taken place, we didn't understand much about it until Darwin wrapped it into a coherent conceptual package. That package, the "Theory of Evolution" revolutionized how we think about ourselves. After reading my book, most readers will say, "Wow! Now I get it." A few readers will say, "Wasn't that obvious?" All readers will gain a shared language and common awareness. Once awareness of spontaneous influence emerges, the grave responsibility of guiding others also arises. Take extreme caution when guiding others during these powerful moments. Read this book in its entirety before testing your new wisdom.

CAUTION WHEN GUIDING OTHERS

Preliminary groundwork enhances safe and productive use of tools. How wise would it be to turn people loose with chain saws before they learned about trees, cutting, safety, and power equipment? The how-to section of this book will tempt many readers to skip the earlier sections so that they can experiment with the practical applications. The strategies presented in the final how-to section of the book appear deceptively simple, yet they are shockingly powerful when used skillfully.

Fruitful applications require as much artistry as methodology. Linguistic know-how, exquisite timing, and the ability to elicit rapt attention are all crucial components of effective, artful intervention. Fertile use of these strategies comes from studying the initial chapters carefully.

✳✳✳

I prepared this book in such a way that the chapters flow in a progressive manner. Earlier chapters provide substance and context for later chapters. Terms and concepts introduced in the early chapters occur regularly throughout the remainder of the text. After reading this book

in its entirety, you may wish to reread earlier chapters with a broader basis for understanding influence.

The beginning section lays a foundation by illustrating the phenomenon of SIEs and Elevated Suggestibility States (ESSs). Once the foundation is constructed, the middle section provides the essential background information needed for deliberately deploying the powerful strategies presented in the final section. The concluding chapters present strategies that show how we can productively manage these inevitable events in others, as well as ourselves. You will recognize several influence strategies you already employ intuitively. By examining these strategies explicitly, you can then use them more deliberately and effectively. You will not only learn how to be more constructive in your own personal development, you will also learn how to be an instrument of healthy development in others, particularly children.

Spontaneous influence occurs throughout our life span. While children are more susceptible in a broader way, adults also have dramatic spikes in suggestibility. The last chapter challenges readers to critique their own way of seeing the world and themselves in it. It then provides strategies to employ these momentary windows of spontaneous influence as opportunities for emotional growth.

Chapter 1

Ignition: How Charged Events Magnify Influence

Think of neural pathways as well-worn paths in a jungle. Initially, an untouched jungle is thick and lush and no routes exist with an easy passage. Methodically, you make your way through the jungle, walking carefully, trying to avoid scratches from the brush, constantly scanning for a trouble-free corridor. Once you've traveled the route safely, you will most likely take the same path again in subsequent trips. After many trips, a worn path begins to emerge. Every time you go through that jungle, the familiar passageway tempts you, and being a prudent person, you never consider going to the trouble of starting a new track. The well-worn path is predictable, easy, safe, and swift.

This time, imagine entering an untouched jungle with a tiger chasing you. Your adrenaline surges, your heart soars as it pumps blood to large muscles, your breathing rate increases as your need for oxygen escalates, and your pain threshold jumps through the roof. You plough through the jungle like a bull, trampling brush, breaking branches, blazing a trail of destruction. You make it through safely, leaving a path of destruction in your wake. It may not have been the best path, but your adrenaline-induced swath left a visible passage for future use. As a matter of fact, it already looks like a well-worn path. This is what extreme emotional arousal can do. If the emotions are powerful enough, the neurons involved become wrapped in myelin, essentially firm-wiring the connections.[1]

SOARING SUGGESTIBILITY

Emotionally charged events frequently activate a brief period of extreme susceptibility to influence. Whether positive or negative, these events indelibly imprint themselves into our neural network. Just as trenches on a slope guide run-off from rain, these emphatic neural pathways instinctively entrain the mind to interpret subsequent experiences in a corresponding manner. The event and its interpretation set the compass of our mind-set and a self-perpetuating cycle ensues. All this takes place automatically, outside any conscious awareness. We may remember the event but only understand its influence much later, if at all. The following stories of Cathy and Peter illustrate how a charged event precipitated a perceptual shift that shaped their lives dramatically.

By the time Cathy reached fourth grade, faith in her ability had plunged considerably. She struggled with learning and felt like the *dumb* kid in class. Efforts to excel only reminded her that she was a failure. She mentally discounted occasional successes by attributing them more to luck than ability. Psychologists tested her, counselors talked with her, and teachers gave her special attention. She spent most of her time at school feeling badly about herself and avoiding any effort. She was afraid that any attempt on her part would only confirm her feelings of inadequacy.

One day, a favorite uncle visited from out of town. Cathy felt special when he was around. The two of them were playing the game Monopoly on the living-room floor when the uncle casually asked Cathy how she was doing in school. Her mood changed immediately and she started to cry. The uncle pleaded with her to tell him what was wrong. She told him that she felt dumb and frustrated with school. She wondered if she would ever add up to anything worthwhile. He then told her something that she would remember vividly for the rest of her life. He said, "Someone who struggles so hard with school will make a great teacher. Discouraged students need a teacher like you." This simple statement stunned Cathy, instantly changing her mind-set.[2]

Outwardly, the change didn't seem dramatic. Neither her parents, teachers, friends, nor Cathy herself noticed a conspicuous change in her behavior, but inwardly, her world changed profoundly. Before that event, school aroused feelings of weakness and incompetence. It now awakened a sense of challenge. School work changed from an impossible chasm to a rocky pathway on her journey to becoming a teacher. She felt ordained to help others like her, those who experienced frustration with learning. Sixteen years later she graduated with a teacher's degree and glowing recommendations.

Her uncle's comment triggered a powerfully positive change in Cathy's self-esteem and outlook on life. It made a sudden impact. Unfortunately, many stories of spontaneous influence are not as rosy as Cathy's. In some cases, they produce crippling effects.

Consider Peter, a high school student with the intellectual capacity to do well in school but a personal achievement level that always fell well below the class average. Like scores of students, he qualified for a resource room designed for students with average to above-average intelligence scores but very low achievement. Educational test scores placed him in the high average to superior range. He always completed his homework, studied extensively for exams, and desperately wanted to succeed in school. However, entering classrooms to write tests always filled him with anxiety and panic. His emotional state played havoc with his concentration and low performance ensued.

In counseling, Peter remembered an earlier event with his third-grade teacher. He recalls, "She was standing very close, right in front of me. She was furious. Her face was all screwed up and full of anger. It was as if she were a witch casting a spell on me, cursing my ability to succeed in school."[3] Before that third-grade episode, Peter had progressed favorably in school, but afterward his demeanor changed, his confidence plunged, and years of disheartened efforts followed. Whenever he felt particularly stressed, he spontaneously flashed back to that traumatic episode. From that event forward he felt anxious about his ability, and developed a gloomy outlook regarding his intelligence and capacity to learn. Peter's metaphor of a witch casting a spell is a frighteningly apt analogy. It appears that the teacher's raging comments, at that time, produced a sudden and momentous negative impact.[4]

Incidents like the two described above are common. If gently prodded, most of us can vividly remember several episodes of critical significance from our youth. Even though we may remember several influential events, we don't usually consider what it was that made them so significant. Until recently psychologists didn't quite understand why some events yielded considerably more influence than others. The process of spontaneous influence seemed unpredictable. Indeed, many of the events that produce the most dramatic effects often appear to be arbitrary and insignificant. To eliminate chance as a factor and gain an upper hand at managing spontaneous influence, we need to gain the ability to notice Spontaneous Influence Events (SIEs) when they transpire.

THE NEED TO RECOGNIZE SPONTANEOUS INFLUENCE

We need to identify the critical elements of spontaneous influence and learn to use them as tools. Only then can we manage these powerful shaping influences. Until now, controlling these precipitous events loomed outside our control. We hoped that those we love, particularly our children, would be lucky enough to experience many powerfully positive influence events, moments that created a positive and self-fulfilling mindset. At the same time we shivered in horror at the thought of our loved ones experiencing a dramatically negative influence event, one that robbed them of vitality, spinning them into a destructive self-perpetuating cycle. When we tried to orchestrate conditions to create positive influence we acted intuitively. Uncertain of our instinctive efforts, we hoped that the sheer will and intensity of our wishes would magnify constructive effects.

Learning to recognize these critical moments enables us to control them prudently to limit potential harm, or take advantage of them to enhance our self-esteem and outlook on life. Let's look at fear as an analogy. We can address fear because we notice it. We know when we are fearful because we recognize the indicators (e.g., increased heart rate, shallow and quick breaths, heightened sensory awareness, and an impending feeling of doom). Fear is easy to detect in ourselves and others. We need to identify the indicators of SIEs as well as their mechanics before we can even examine them, let alone control them. The first step in the process of examination is to find vivid examples. At least we know where to find them: our childhood. This is one reason that many of the anecdotal illustrations throughout this book are from reflections on childhood.

STARTING AT THE BEGINNING

Childhood anecdotes work like magnifying glasses, illuminating what we need to examine in ourselves. As many readers are also parents, these illustrations will help you gain confidence in your own development in that critical role.

Children show much less sophistication than adults as they are not yet practiced at concealing their thoughts and feelings; hence, their actions, reactions, and patterns appear more deliberate and obvious. The mechanism of spontaneous influence remains just as compelling with adults, but adults typically develop psychic armor that makes reading them more difficult. Once you begin to see the most vivid and dramatic examples in childhood, you'll continue to see them throughout your life span.

Society charges parents with the responsibility of raising children, to socialize and influence them to be constructive members of the community. However, parents and family members aren't the only ones who profoundly influence children. Teachers, youth workers, coaches, and other significant authority figures in the child's life also play a critical role in the psychological development of a child. Influencing someone's self-esteem and outlook on life is serious business and many would ask, "Should you be revealing powerful tools for molding children's behavior, their character, and their self-esteem?" My response is simple. Influence events happen to children arbitrarily whether we like it or not. As we can't avoid this influence, we should enlist every means at our disposal as a resource and make the best of it. The concern then changes to, *How can I ensure that children receive only positive influence, the kind that fosters healthy functioning and fulfillment?*

Obviously, we can't protect our children from all the negative aspects of life, but we can inform ourselves about the mechanism of spontaneous influence and the nature of a child's suggestibility. We can learn to recognize these moments when they happen to react constructively. Armed with this knowledge, we can sustain the positive influences, endeavor to reverse harmful perceptions, and deal earnestly with negative effects.

We educate ourselves and our children in *good touch* and *bad touch* because we realize the long-lasting and devastating effects of sexual abuse. We also need to educate ourselves and our children about *good suggestions* and *bad suggestions*. Maybe even more so; unlike touch, with a physical and alert component, suggestions during brief windows of soaring suggestibility can critically influence someone without any conscious awareness.

Destructive suggestions generate low self-esteem, self-defeating out-looks, and problematic behavior. Consider Jewel's experience. I met Jewel when she was in her early forties. She is a striking woman except for one feature; she always carries a stern look on her face. When I described my thesis of spontaneous influence she instantly recalled an episode from her youth. She said she used to smile all the time as a happy-go-lucky child, until age eight. She remembers the episode clearly. Her third-grade teacher asked her to take a note down to the office. She skipped happily down the hallways, humming a favorite tune. When she got to the office, a bitter school secretary wearing a scowl, snapped at her, "Wipe that smile off your face. You've got nothing to smile about." She froze, stunned in shock. She walked back to her class impassively with a new outlook on life. Now, more than 30 years later, Jewel claims that her friends frequently comment about her stoic demeanor.[5]

Self-esteem in children develops largely as a result of interactions with adults whom they encounter regularly. The building of a child's self-esteem and personal outlook is retained largely at nonconscious levels; it plays out automatically and sustains itself through daily interactions. High self-esteem in children enhances eventual success as an adult. Consider the story of Stephen Glenn, a famous research scientist who's made several very important medical breakthroughs. A newspaper reporter interviewed him. The reporter asked Glenn why he thought he was able to be so much more creative than the average person. Glenn responded that it all came from an experience with his mother that occurred when he was very young. He recalled a critical moment when he spilled an entire carton of milk. Fearing a scathing rebuke, his mother surprised him by treating the spill as an opportunity for play and learning. They played in the milk, making splash patterns, cleaned it up together, and practiced carrying the carton properly. His mother referred to the spilled milk as a failed attempt to carry milk cartons carefully. Glenn claims that his mother's reaction taught him that he didn't have to be afraid of mistakes. He learned that mistakes were opportunities for something new.[6]

As children grow, their experiences broaden. Very early in their impressionable lives, children move to a new forum of influence, school. In this new arena, children face a host of new influence agents.

CHANGING THE GUARD: SCHOOLS

The home lays the fundamental building blocks for a child's personal development, but SIEs often crop up elsewhere as well. Once children begin school, the majority of them spend more time with their teachers than they spend with their own parents. No other activity occupies the child's time as much as school, and a child spends more waking time in the classroom than any other place. Consequently, many of the critical events that shape children's development occur at school. The teacher's influence, at this time, may entrench itself in the character of the child.

Learning about spontaneous influence is not just critical for parents, but also for all those who work with children, especially teachers. Consider Nancy, now a proud mother of two. She credits a gentle, supportive squeeze from her high school art teacher as a turning point that saved her life. Suffering prolonged physical and sexual abuse at home, she finally planned to commit suicide one Friday after school. The previous day she made methodical arrangements to gas herself in the family garage. During the last class on that fateful Friday, her art teacher's caring squeeze on her shoulder gave her a strong sense of self worth. With her bolstered self-esteem, she changed her mind, reported the abusive home to the police, moved out of the home for good, and has since flourished.[7] How could a gentle squeeze, signifying "you are important" create such a profound effect? Other teachers had expressed similar sentiments, without extraordinary results. This time it was different; the emotional arousal from anticipating her suicide propelled her into an Elevated Suggestibility State (ESS).

Imagine being in a highly suggestible state and receiving the following suggestion: "You sure learn things quickly." Imagine further that you then go around acting out this suggestion proudly, *as if* it was real, finding or creating evidence in your interactions with others that support this belief. Your newly inspired confidence will create a self-perpetuating cycle. Your self-assurance in "learning quickly" encourages you to challenge new opportunities, which in turn generates similar comments from others, which make you even more eager to learn quickly, and so on. Any comment, if accepted as a core belief, will similarly create a self-perpetuating cycle: "You sure find creative solutions."

The fortunate among us, those with fond memories of childhood and school, will gain a sound appreciation for those critical encouraging moments from their past. Stephen's dyslexia created learning difficulties in his early years at school. He felt intimidated by the learning process. As a consequence of his uncertainty, he developed a stutter. He learned to sit in the back of the room to avoid embarrassing attention from teachers. Stephen vividly recalls his turning point in the fifth grade. His teacher, discussing Stephen's situation with the school nurse, bellowed, "He's not learning disabled, he's eccentric." His surprised reaction to hearing the nurse's pronouncement created an ESS. He then accepted the statement uncritically. This allowed a much more optimistic view by himself and others. Since that time, with the help and guidance of a stellar teacher, he developed feelings of confidence and significance. He didn't magically become studious overnight, but the long road to success became paved by his teacher's comment.[8] How can such seemingly innocuous comments produce such a profound impact? The mechanism of spontaneous influence answers this riddle.

For those of you who suffered an unpleasant schooling and childhood, reading this book may be a courageous journey filled with painful memories, and in some cases anger. How many of us, during a spontaneously charged moment of elevated suggestibility, unconsciously accepted one of the following suggestions *as if* it were real: "All you do all day is make trouble for others!"—"You'll never understand!"—"You're stupid!"—"You'll never add up to anything!"—"You're more trouble than you're worth!"—"You're fat!" These suggestions will find self-affirming evidence and create interactions that perpetuate themselves.

Consider Alicia who has had difficulty voicing opinions for the last 20 years. Up until her sophomore year, Alicia was an avid actress, in every school production. She loved acting and being the center of attention when she was playing her part. It all changed in one explosive moment. A popular boy gave her a sweet compliment. Surprised and elated, she floated on clouds to her next class. In class, still beaming with confidence and delight, she eagerly answered the teacher's question. "The teacher gave me the equivalent of a shotgun blast to the gut. I went reeling back in time and emotions. She thought I was being a show-off and embarrassed me in public. I truly wish I could remember what she asked and how I responded because it surely had a long-lasting effect." She credits her subsequent reluctance to voice opinions to her teacher's angry comment, "Be quiet! Nobody wants to hear your opinion."[9] Alicia's shocked response produced a brief moment of soaring suggestibility whereby she uncritically accepted the teacher's insensitive comment.

Children's battered spirits are like broken bones that don't heal properly; the wound needs to be reopened to be correctly set. Whatever your personal history, this book provides an innovative perspective for examining critical influence events in your life. Now that awareness of spontaneous influence exists, you'll find that these events occur within a broad range of age and intensity.

SPONTANEOUS INFLUENCE: AT ANY AGE, IN VARYING DEGREES

Spontaneous Influence Events continue to operate throughout the entire life spectrum. Some are monumental in scope, initiating a sudden and radical change in perspective that affects a person's total belief system.

Popular literature and cinema abound with dramatic moments when the protagonist or antagonist suddenly undergoes a massive personality change during an emotional crisis. We loosely call these events *conversion* experiences.

Comedian Billy Crystal recalls a time early in his career when he just finished wowing the audience at a comedy club. After the show he joined a highly respected manager in the business for coffee and a chat. Glowing, from what he thought was a dynamite act, Crystal asked the manager what he thought of the performance. The manager replied, "Effective? Yes. Good? I don't think so." Reflecting back on that time in his life, Crystal said he was dumbfounded. He credits that moment as a turning point in his career, ". . . ultimately, this singular piece of advice vaulted me into a whole different state of mind. I began to change the way I looked at the world." Crystal claims, "That's when I became a comedian." In one moment, Crystal's emotions went from the thrilling high of elation to the dismal low of anguish, creating a sudden window of influence.[10]

Critical events can also be smaller in scope, relating to some detail of behavior rather than a full-scale personality change. I used to smoke a pack of cigars each day. Most of my friends and family didn't smoke and found my habit disgusting. I acted self-conscious and defensive when they were around. One particular evening, I stayed up late, playing cards with friends as I smoked an entire pack of big cigars. I smoked so many, I filled a large ashtray with ashes and butts and had to empty it before lighting my last smoke. The next morning, sitting at breakfast, my five-year-old daughter rushed up to me, eyes wide with excitement. She said, "Dad," pointing at the ashtray on the counter, "You only had one cigar last night. Wow!" She wrapped her arms tightly around my neck and ground her lips into my cheek with an enthusiastic kiss. Stunned by the sudden outburst, I gently hugged her back, feeling somewhat sheepish at her mistaken excitement. Instantly, my self-image changed from smoking pariah to proud role model. I quit smoking then and there. Previous failed attempts were short-lived, but this time each subsequent urge to smoke activated that vivid scene in my mind, along with the gratifying feeling of being a virtuous parent.

You might be thinking, how does such a simple episode qualify as spontaneous influence? The essential dynamics are present. My stunned, sheepish reaction activated an ESS whereby my daughter's comment immediately changed one aspect of my self-image. This event also made an indelible impression on my memory. I still recall that episode vividly. An extremely vivid memory, one that produces images and sensations as if it just happened moments ago, is called hypermnesia. Hypermnesia, often triggered by emotional arousal or personally significant events, frequently accompanies these critical moments.[11]

Those who listen to my presentations on spontaneous influence frequently report that they experienced several flashbacks to earlier episodes when they had experienced their own key episodes. They uncovered the origins of many critical values and beliefs that dramatically affected their self-esteem and outlook on life. They also began to recognize sudden impact events as they continue to happen in their lives and the lives of those around them. They now see these moments as opportunities to create healing or empowering suggestions for themselves and others.

Recent developments in emotional and cognitive development make the previously mysterious process of spontaneous influence accessible. When you understand spontaneous influence, you see SIEs everywhere. You also see opportunities to handle them. Spontaneous influence is much like fire. When managed properly, it is our intimate friend; when left on its own, it can be devastatingly destructive. The catalyst for spontaneous influence is elevated suggestibility, which we explore in the next chapter. Examining this special window of influence brings us closer to our goal of managing spontaneous influence.

Chapter 2

Windows of Influence

Emotions guide our moment-to-moment decisions, working hand-in-hand with our rational thought processes. When the brain senses a matter of import (opportunity or danger) emerging, powerful emotions override the rational processes. These charged events then become encoded in memory with a greater than normal degree of strength, like the way we use **bold print** to highlight notes.

Acclaimed actor, Martin Sheen, vividly recalls a comment that he says, "... hit me like a thunderbolt." During a Vietnam peace rally, activist and catholic priest, Father Berrigan, suggested that it was better to go to prison than to fight an unjust war. A reporter challenged him, indicating that prison was acceptable for a priest as he had no children. The reporter then posed the question, "What's going to happen to our children if we go to prison?" Father Berrigan calmly replied, "What's going to happen to them if we don't?" Sheen credits that statement as a trigger that caused him to reevaluate himself and his world. In Sheen's words, "... he [Father Berrigan] became an ideal and an inspiration as his one comment forced me to reevaluate everything about myself and the world in which I lived." He refers to that remark as his guiding light, "... and that light illuminated every political and social stand I would take for the rest of my life." Since that time, authorities have arrested Sheen not less than sixty-four times.[1]

It's as if critical events are encoded with a neural highlighter. Highlighting charged events makes evolutionary sense because learning from these moments is crucial to survival. Our emotions evolved to protect us from danger and guide us to opportunities. If the organism survives a dangerous incident or benefits from a golden opportunity, the now-highlighted response becomes automatic in subsequent similar events.[2] When describing what strong emotions can do, Daniel S. Janik, author of *Unlock the Genius Within*, writes, "We simply learn what we have to learn, quickly and efficiently; if we don't, we die. Those who live have a new set of reflexes hardwired into them."[3]

Most of human development takes place after birth; subsequently, we are extremely susceptible to environmental tuning. Our genes don't determine our behavior; genes regulate how we respond to the environment. Our unique life experiences remain the most important factors in forging our personality. Even genetic predispositions in temperament may be amplified or muted by experiences.[4]

For learning to take place instantly and ingrain subsequent automatic responses, a special condition must exist. This special condition is elevated suggestibility, triggered by emotional arousal. Events that startle, overwhelm, or emotionally charge us in any way, activate what I term an Elevated Suggestibility State (ESS). This state creates a window for spontaneous influence, but these critical events don't happen every time. Many times we just experience a spike in suggestibility without any extraordinary change in our outlook or self-esteem.

TRIGGERING ELEVATED SUGGESTIBILITY

In the following story, a teacher's explosive response during an art lesson shocked eight-year-old Bob out of a reflective moment, triggering an ESS. The jarring disruption probably magnified his state of fear and confusion. His final project, completed with large loops of red and black, indicates an emotional response of anger.

On that fateful day, Bob's teacher roared at him for not following directions during an art project. The teacher had instructed the class to close their eyes and draw random rings on a large sheet of paper. The next stage focused on filling in the loops with different colors. Bob had opened his eyes while drawing, staring blankly at the high right-hand corner of the ceiling.[5] His teacher stomped across the room, ripped up his paper, threw it on the floor, and screamed, "Can't you ever do anything right!" The teacher then picked up the paper, marched back to her desk, threw the paper in the garbage, and returned with a clean sheet. Bob completed his second attempt with compliance, using red and black for the two largest colored loops.[6]

Of course, Bob wasn't faced with a life threatening situation, but driven by a primitive automatic fear response, he responded as if he was. He was probably shocked by the teacher's explosive response, asking himself, "What's going on? Why is the teacher angry? What happened? What did I do?" His state of fear and confusion would have been magnified because of the jarring disruption from his mental imagery.

When these naturally occurring meteoric rises in suggestibility occur, they typically take place suddenly, profoundly, and momentarily. Bob felt and acted differently ever since that day in class, but others, even his parents, may not have noticed a dramatic shift in behavior.

Since that time, Bob became overly concerned with making sure assignments were perfect before handing them in to teachers. Sometimes he felt angry toward teachers, particularly those with rigid guidelines or extremely high standards of neatness. He procrastinated on large projects, sometimes feeling powerless to produce respectable work. When he didn't complete projects for teachers he liked and respected, he felt guilty and ashamed. As an adult, his aversive reaction to rigid guidelines imposed by authority figures (bosses, supervisors, colleagues) continued to play emotional havoc in his life, often interfering with opportunities to succeed.

Years of behavior patterns following this event suggest that Bob accepted the teacher's pronouncements uncritically. He responded automatically to the teacher's comment, "Can't you ever do anything right!" in the same way that a hypnotized subject responds to a hypnotic suggestion. In his own words he stated he often felt, "a really good job was hopeless." Subsequently, the ensuing vicious negative cycle all but ensured that his inevitable frustration would hamper his ability to excel at his work.

This Spontaneous Influence Event (SIE) took on a negative tone, shifting Bob's emotional compass in a subtle, yet powerful manner. Emotions steer crudely. When a key element of a present event appears similar to the past, our emotional systems call it a match. Subtle emotional prodding, in the form of *gut instincts*, then urge us to respond to the present in ways that were imprinted long ago, even if current events are only dimly similar. In Bob's case, subsequent demanding authority figures or rigid requirements triggered responses of fear and anger that sabotaged his efforts. Bob's nonproductive reactions remained the same for more than thirty years until he visited a therapist in an attempt to resolve his self-defeating behavior patterns. Bob's soaring suggestibility during that early event enabled the teacher's comment to generate a self-perpetuating negative belief about his ability.

THE POWER OF BELIEF

The impact of a communication does not reside in the words themselves but in the receptiveness of the listener. To produce profound influence in communication, the receiver must enter an ESS. Simple words can yield dramatic effects under these conditions.

Bob's fateful experience initiated a damaging cascade of events; however, liberating and constructive suggestions during elevated suggestibility can launch powerfully positive results. Les Brown, a world famous author and speaker on inspiration, motivation, and self-esteem, remembers how a critical episode in his life sent him in a new direction of growth and empowerment. In his early years at school, his consistently low achievement scores prompted a series of tests for learning disabilities. He subsequently received the label Educationally Mentally Handicapped (EMH). This label gave him a new identity, an explanation for failing, and a reason for giving up with classwork. He convinced himself that trying was futile: Failure was inevitable.

One day an episode with a new teacher changed his life. The teacher put a problem on the chalkboard and asked Les to come to the front of the classroom to solve the problem. Les said that he couldn't. The teacher questioned him. Les replied matter-of-factly, "Because I'm educationally mentally handicapped." The teacher responded angrily, "Don't ever say that again. Someone's opinion of you does not have to become your reality." When Brown reflects back on that moment he says, "Mr. Washington restructured my own picture of who I am. He gave me a larger vision of myself, beyond my mental conditioning."[7]

The teacher's response shocked Les, creating a momentary ESS, whereby he accepted the teacher's pronouncement uncritically. The world, and his place in it, looked different now. A seed for success rooted itself during his soaring suggestibility, resulting in a positive SIE. Friends and family probably didn't notice an immediate change, but Les's internal bearing changed that day and a new path emerged. Several decades later, he now speaks internationally on motivation and owns a multimillion dollar empire created by his will to succeed and faith in his own ability.

Who hasn't heard the worn expression, "You can do anything you want if you put your mind to it"? If the words themselves produced the effect, we'd all be achieving to the best of our abilities. You need the special condition of elevated suggestibility to spontaneously adopt a belief.

At this point you may be asking yourself, "What's the difference between a Spontaneous Influence Event (SIE) and an Elevated Suggestibility State (ESS)?" An ESS refers to the natural process whereby a person's level of suggestibility soars due to extreme emotional arousal, profound confusion, or shock. ESSs happen regularly in our day-to-day lives. Usually these events pass without dramatic changes in our character. However, if a person's self-esteem, belief system, or outlook on life changes spontaneously and dramatically during an ESS, it becomes a SIE. Bear in mind that the word spontaneous refers to the sudden change itself, not to the visible results. Even when people spontaneously adopt a new belief, close friends and family may not notice a dramatic shift in behavior.

HOW BELIEFS MOLD IDENTITY

Once we genuinely adopt a belief or value, it then coordinates our behavior and decision making. It unconsciously and automatically guides our thoughts and actions. We rarely search for the origin of values and beliefs, instinctively defending these aspects of ourselves whenever we feel challenged. Most of us just accept our values and beliefs as "That's just the way I am" and go on living life unquestioned, mainly because we aren't sure how our character and personality developed.

We may believe we're like Dad, Mom, Uncle Joe, or Cousin Allissa, but we really do not comprehend the depth of these similarities, or understand how we evolved that way. Could it be that we act like Cousin Allissa because someone dear to us said, "You act just like Cousin Allissa"? If this was stated during an emotionally charged ESS, with our impressionable identity exposed, we might then accept this pronouncement uncritically, subsequently acting out this suggestion as *if it* were etched into our personality. It would perpetuate itself by eliciting additional comments about further similarities with Cousin Allissa. Consider the following anecdote.

Nine-year-old Andy found himself continually in trouble at school for his uncontrolled violent outbursts. His teachers referred him to me for counseling. He didn't like his behavior, but in spite of his best intentions he felt unable to manage it. As we talked, he made several references to his deceased father. His father had a fierce, uncontrollable temper that led to a violent death. Andy, a big boy for his age, resembled his father's appearance in many ways. His mother and several other family members often told Andy that he was "just like his father." Andy accepted these comments uncritically. He convinced himself that his temper also matched his father's: fierce and uncontrollable. Andy spoke about his father tearfully. I encouraged him to tell me about his father's good qualities, and as he did I associated them with Andy's current beliefs, values, and behaviors. He told me his father had been athletic; I commented on Andy's ability to play baseball. He told me his father had loved to laugh; I commented on Andy's warm and contagious laughter (he laughed). I emphasized the connection between his father's temper and his father's abuse of alcohol. I asked Andy if he drank alcohol or consumed illegal drugs. He assured me that he didn't.

Andy entered an ESS triggered by a tearful recollection of his father. He conceded that comments from others about similarities to his father were merely references to his father's good nature, large size, hair color, interest in fishing, athletic ability, and other positive qualities. I stressed how his temper would soon be manageable because he didn't abuse drugs or alcohol. With subtle direction on my part, he elicited examples of ways he and his father differed in how they handled stress, noting that they were actually opposites in this regard. At the height of his suggestibility, I told him that the violent outbursts would soon subside because in that way he paralleled his mother. I then underscored similarities between his sensitivity and his mother's effective manner in dealing with anger.

Before counseling began he exhibited up to four outbursts a day, almost twenty per week. The following week he dropped to only three small outbursts for the entire week. Teachers reported that he frequently calmed down by walking away from other students who annoyed him; this was how his mother responded in similar situations. The next week he eliminated all outbursts. I assured him that he was one of those lucky people who ended up receiving the best of both parents' qualities. Andy's ESS during therapy provided fertile ground for seeds of hope. Even hardy seeds benefit from continued nourishment. Accordingly, I instructed Andy's mother to continue positive associations between Andy and his deceased father, and to also refute any negative references others might make about similarities in expressing anger.[8]

When life goes smoothly we usually pat ourselves on the back and credit our success to hard work, luck, God's will, or karma. When life doesn't turn out the way we like, we look for the origin of our discomfort and often blame others. For this reason, it's usually easier to discover stories about ourselves and others where spontaneous influence had a negative effect. Rarely do we say to ourselves, "I function so well. I wonder who planted the seed of my actualization?" Negative stories are simply more common and illustrative. Once we learn how to examine our past more prudently, equipped with the understanding of spontaneous influence, we may begin to look more earnestly for positive influences in our lives—the seeds of growth and healthy living. Whether these beliefs are positive or negative, they generate their own confirming evidence to support themselves.

THE CONUNDRUM OF SELF-PERPETUATING BELIEFS

The effects of critical incidents that help form personality and behaviors are extremely difficult to predict accurately. We usually sort them out through reflection on past experiences. Consider the cases of Sarah and Carol, both aged 10. They started school at a very early age and struggled with schoolwork. Although both shared nearly identical scores on intellectual profiles, they ended up on completely different paths. Sarah, although popular with other students, developed a low self-image regarding academics, leading to low achievement. Carol developed a positive outlook toward academics, leading her to high achievement status in the same class.[9]

Could it be that a major cause of the differences between Sarah's and Carol's experiences in school stemmed from SIEs during ESSs?

Indeed, both Sarah and Carol responded to parental pronouncements by reflecting the parents' corresponding beliefs. Sarah's low self-image in academics reflected her parents' comments: "Sarah's early start got her off on the wrong foot. I don't know if she will ever catch up." Carol's academic confidence reflected her parents' comments: "Carol's early start made her work hard to keep up. Her hard work made her a superior student." Once children accept an idea, they automatically respond in a way that perpetuates it. Their beliefs about themselves become reflected in their behavior because beliefs are unquestioned commands that direct how we think, act, and feel.[10]

Sarah's and Carol's illustrations generate some intriguing food for thought. The outcome implies that the girls adopted and subsequently played out their parents' views. Most of us tend to presume the opposite, that we don't generate behavior in others, we just describe it. A chicken-and-egg conundrum arises. Which came first? Did the children's behavior generate their parents' comments or did the parents' comments generate self-perpetuating beliefs in their children?

We rightfully believe that other people's behaviors elicit descriptive responses from us. If Sarah's parents saw her continually struggling at school, they could perceptively comment that her early start may have put her at a disadvantage from which her confidence never recovered. They would also be correct in believing that their comment did not create her low achievement or lack of confidence. Yet, the parents' comments perpetuate her belief, a belief that may well have originated during an ESS.

Once a belief embeds itself in a person's mind, it drives subsequent behavior. The subsequent behavior then generates corresponding comments from others and perpetuates the person's belief. With Sarah and Carol, we don't know for sure how their beliefs emerged, only that their behaviors reflect them. We can never be sure unless the initiating event is remembered vividly.

Most of the examples I use clearly show the critical moment of elevated suggestibility when the seed of a belief became fertilized. They leave little doubt about the origin of beliefs. However, my clear examples show only the tip of the proverbial iceberg. Until now, we lacked the conceptual ability to find these seeds in the past and recognize them in the present, keeping most of our critical events below the surface of awareness. Comparing spontaneous influence to other forms of sudden change will help uncover some of the mystery.

COMPARED TO WHAT

We understand something more clearly when we learn about it in terms of something we already know. For example, if we think of our body as a car, and food as its fuel, we get a better appreciation for the importance of good nutrition: high-quality fuel improves performance. We could also note that newer cars (youth) will run reasonably well on any fuel, though adding further that those older cars in good shape are reliable because they were cared for consistently. We could also make car–body analogies regarding hygiene, regular maintenance, and cosmetics.

Essentially, we only understand new concepts in terms of previous knowledge. For example, the locomotive was seen as an iron horse, the electric light as a powerful candle, and the radio as a thundering megaphone. Although metaphors are fundamentally flawed (a human body is not a car), they do provide a framework for understanding. The well-researched field of clinical and medical hypnosis provides us with a ready-made framework for discussing elevated suggestibility and spontaneous influence. In later chapters, I borrow some of its terminology and conceptual principles to illuminate similarities through comparison. To compare spontaneous influence to hypnosis, I must first dispel some myths about hypnosis and build a more knowledgeable framework for comparison.

It's unfortunate that much of hypnosis is shrouded in mystery, trickery, and entertainment illusion. Entertainment hypnosis has as much to do with clinical hypnosis as WrestleMania has to do with Olympic wrestling. Regardless of your opinion of hypnosis, the fact remains that the clinical use of hypnosis creates real and measurable benefits more often than many people realize.

A recent article published on Time magazine's website titled "Mind Over Medicine"[11] reported that a prestigious Belgian hospital logged more than 5,000 surgeries with hypnosedation, a technique that replaces general anesthesia with hypnosis, a local anesthesia, and a mild sedative. Patients come from all over the world. These patients actually get by on less than 1 percent of the standard medications required for general anesthesia, helping them avoid many negative aftereffects. Accordingly, patients recover at almost twice the rate. Doctors in the United States have been using hypnosis since 1958 when it was sanctioned by the American Medical Association. Dr. David Spiegel, associate chair of the department of psychiatry at Stanford University, hypnotizes Parkinson's sufferers during implantation of deep-brain electrodes because it requires the patient to remain conscious and calm.

In reality, hypnosis wouldn't work if it didn't tap into aspects of our existence that weren't already present and common. For instance, you can not hypnotize a dog because it has neither the neurology nor the consciousness needed to experience that condition. Hypnosis is merely a procedure that magnifies an already present human potential.

So then, is an ESS a hypnotic state? Scientific researchers and clinicians in hypnosis are reluctant to call such a common state *hypnosis* because a formal induction procedure did not take place. Debates about the essential elements of hypnosis and hypnotic states are mostly academic.

While these discussions are critical for theoretical consideration, they serve no purpose for our practical needs. Despite ongoing debates about the technical definition of hypnosis, clinicians generally agree that elevated suggestibility may take place at any time or place, without a formal induction, if conditions are conducive for its presence. The results of my intensive research clearly indicate that we regularly experience situations that initiate ESSs.[12]

Think about planning a party. How can one be assured of staging a successful party? It would seem that the necessary ingredients are (a) people who are ready to celebrate, (b) people who savor each other's company, and (c) an enjoyable environment. These three ingredients represent the personal, relational, and contextual dimensions of hosting a successful party. If each of these dimensions is present to a considerable degree, the likelihood of staging an enjoyable party is high. Even if some of the ingredients are only partially present or intermittently present, the likelihood of staging a successful party is still high. Similarly, the personal, relational, and contextual dimensions of spontaneous influence are regularly present in our lives. It would be absurd to say that we don't experience the sudden impact of SIEs during our periodic ESSs.

✳✳✳

Strong emotions seize our attention and generate the neurological machinery to create instant learning. However, this learning reflects our perception of events, and not the objective world. Beliefs about ourselves (self-esteem) and the world we live in (outlook) emerge, sustaining themselves with self-perpetuating interpretations. Some beliefs cultivate a fulfilling and positive mind-set while others produce destructive or self-defeating behavior. Right or wrong, good or bad, we forge ahead blindly on the basis of those beliefs. To a large degree, we live our lives validating our own ill-formed ideas. So what then is the evolutionary advantage of a belief system when the price is typically self-delusion? Beliefs, held with conviction, allow us to build a stable mental model of the world, providing us with the comfort of order and predictability in our existence.

The next chapter describes how learning takes place and how children inherently construct a highly subjective mental model of their world to interpret their experiences. Adults do the same, but this process is easier to examine in children because of its elementary nature, just as it is easier to understand the mechanical workings of a typewriter than the sophisticated operation of a word-processor. Chapter 3 illustrates how our mental models, the beliefs we have about ourselves and the world, tend to validate themselves by creating their own support. Learning how children experience themselves and the world is the key to understanding spontaneous influence.

Chapter 3

The Foundations of Reality

We have an innate need to find order, structure, and predictability in our existence. If we don't find it, we impose it. To do this, we instinctively construct and maintain a reliable mental model of reality, a basis to understand ourselves and the world we live in. Creating and renovating this mental model is what we commonly refer to as learning. Our representations of the world are as personal as our fingerprints.

This inherent model-building and renovation process provides psychological comfort by making our experiences stable. Once established, we hold on to our beliefs with conviction, often in spite of contradictory evidence. We identify new experiences according to how we associate them to previous experiences, instinctively adapting conflicting information in order to maintain our personally constructed understanding. For example, many adults still refer to dolphins as fish rather than mammals because that was how they first labeled them. While all of us operate like this, the process is more visible in children.[1]

CONSTRUCTING A PERSONAL REALITY

I observed a first grade class participating in a lesson on gravity.[2] The teacher had collected several objects of different sizes, densities, and weights. To begin, the teacher held up two objects at the same distance from the floor, one in each hand. She then asked the students to identify which object would land on the floor first if she let them drop from her hands simultaneously. For the first demonstration she held an inflated balloon in one hand and a large button in the other. The students unanimously agreed that the button would hit the ground first. She dropped the objects, confirming the students' predictions. The teacher then asked the students why the objects had fallen at different rates. One student declared that the button was obviously heavier; the other students nodded in agreement. Clearly, the students' conceptual rules for gravity reflected an incorrect belief that heavier objects fall at a faster rate.

The teacher then held out the next two objects: the same large button and a small solid block of wood students played with regularly. Again she asked the students to predict which object would land first. The students remained unanimous; they predicted that the building block would land first. She let them drop simultaneously. Immediately, disagreement arose among the students about whether the block landed first or whether both objects landed at the same time. The teacher simultaneously dropped the button with the block several more times until all the students agreed that both landed at the same time.

The teacher cleverly designed the lesson to challenge the students' incorrect concept of gravity. The first demonstration appeared to confirm their incorrect assumption that heavy objects fall faster. The teacher fashioned a second demonstration to intentionally challenge their assumption. A discrepancy now existed between the students' preexisting understanding of gravity and their current experience.

The teacher asked the students to explain why both objects had landed at the same time. One student suggested that both objects must be the same weight. The other students cheered their approval and nodded in agreement. Here the students reasserted their incorrect concept of gravity in an attempt to solve this apparent discrepancy. One young boy even put the button and block in separate hands, moving them up and down in an apparent effort to decipher their respective weights. This student then confirmed (incorrectly) that the objects did indeed weigh the same. Once again the students cheered, thinking they had solved the puzzle. This hypothesis was another desperate attempt to protect an existing incorrect image of the world. In order to maintain the integrity of the incorrect model of gravity, this boy actually experienced a sensory distortion. He firmly believed, incorrectly, that the block and button weighed equal amounts.

The experienced teacher did not waste time explaining the complexities of gravity to this first-grade class.[3] Indeed, several hundred years earlier, Galileo had experienced a similar difficulty in attempting to convince intelligent adults that all objects fall at the same rate, air resistance acting as the only mediating factor. The teacher only intended to challenge the students' notions of the world by introducing experiences that conflicted with their preconceived ideas. This challenge created a readiness for new information.

Although the construction and renovation of our mental models of the world continues throughout our lives, this endless process shows itself most visibly in children. For example, a toddler who is familiar with puppies, but not yet cats, will mistakenly identify a cat as "Puppy!" This toddler has no concept of cats. He recognized the cat as similar to its experience of dogs and labeled it accordingly. As children acquire experiences they tend to order and categorize them to fit what they already know within their own mental reproductions. These models then filter subsequent perceptions.

When we're observant, we can see this in adults too. On a recent trip to the family farm, several of us went on our traditional afternoon walk. We hiked to the spot we call Coyote Hill. I decided to search for evidence that this was indeed a hill frequented by coyotes. Shortly thereafter, I found coyote tracks and some coyote feces. The evidence confirmed my suspicions. Yes, this was definitely a coyote hill. Or so I thought. My niece casually remarked that the tracks and feces were probably from the local farm dog, out with the cattle. My doubt returned. I don't actually know what coyote feces or paw prints look like, although they are undoubtedly distinct from dogs as their respective diets and activities are clearly different. Nonetheless, I had unconsciously imposed my concept of *dog* feces and paw prints on the evidence I found because coyotes fit so nicely into my existing *dog* category. We instinctively impose our model of the world effortlessly.

When we experience anything for the first time, we identify it according to how we associate it to previous experience. For the same reason that most of us still refer to dolphins as fish, students in the gravity experiment imposed their flawed conceptual framework onto their experiences and understood those experiences from that faulty point of view. Many of our misconceptions remain intact, leaving us with faulty models full of square pegs squeezed into round holes.

MAKING THE WORLD MAKE SENSE: SQUEEZING SQUARE PEGS INTO ROUND HOLES

The need to make sense of the world and feel skillful in it is as strong as the need for food or sleep. When our experience confirms our ideas about how the world functions, the world makes sense to us and we feel settled. We feel the undeniable comfort of being in control. In the gravity experiment, the children cheered during the first demonstration when the button landed before the balloon because that result confirmed their representation of the world.

When ideas about the world clash with our experience, we suffer a mental state of uneasiness. To rid ourselves of this uneasiness, one of two possibilities occurs. First, we can adapt our model of the world to fit the circumstances. In the students' case, that would mean reconceptualizing gravity. Second, we can adapt our experiences to fit our existing framework. The students' assertion that button and block weighed the same reflects this second possibility. We rely on one or the other of these inherent processes to regain a sense of security about our world. Psychological security returns when our model and experiences complement each other.

We are intrinsically motivated by a drive to understand the world, and the mechanism we use to interpret our experiences is our personally constructed mental facsimile of reality. Brain systems resist meaninglessness by constructing patterns and categories, often imposing connections where none exist. Building our mental replicas is a creative process, often trimming round pegs to fit square holes. Consequently, the beliefs we form and the knowledge we acquire does not reflect reality itself. Our beliefs and knowledge merely reveal personalized accounts of how we interpret events according to our perceptions.

The construction process of our mental model of the world is similar to the construction of any concrete structure. The only difference is that we use our experiences as the materials to build our mental simulations. We all have different experiences; hence, different representations. Our most dramatic experiences, Spontaneous Influence Events (SIEs), make the most formative materials. We favor materials that fit effortlessly or appealing ones that can be modified easily to fit into the existing framework.[4] However, we will go to drastic lengths to ply new materials rather than tear down the existing foundation and start over.

I KNOW WHAT I KNOW. DON'T CONFUSE ME WITH THE FACTS

Like the kindergarten students, resistance to changing our interpretive mechanisms is so high that our mind finds it more prudent to adapt our experiences. This is why several people, while referring to a similar event, will often provide wildly differing interpretations. Consider the notorious Chowchilla kidnapping ordeal when *three white males* abducted a busload of children, temporarily burying them alive in their bus.[5] Having survived this ordeal, most of the children remembered their terrifying experience vividly. However, regarding the identity of the abductors, one child remembered a black man, another remembered a bald man, still another remembered a lady, and one child even remembered an old man who used his shotgun as a crutch to support a missing leg.[6] Research by an award winning professor in the Center for Neural Science at New York University, Joseph LeDoux, tells us that explicit, conscious memories are "reconstructions that blend information stored in long-term memory with one's current frame of mind."[7]

Events are encoded in memory according to their significance and the interpretation they received at that time. The perceived level of significance and how the event was interpreted was different for each person.

When recalled later, the interpretation and level of significance color the memory. It is more accurate to say that we remember *our experience* of the event, not the event itself. Current brain research shows that we construct our memories from perceptions of the event itself, expectations of how the world works, and past experiences.[8]

In the act of recalling past events, people often delete some details and embellish others. This innate process helps maintain a consistent grasp on *reality*. Whether accurate or not, this consistency provides emotional security. We don't just tell self-serving stories; we actually believe them.[9] Parents regularly break up fights among their children. Each child renders his or her own interpretation of events with conviction, yet the interpretations rarely match. We frequently throw our hands up in surrender when trying to sort out who is responsible.

How you experience an event effects how it is remembered. Therapists who conduct marriage and family counseling quickly discover that no objectively *true* version of an interpersonal episode exists. Members of the family convince themselves of the authenticity of their own versions. I remember asking separate family members to recall an earlier argument.[10] The father felt the daughter acted insolent and aloof. The mother thought the daughter attempted to lighten the tension with some light-hearted comments. The daughter herself remembered feeling condemned and anxious, withdrawing into sadness. Each experienced the argument according to his or her interpretation. Memories of life's events aren't as accurate as we may like to think, nor do we observe events as objectively as we like to think we do.

Attempts to change a person's schemata meets innately programmed resistance. If events don't fit neatly into the existing framework, the person can reject them outright, or redefine them to make them more compatible with the existing model. Redefinition takes place automatically and unconsciously to maintain a consistent representation of the world. Here again, illustrations from childhood are more demonstrative. For example, Dad tells Jonathan he is smart. If Jonathan believes he is smart, he will accept this as validation. If Jonathan thinks he is not smart he can reject it outright by thinking, "Dad is just saying that to make me feel better." Or, he may redefine the statement and think to himself, "I'm not smart, I'm just lucky sometimes." He gently redefined smart to lucky. Smart is permanent; lucky is temporary. Redefining keeps us trapped within our personally constructed worlds.

Jonathan's schemata instinctively spins interpretations to confirm itself. Models perpetuate themselves by generating a sense of self, generally referred to as a self-image, and a sense of the world, commonly called an outlook. These two aspects work together to keep our representations secure.

A COMPLEMENTARY REALITY: WHAT WE SEE IS WHAT WE GET

Essentially, models of reality have two aspects that work together to screen information and initiate experiences. One aspect is how we experience ourselves (internal) and the other is how we experience the world (external). These aspects complement each other in that our self-image helps mold our outlook, and our outlook helps shape our self-image. For example, those that experience themselves as a victim (internal), typically experience the world as oppressive (external). Those who see themselves as competitors (internal) experience the world as challenging (external). Hence, a self-image of conqueror yields an outlook of immense opportunity. A self-image of successful adventurer prompts a view of mistakes as temporary setbacks and the person trudges on. A self-image of hapless pawn fosters the perception that mistakes are failures and the individual ultimately gives up.

In each of the instances above, I implied that a self-image generates a complementary external outlook. The opposite may also occur: external outlooks (the world is oppressive) can also generate complementary self-images (I'm a helpless victim). These complementary aspects affirm each other in an endless cycle by activating validating interpretations.

I used highly simplified examples to illustrate how these two complementary aspects work together to confirm our assumptions of reality. The majority of us fall between these extremes and we may not display such clear representations. So, whether we find the world oppressive or full of opportunity depends on our perception. We all believe we experience the world the way it really is. This belief itself is a product of a self-confirming delusion. In *Stumbling on Happiness*, Daniel Gilbert states, "The problem isn't that our brains fill in and leave out. God help us if they didn't. No, the problem is that they do this so *well* that we aren't aware it is happening."[11]

THE SELF-CONFIRMATION DELUSION

Early impressions of ourselves and our world fortify as we mature. Self-confirming evidence piles up. If faulty views are not corrected or if they go unchallenged, they become entrenched as the child matures to adulthood. Indeed, many firmly held convictions may be remnants of ill-conceived notions from our youth. The following example illustrates how our conceptions, once etched into our neurological fabric, drive subsequent interpretations. In the example, the expectation of a response not only triggers a self-affirming interpretation, it actually creates a situation that prompts the expected response.

Imagine a teacher walking the aisles between students' desks, monitoring their work, and peering over them as they work at their tasks.

Brendan likes this teacher and accepts the monitoring as diligent attention from a caring teacher. Brendan looks up fondly at the teacher and smiles, and in so doing elicits a return smile from the teacher, confirming his belief. Another student, Chris, doesn't like this teacher nor schools in general. Chris interprets the teacher's attention as vigilance from a vindictive teacher trying to catch students making mistakes. Chris behaves defensively, eliciting a confused and suspicious look from the teacher; consequently, the teacher checks Chris's work and admonishes him to work carefully.

It is critical to note that the teacher's behavior did not confirm the students' beliefs. The *students' interpretations* of the teacher's behavior confirmed their beliefs. The teacher's behavior itself is inconsequential. Inherent in our model is a built-in feedback mechanism that confirms its own validity. Even an unexpected response from the teacher would likely be squeezed into the students' preconceived notions. Consider the following examples. Brendan's belief predicted an encouraging, supportive encounter. If the teacher had surprised Brendan with a scowl instead of a smile, Brendan would probably dismiss it as an anomalous sour mood on her part, or worse, look to himself as a *bad* child who deserved the wrath of an otherwise nice teacher. Such an interpretation might not reflect reality, but it would keep Brendan's belief intact. Chris's belief predicted a disparaging response from the teacher. If the teacher had surprised Chris with a soothing and encouraging response, Chris would probably have dismissed it as anomalous or interpreted it as a thinly veiled attempt to slyly manipulate him with phony congeniality. Such an interpretation, while not necessarily reflecting reality, would keep Chris's belief intact. I can't stress this point enough. *The existing belief, not the actual event, drives the interpretation.* As Aldous Huxley proclaimed, "Experience is not what happens to you; it is what you do with what happens."[12]

ADULTS DELUDE THEMSELVES TOO

Children aren't the only ones who embrace flimsy evidence to support ill-formed and preconceived notions, while simultaneously dismissing any contrary evidence. It is actually the pervasive logic of everyday thought. Several studies by sociologists show how teachers tend to label students into categories such as independent worker, bright child, immature child, and so on.[13] However, children's behaviors occasionally conflict with the attributes teachers assign them. Teachers, like all of us, unconsciously find ways to account for or dismiss contrary behavior. The studies showed that teachers perceived a poor test performance by a *bright child* as evidence of the student's rattled state of mind or a poorly constructed test. The low test result did not challenge the teachers' assignment of the child to the category of *bright student*. Talking out of turn by a *bright child* was termed eagerness, while talking out of turn by an *immature child* was considered a lack of self-control. Our predisposition to confirm our perceptions affects all of us, not just teachers.

Along similar lines, we often mock primitive cultures and their superstitious beliefs. One such culture believes that going out at night alone during a full moon is dangerous. However, when someone returns unscathed after a full-moon outing, villagers naturally attribute the safe return to a special amulet, prayer, or forgiving gods. Questioning their own beliefs simply never occurs to them. The primitive villagers and educated teachers exhibit the same underlying logic. Anomalous behavior squeezes itself into the existing belief framework.

The world of purely physical objects and their properties produces relatively reliable and predictable results. Experiences with a balloon or button typically yield the same results independent of when or where they occur. The world of human behavior is passionately different. Emotional and psychological factors play a critical role, making human interaction inherently ambiguous. Beliefs, hopes, and prejudices create predispositions that have the remarkable ability of generating their own justification.

The teacher and primitive villager examples illustrate how beliefs about the world trigger self-affirming interpretations. Beliefs about the self operate the same way. Congratulate a self-assured and confident worker for a good job and you'll get a smile of acknowledgment for recognizing the inherent ability (that co-worker sees success as internal). Criticize that same worker and you'll get excuses or explanations citing external factors (e.g., not enough time was provided, poor materials, lack of support, etc.). The opposite is true for the hesitant and insecure worker. Such a worker attributes compliments to luck or other external factors (e.g., strong leadership, good support, excellent materials, etc.) and accepts criticism by internalizing (e.g., isn't skilled enough, didn't prepare well, lacks ability, etc.). This second worker sees success as externally driven and failure as a personal weakness. Attributions by both workers keep each of their views of themselves intact.[14]

Deluding ourselves by spinning interpretations keeps our models reliable, providing psychological comfort. Our mental representations also screen perceptions, guiding us to unconsciously select information that fits nicely into our already existing schemata.

PERCEPTION IS LIMITED

The mind can only pay attention to a limited number of elements in the environment at any one time. Simply put, we typically notice aspects of the environment that have significance to us; we miss or ignore sensory information that we don't understand, value, or need. We literally have a preconscious bias to focus on parts of the environment that emotionally interest us. This operates continuously, outside consciousness.[15]

Arguments and public debates stem from opposing models of the world. An environmentalist, a developer, and a logger view a magnificent vista differently. The environmentalist sees an unspoiled habitat with a vast array of wildlife and a legacy of natural beauty for future generations. The developer gazes at the landscape, seeing the possibility of a comfortable family-oriented community with affordable housing, beautiful park lands, wonderful recreational opportunities, a small shopping mall at the foot of the valley, and a tremendous opportunity for investors. The logger sees several million board feet of prime lumber, a renewable resource to be harvested with minimal ecological disruption, housing for many families, and two hundred jobs for a slumping economy. Each present what they assume is a rational discussion, while opponents are appalled by what appears to them as a narrow, self-serving perspective. Emotionally laden debates often escalate hostilities rather than resolve them because when people on the opposite side don't immediately concede, it only proves they are unreceptive to reason.[16]

Our simulations give us a *sense* of ourselves and our world. This sense allows us to predict outcomes and form expectations. Expectations provide psychological comfort by anticipating outcomes.

MODELS MAKE THE WORLD PREDICTABLE: HOW THE FUTURE DETERMINES THE PRESENT

Our models of reality screen our experiences and determine what behavior is appropriate for a given situation. This screening generates expectations that unconsciously elicit behaviors, producing self-fulfilling prophecies. In this very real sense, your anticipated future, in the form of expectations, activates your present behavior. An expectation is a mindset that unconsciously directs our senses to search for confirming evidence that we were indeed correct in our anticipation. Thinking of something is literally the start of doing it.[17]

When you expect to do well at something, you behave much differently than when you think you will do poorly. When you expect a poor outcome, you are more likely to exhibit behavior consistent with a poor result. If someone asked you to sing the national anthem at an event, and you have a self-image as poor singer, expectations of doing poorly and embarrassing yourself will interfere with your performance. Your anticipation of a poor performance will create anxiety triggered by images of embarrassing yourself. Distress sends adrenaline surging through your body giving you the sensation of butterflies in your stomach. Your anxiety escalates, likely sabotaging your performance by interfering with proper breathing, correct posture, and voice projection. You warm up with a note. It sounds off key and hesitant which confirms your fear and also raises your anxiety one more notch. On the other hand, if you anticipate doing well, you will breathe deeply, stand erect, and project your voice effectively, thereby enhancing your performance. You warm up with a note. It sounds off key but you brush it off as a necessary exercise to find your tone. In essence, your expectations enlist corresponding responses.

This explains one psychological effect of practice. Practice not only increases performance through rehearsal, it also increases positive expectations, diminishing the anxiety that frequently interferes with a peak performance.

Children who feel like hopeless failures act in a manner that corresponds with their expectations. Self-defeating behavior illustrates the effect negative expectations can have on behavior. In school, expectations of low achievement often lead to the unconscious sabotage of a competent performance. Such students often produce poorly organized and incomplete notes, are easily distracted, forget to take books home for study, find themselves busy during study time, stay out late, or sleep in. Teachers and parents pull their hair out, knowing that these children would improve measurably with the right attitude. On the other hand, expectations of doing well usually generate optimal achievement behaviors such as practice, study, homework completion, and pride in organization. Students' attitudes reflect their expectations, generated by their views of the world and themselves in it.

Do you see evidence of this in your adult friends too? Some challenge new opportunities boldly, dismissing failures as a bump in the road, *expecting* inevitable success. Others don't even attempt new experiences or give up easily with the first setback, *expecting* that they will eventually fail anyway.

Under normal conditions, changes in expectations and their corresponding conceptual frameworks progress extremely slowly if it happens at all. Have you ever tried to convince a pessimist that the world is a bed of roses? Under special conditions, such as during an Elevated Suggestibility State (ESS), change can occur spontaneously. Attacks on mental models can create these special conditions.

ATTACKS ON MODELS CREATE TEACHABLE MOMENTS

There are three fundamental truisms about learning and understanding the world. First, we interpret our experience in accordance with our concept of reality. Second, we can easily distort sensory perceptions to accommodate our interpretation of events. Third, upon awareness of a discrepancy between our representation of the world and experience in it, we begin to question the experience. This uncertainty creates teachable moments.

During a Disneyland vacation, our family went on a ride named, "Journey Through the Human Body." While waiting in line, we watched the loaded cars ahead of us enter a dark tunnel, turning out of sight as they entered the *shrinking zone*. The shrinking zone was a winding conical tube adorned with hundreds of flashing lights. Miniature cars with human figurines emerged from the small end of the tube, off in the distance, too far away to see clearly. It created the cute illusion that the people on the ride shrank. These miniature cars then proceeded to enter another shrinking zone, which in turn entered a large hypodermic needle. Now that the cars and people had presumably shrunk to minute proportions, they could easily enter a human artery.

My family boarded a roller-car, began a journey into the dark tunnel, apparently shrank to molecular size, and eventually made our way through a *human* artery. At the end of the trip, we jumped out of the car and began walking toward the next exhibit. My six-year-old daughter tugged at my sleeve. With furrowed brows, she begged answers to some burning questions: "Are we still tiny? I remember *the shrinking feeling* but I don't remember growing big again. When did I get big again?"

Her interpretation of the experience reflected her notion of reality. The harmless illusion had fooled my youngest daughter, because the concept of human-size-constancy did not yet exist in her model of the world. Her mental representation, based on Saturday morning cartoons, allowed for humans to shrink to minuscule dimensions.

She distorted her sensory perceptions to seamlessly accommodate her interpretation of events. My daughter undoubtedly experienced some physiological arousal due to the excitement and anticipation of the ride: that tingly feeling we get when excited. The motion of the ride enhanced this physical sensation to the point where she interpreted this vague, visceral, tingly experience as the *shrinking* sensation. This matched her visual perception and expectation of shrinking. Our models are so pervasive, they can even affect our sensory experiences.

Once aware of the contradiction between her experience and her simulation of the world, she began to question her experience. Accordingly, when the ride ended and she hadn't felt a *growing* sensation, she started to wonder when it had happened and why she had missed it. To her, the act of shrinking and growing were unquestioned, because they fitted gracefully into her model.

This moment of wondering can be loosely coined the "teachable moment." It is characterized by an increased receptiveness to new interpretations, a slightly elevated suggestibility state. At this precise point in time, the youngster will eagerly accept almost any interpretation uncritically, especially from an authority figure. When my daughter's awareness of discrepancies between her mental representation and her experience surfaced, it generated several questions. These questions displayed her earnest desire to integrate this recent experience into her understanding of the world. These questions also illustrate a heightened receptivity to any new information that would aid her in the integration process.

I could have addressed her questions in a variety of ways. I could have told her the truth about the illusion. Developmentally she was ready. She would have understood and adapted her model accordingly. More dramatically, I could have taken her back on the ride, excitedly exclaiming the following as we made the last turn before the exit, "See . . . see . . . There it is . . . That's the growing feeling!" Most certainly she would have experienced an arousing sensation triggered by the exhilaration in my voice. She would have subsequently labeled that arousing sensation as the "growing" feeling. She would have accepted this information eagerly because of her trust in me, her ESS, and because my response would have effortlessly fit into her already existing schemata. Alternatively, I could have handled her question expediently by saying, "We don't get a growing feeling because *big* is our normal size. We only feel the shrinking because *tiny* is not our normal size." That would have solved her mystery and she could have kept her model intact. Finally, I could have proceeded, like many wise parents and teachers do, by reflecting the question back to my daughter, "What do you think happened?" gently prodding, helping her renovate her concept herself.

Conditions similar to the ones my daughter experienced at Disneyland take place during an ESS. In my daughter's case, loud sounds, flashing lights, and excitement about the ride triggered a state of emotional arousal. Emotional arousal triggers an all-alert in the brain that increases receptiveness to incoming information, and produces an ESS. Her confusion also increases her receptiveness.

In her precarious mental state, my daughter created a sense of shrinking to match her model of the world. When she exited the ride, she missed the sensation of growing large again. A discrepancy between her experience and her model of reality caused confusion. The resulting confusion produced an eagerness to accept anything that solves the uncertainty. New information is then either squeezed into the existing framework or the challenging information initiates a renovation process. Obviously it is more expedient to change one bit of information than to renovate a whole mental infrastructure, but sometimes the information is so demanding that the model crumbles and a new form takes shape. When this happens suddenly in the area of self-image, general outlook, or any underlying personal beliefs, a SIE occurs. Although ESS and spontaneous influence occur throughout our lives, they appear more often in our early years because of the nature of children's suggestibility.

THE NATURE OF CHILDREN'S HIGH SUSCEPTIBILITY TO SUGGESTION

Tens of thousands of years ago, the environment was considerably more dangerous. To survive, important lessons had better make an indelible impression and last a life-time. Only those children who learned critical lessons quickly and effectively survived to pass their genes on to the next generation. If the lessons worked, the child survived and his genes marched on. Hence, a drive to learn, particularly from authority figures, developed in humans. If you don't know much, you wonder a lot. The more you wonder, the greater the drive to learn. Simply put, children don't know very much about anything. (Until they become teenagers and then they know everything.)

Children's models are only partially developed, and this subsequent deficit drives them to continually adapt to vast amounts of information. When children wonder about things, interpretations presented by authority figures are eagerly accepted because they solve the child's perplexity. Whether the information is accurate and healthy for the individual is not as important to the child as whether the information works. Does it solve the mental uneasiness by fitting into the child's scheme of things? Humans have the ability to learn symbolically, through explanations. Other animals must learn from experience, observation, or innate ability. Our symbolic learning capacity is double-sided. Our tendency to learn symbolically does not screen out wrong or misleading information.[18]

Recall the Disneyland story and the variety of explanations I could have provided for my daughter regarding her shrinking experience. All she wanted was a solution to her puzzle. If I spoke with conviction, she would have believed me regardless of what I said. The prospect of questioning my explanation would never even occur to her. With maturity, our mental representations strengthen, confusion diminishes, and challenging authority increases.

OUR MODELS STRENGTHEN WITH AGE

As we grow older, models of the world fortify themselves and we defend challenges to our beliefs. We begin to question and explore explanations to determine if they are plausible. Our basis for examining new explanations is our already-flawed conceptual framework. We also develop skepticism for some sources (like the kid down the street who tried to convince us that he had an alien in his basement). Some sources remain infallible for a long time. Parents, teachers, older siblings, trusted friends, and relatives play special roles in our development. Authority figures have a particular edge in the influence sweepstakes. Children who listened to parents and elders in our ancestral communities probably had a higher rate of survival.

As adults, threats to our greater body of experience and more highly developed models occur less often. Fewer threats occur because a more sophisticated understanding of the world provides a security for our existence, a way to successfully predict events in our lives. Our schemata commands a defensive posture. After all, we've made it this far. Right or wrong, we feel better when we think we have a handle on things. We often hear the expression, "You have to do what feels right." What *feels* right is that which matches our mental simulation. It has nothing to do with what *is* right.

Children don't have an accumulated wealth of relevant knowledge and associations to assemble a wider context of understanding. They haven't yet "been around the block." During the regular course of day-to-day living, adults have an enormous amount of previous experiences that provide clues for interpreting events. When events take place, relevant knowledge and associations from similar events provide a context that helps us decide how to deal with the situation. For example, as you walk down the street you look ahead and see a circle of people shouting. You pause for a moment to discern the nature of the crowd. Your accumulated knowledge and associations from similar incidents help you recognize that this is a fight and not a street entertainer. Several clues in the environment enable you to differentiate between an excited, joyous audience and an aroused, callous crowd. These associations occur so rapidly that we do not usually notice them. A young child would be unable to make the subtle distinction.

We know how children's models of reality perpetuate themselves. We also know that socialization by authority figures, particularly parents, creates a predictable degree of influence in the molding of children's conceptual frameworks. What then is the role of SIEs? Pulitzer Prize finalist and MIT professor Steven Pinker believes that life's serendipitous events may be the determining factor for our personalities.[19] Self-image, outlook, and personal beliefs create our distinctive personalities, and nothing shapes these elements more profoundly than a SIE. ESSs can turn our rigid mental structures into malleable putty, whereby some agent of influence can dramatically shape subsequent behavior and perceptions.

✳✳✳

We instinctively squeeze new information into our existing representations of the world and don't even consider the possibility of being wrong until some event or piece of information challenges that conviction. You, the reader, will undoubtedly go through this same process as you try to make sense of spontaneous influence. You will attempt to understand this new concept in terms of your current model of understanding similar events. In the next chapter, I take an active role in guiding you in this respect by comparing hypnosis, a procedure most of you are at least marginally familiar with, to spontaneous influence.

Chapter 4

More than Hypnosis

Some of you may be thinking, "Heightened suggestibility, influence agents, and sudden change sure sound like hypnosis." Many obvious similarities exist. Although spontaneous influence is exponentially more powerful and longer-lasting than hypnosis, both share some fundamental features. A brief comparison provides extraordinary insights into how we learn and change. Enriching your understanding of both will aid you in learning how to deal constructively with spontaneous influence.

This chapter begins with a broad description of the hypnosis experience. It then moves to a carefully crafted event that blends spontaneous influence with hypnotic strategies. The following section illustrates positive and negative examples of Spontaneous Influence Events (SIEs). The chapter finishes by highlighting the subtle aspects of spontaneous influence that make it so powerful and difficult to defend against.

A LITTLE BIT ABOUT HYPNOSIS

Traditionally, the hypnotist induces high suggestibility in the patient through physiological relaxation ("Take a couple of deep breaths and let yourself relax") and mental focus ("Stare at a freckle on your hand"). Once a highly suggested state is induced, the hypnotist creates a model of the world for the hypnotic subject. If the induction process is successful, the patient responds by creating experiences consistent with the hypnotist's fashioned suggestions. Imagine that your doctor is about to perform a minor surgery. She hypnotizes you and constructs an imaginative journey to a warm and tranquil beach. You become totally immersed in the experience and feel *as if* you are on that beach. Your newly created model of reality generates the sensations of warmth and relaxation, making the suggested model *seem* real. Painful sensations from surgery do not fit into your fashioned experience; accordingly, you manage to get through the surgery without any awareness of pain. Research shows that while your mid-brain registers pain, the "ouch" message never gets to your cortex where conscious experience takes place.[1] While it is only recently that we could measure the brain patterns of hypnosis, the process itself emerged long ago.

Early in our human history, teachers, healers, and storytellers used concentration and imagination to invoke a particular reality for their students, patients, and listeners. Over the years, the practice of engrossing someone in thoughts and images became honed and refined. Inevitably, healers ritualized this practice and mystified it with sensational claims. Primitive people still use similar methods of concentration and imagination for healing, but they don't view it suspiciously or refer to it as hypnosis. Modern civilization eventually coined this natural process hypnosis.[2] Today, hypnosis is the formally defined system designed to reliably induce a high state of suggestibility.

The next few sections illustrate the experience of hypnosis. Learning how hypnotic phenomena emerge and how they activate subsequent behaviors will help you understand similar but more powerful phenomena operating during SIEs. We start with compulsions. Hypnotic suggestions initiate compulsions to act in a way that corresponds with the suggestions.

COMPULSIONS

Most of the time we give in to our compulsions and we usually do so without examining or analyzing our motives, thoughts, or the circumstances. Such automatic behavior is driven by gut reactions.[3] Gut reactions stem from biological urges (e.g., run or fight back when threatened) and our deep-seated beliefs (e.g., apologize when we bump into a fellow shopper). It just isn't expedient to examine every choice we make, all the time. These biological urges and learned instincts guide us subtly, most times so subtly that we aren't even aware of the choices we automatically make. If we consciously go against our gut feelings, it's as if the gut fights back by boosting our anxiety in a further effort to nudge us to do its bidding. A feeling of satisfaction comes from following our subconscious prompts.

Those who have experienced deliberate hypnotic inductions provide us with broad information about how it feels to be *compelled*. The following anecdote reveals the typical feelings associated with responding to hypnotic suggestions: satisfaction for behaving *correctly* and anxiety for behaving *incorrectly*. Feelings of behaving *correctly* are akin to those we experienced when we eagerly followed the instructions of our parents or like the feelings of satisfaction we arouse when we cooperate with a loved one. Feelings of behaving *incorrectly* are akin to the anxiety experienced when being naughty in childhood. When research subjects respond appropriately to suggestions, they report a feeling of satisfaction. When hypnotized research subjects resist a suggestion they usually report a feeling of anxiety, as if they are doing something wrong.

In his book, *Surely You're Joking Dr. Feynman*,[4] the acclaimed Nobel Prize winning physicist Richard Feynman described his experience during a hypnotist's performance at a university where he taught. During the induction of the hypnotic state he felt no different than he did before he went into the hypnotic state. He followed the induction procedure dutifully and produced all the typical signs of a good hypnotic participant while feeling that he was merely being compliant (acting correctly). For the last suggestion, the hypnotist instructed him to leave the stage and walk all around the gymnasium to get to his seat. He thought this was odd because his seat was directly in front of him. He decided to ignore this last suggestion and go directly to his seat in the audience at the end of the show.

At the appointed signal he left the stage, but as he moved to go directly to his seat he felt apprehensive about taking that route (anxiety from acting incorrectly). He was aware that he was supposed to go all around the gymnasium, and that the instruction was given to him by a hypnotist. After a moment's hesitation he submitted to his unease and decided to walk around the floor to get to his seat. His *gut* reaction urged him to take the long route. Like Feynman, we typically behave in a similar manner, usually submitting to our anxiety. But that isn't harmful. We would never get anything done if we continually reflected upon the hundreds of decisions we make on a daily basis. Most of the time we operate automatically without thinking about our actions.

The goal of hypnotic inductions is to raise a person's suggestibility to such a degree that the subject accepts the hypnotist's command and subsequently responds automatically, without using any intervening rational process. Hypnotists do this through a highly ritualized process called a hypnotic induction. When the hypnotic subject's suggestibility rises significantly, we say they are in a hypnotic state. Most readers will associate special features with hypnosis that are commonly referred to as "deep trance phenomena."

DEEP TRANCE PHENOMENA DISPELLED

Experiences of *deep trance phenomena* are hardly mystifying. Indeed, they occur so regularly and naturally that we hardly take special notice of them. We have all experienced them at some time or other. They are not uncommon, merely unnoticed. Entertainers and others who wish to mystify hypnotic phenomena may exaggerate them in an effort to awe an audience. They are common conditions that just look exceptional when produced on command and clustered together deliberately for amusement.

Many of us experience a form of age regression when hearing a favorite song from our past. We take a mental trip back in time and re-experience some of the emotions and reactions from that period. Have you ever been frustrated by trying to remember something you are sure you know: the tip-of-the-tongue phenomenon? That's temporary amnesia. Why is it that when we lose our keys we sometimes check our jacket pocket several times as if they would suddenly reappear? Because past experience tells us we often lose something right under our noses. This is called a negative hallucination: not seeing (sensing) something that is physically present. Think of common expressions such as, "A watched kettle never boils" (time moving inordinately slowly) and "Time sure flies when you're having fun" (time speeding up). The experience of time distortion is so common that we even have day-to-day expressions for them. Can you remember details from some events early in your life that are as vivid as if they happened yesterday? That phenomenon is called hypermnesia: extremely vivid recall. Have you ever had to call someone's name several times even though they were right in front of you, seemingly awake and aware? The person was engrossed in deep thought, oblivious to the concrete surroundings. That's either a sensory distortion of deafness, or a mild dissociation from the physical environment. These familiar experiences, when created intentionally in the context of hypnosis, seem more extraordinary than they really are.

Deep trance phenomena tend to occur during moments of extreme emotional arousal (ecstasy, panic, rage), deep concentration (immersion in a task), or during extreme relaxation (daydreaming, pre-sleep nodding off). The following story, recalled by a graduate student, reveals several deep trance phenomena that arose together during a spontaneous mental state of alarm, characterized by confusion and anxiety.[5] I use parenthesis throughout the text for illustration purposes.

> One night, before drifting off, I heard a troubled sound from the room where my twin boys were sleeping. Immediately I sensed that something was wrong. My adrenal glands kicked in, my heart rate soared, and my breathing quickened. I was anxious and frightened; there was a sense of urgency (extreme emotional arousal). I raced down the hall to the boys' room. Shaking, I reached for the light in my sons' bedroom and failed to locate it (amnesia). I focused on the sound and it intensified (sensory distortion: heightened auditory acuity). My wife turned on the light. My son was having some sort of seizure.

My son's body rapidly jerked around in a contorted twisted movement, and froth formed in his mouth. I tried to remember what I had heard about seizures. I didn't know what to do next. I was in a situation that I had never encountered before. My normal reality references were shattered. It was like a nightmare (a form of dissociation: a feeling of other-worldliness). I focused on one thing only: helping my son. My wife was speaking to me but I didn't hear her (sensory distortion: deafness). His body twisted unnaturally to the left. In a panic, I yelled for my wife to call 911.

My wife returned moments later saying that an ambulance was on the way. It seemed to take forever (time distortion). Finally the medic appeared at the door. At last, help had arrived. I hadn't noticed the sirens (sensory distortion: deafness). I didn't even recognize one of the attendants, a neighbor whose son played regularly with my boys (amnesia). I was asked which side of the body was affected. All of a sudden I couldn't remember (amnesia).

The whole event seemed to take hours (time distortion). Our distress call and the ambulance arrival were all documented. The gap between the call and the arrival was only four minutes. Could so much have happened in that time? It seemed like an eternity (time distortion).

Much of the public views hypnosis as an aberration of the human condition, a rare and mysterious phenomenon, dangerous in the wrong hands, and seductively powerful. Clinicians and researchers who work with hypnosis know that it is typically much less sensational. The reality is much less dramatic.

Mentalist and entertainer, The Amazing Kreskin, offered $100,000 to anyone who could definitively produce any "hypnotic" behavior that he couldn't also produce outside the supposed hypnotic state. For three decades, Kreskin successfully defended his challenge. He frequently demonstrated to live audiences that he could produce any so-called "hypnotic phenomenon" without a hypnotic induction or deep trance of any sort. According to Kreskin, there is nothing extraordinary about hypnosis; it is a natural phenomenon.

In the example you just read about the young boy's seizure, the father's extreme emotional arousal didn't just produce so-called extraordinary phenomena, it also put him in a naturally Elevated Suggestibility State (ESS). Our suggestibility soars during emotional arousal just like it does in hypnotically induced states.

OUR SUGGESTIBILITY

Suggestions occur everywhere, often in the form of unplanned comments. The following personal anecdote illustrates that even professionals trained in influence are vulnerable. I broke my leg several years ago. Upon removal of the cast, I turned to swimming to rebuild the atrophied muscles. I swam four or five mornings a week before leaving for work.

Early one morning, before leaving to swim, my wife approached me with a grim look on her face. Concern swept through me. I trained my attention on her, awaiting an important pronouncement. She said, "Doesn't your leg hurt when you swim in the morning?" I laughed with relief, commenting that her dour expression had alarmed me. We both laughed and made light of the inadvertent nature of her suggestion, returning to our morning routine.

Later that morning, while swimming, letting my mind take me where it may, I started to get an ache in my leg. It surprised me. I hadn't experienced pain during previous swims. I did a quick mental search for reasons my leg might be aching, and then the morning conversation flashed back to me. I spent the next few laps grinning to myself while marveling at my suggestibility.

Looking back at the morning incident, I realize that I was particularly vulnerable to my spouse's suggestion because her serious expression riveted my attention. Her grim look triggered emotional arousal, creating a subtle ESS. I didn't consciously counter the suggestion for two reasons. It didn't seem serious enough to warrant deliberate intervention, and I became distracted by my morning regimen. Had I felt the comment was a seriously negative suggestion I would have countered it right away, but I'm mentally equipped to do that. Most of us, and particularly young children lack the sufficient awareness to defend against many of the self-defeating and destructive suggestions that unwittingly, and some times intentionally, fall their way.

Once the mind accepts a suggestion, consciously or unconsciously, it finds a means for expression or validation. Those who exercise regularly have learned to ignore minor aches and pains unless they become persistent or debilitating. Minor aches and pains become mental background unless something nudges them into the foreground of conscious awareness. That was certainly the case with my leg while swimming. That morning, my mind accepted an inadvertent suggestion and rather than ignore slight discomfort as it usually did, it became vigilant for signs of pain. My mind was ready and eager to alert my conscious thoughts at the earliest opportunity.

The previous illustration, while not very dramatic, shows how comments during an ESS can change the landscape of someone's thoughts, by changing what they attend to. What you attend to influences your behavior. All this typically goes on outside your everyday awareness. Was I hypnotized? After all, I responded to a suggestion during elevated suggestibility.

IS ELEVATED SUGGESTIBILITY HYPNOSIS?

Are all forms of elevated suggestibility hypnotic states? Scientific researchers and clinicians in hypnosis hesitate to call the common condition of elevated suggestibility "hypnosis" because a formal induction procedure did not occur. However, clinicians generally agree that impressive surges in suggestibility may take place at any time or place, under the right conditions, without a formal induction. Extreme emotional arousal, profound confusion, and shock are the three most common conditions that initiate ESSs.

Suggestibility is not a single condition with clearly marked boundaries. Rather, it encompasses a continuum ranging from slightly more suggestible than usual to dramatically more suggestible. We all experience a range of suggestibility. Just as some people possess more patience than others, some people possess a broader range of suggestibility. Like patience and many other traits, suggestibility depends on the context and your mood.

At the high end of this suggestibility continuum, many of us can absorb ourselves in an idea to such an extent that we experience a hypnotist's suggested image as real. For example, imagine that a hypnotist has managed to raise your suggestibility. In this state you accept the following suggestion about an inability to bend your arm: "Your arm is enclosed in a steel sleeve, and you know how difficult it is to bend steel . . . It is impossible to bend it . . . Just try . . . and you will see how difficult it is to bend your arm." All of us can imagine a steel sleeve over an arm, and we can all imagine how futile it would be to try to bend our arm in such a situation. You certainly don't need hypnosis to experience this suggestion; it just makes it more vivid. Try it yourself right now. It's easy. See how deeply you can imagine your arm encased in a steel sleeve. Children do it quite easily. Those who can engross themselves in this image to such a degree that they experience it as authentic are called deeply hypnotized. Some hypnotists say these people are in a deep hypnotic trance because their images of a steel sleeve govern their behavior instead of their true situation. Such people temporarily operate *as if* the suggested condition is their actual experience.

ACTING AS IF

Hypnotized subjects actually create a mind-set that perpetuates a suggestion, making a purely fictitious suggestion *seem* genuine. For example, if I tell hypnotized subjects that imaginary spiders are moving slowly up their arms, they actually experience that sensation. This is similar to the experience we have when someone describes a nest of snakes; it makes us feel creepy. The description triggers involuntary muscle spasms and literally makes our skin crawl. The mind, if it believes something to be true, will find or create evidence to support it.

At some conscious level, formally hypnotized subjects know they are playing out suggestions, but they manage to keep it out of current awareness. We engage in a similar but less dramatic form of mental escape whenever we engross ourselves in a good film. We experience the authentic thoughts and emotions triggered by our movie experience (e.g., crying during sad moments), but we know we are sitting in a theatre, watching actors perform scripted parts. When a formal hypnosis session ends, the subject knows hypnosis took place. This is similar to when we exit a movie theatre. We may still be moved by the experience, but we know it was a movie that stimulated us.

Hypnotic suggestions will only last while the hypnotic state exists. This frequently takes place at hypnosis stage shows where some audience members drop into a hypnotic state. At the end of the show, they wake up and understand that they were hypnotized. They experience no side-effects and are not walking around later with unexpressed or continuing hypnotic suggestions. In other words, they won't crow like a rooster every time they hear the word "farm."

Even though hypnotic subjects act *as if* the suggestions are authentic, the thoughts and images produced by the suggestions are themselves genuine. Our thoughts and images produce actual emotional and physiological responses.

THOUGHTS AND IMAGES ARE REAL

To illustrate how common it is to experience thoughts and images as real, a hypnosis instructor of mine assigned us the following exercise. Consider trying it discreetly with a friend. The object of the exercise was to have the leader (X) make the receiver partner (Y) produce some form of unconscious behavior without requesting it directly (e.g., rubbing eyes, scratching a nose, shaking a head, shrugging shoulders). To do this, person X was to create thoughts and images that would produce a predictable reaction in person Y. Person X must do this without telling person Y what action they wish to exhibit.

Acting as a leader (person X), I secretly attempted to get my partner (person Y) to shrug his shoulders and pull at his collar, the way we do when wearing something uncomfortable around our necks. I began by recalling my recent down-hill skiing excursion. I described in detail how my new wool scarf continually irritated my neck. During my descriptively vivid delivery, I subtly pulled at my shirt collar, rolled my head, and rubbed my neck continuously, as if re-experiencing my own discomfort. Shortly thereafter, my partner rubbed his neck and pulled at his collar, vicariously experiencing my described discomfort and unconsciously mimicking my behavior. His thoughts and images induced a tangible experience in him with a subsequent physiological response.

In a sense, we experience the same phenomenon every time we see someone suffering raging cold symptoms: watery eyes, inflamed and itchy nose, and a muffled voice caused by congestion. Instinctively, we often rub our own eyes or nose as if we ourselves were experiencing similar symptoms. You may even be twitching your nose or rubbing your eyes right now, as you read these symptoms. These sensations are generated within our mirror neuron system.

Recent experiments on brain imaging uncovered a complex mirror neuron system. Mirror neurons reflect back an action we observe, hear, or read about. In other words, the same part of our brain is active when we perform an action and when we observe, hear, or read about that action. When you see a spider crawling up someone's leg you get a creepy feeling because your mirror neurons are firing. In the brain, simulating or viewing an act is the same as performing it.[6]

When I taught hypnosis to graduate classes at the University of Oregon, one of the most common questions I'd get during orientation was, "What if you hypnotized someone and they never came out of it?" Decades before, as a young student in undergraduate studies, I often pondered the same question. In part, that intriguing question led me to my graduate studies and this book. I researched all forms of hypnosis as well as related forms of mind/thought management such as the relaxation response,[7] meditation, yoga, and suggestopedia.[8] I eventually found the answer to the question: spontaneous influence.

SIMILAR, BUT DIFFERENT

While spontaneous influence and hypnosis share the primary feature of heightened suggestibility, profound differences also exist. SIEs prove substantially more powerful and longer lasting than any hypnotic suggestion because we have no defense against spontaneous influence.[9] Hypnosis is less potent because clients openly consent to the process; goals are mutually agreed upon; the client can terminate the session at any time; it is time bound to a specified period; and is usually performed by a trained professional. Hypnosis is a rational and deliberate process with commonly identifiable features.

A SIE differs in that it is sudden, often unintentional, frequently unnoticed, and devastatingly effective because it knocks out or severely limits our usual rational processes. You can arm yourself against hypnosis and dispute the suggestions because it is a consensual and discernable process. Defending yourself against a SIE is futile because most of us don't know the signposts to alert us and the effects are elusive. Our only defense is to learn about spontaneous influence so that we can manage them when they inevitably occur.

The next section describes an episode of my daughter's surgical treatment and recovery that occurred during my doctoral training. This story illustrates how my practical knowledge of hypnosis and spontaneous influence blended together to create a magnificent healing event. The only training necessary to produce similar results yourself, is a sound understanding of spontaneous influence. Everything I did to precipitate and manage this event is easily within your grasp once you learn about spontaneous influence and practice the strategies I present in the final chapters.

MORE POWERFUL THAN HYPNOSIS

The following series of events underscore two critical features of SIEs. First, suggestions during moments of naturally elevated suggestibility states can produce extraordinary results, even more powerful than traditional hypnotic suggestions. Second, informed authority figures (e.g., parents, teachers, counselors, physicians, experts, or anyone who speaks with conviction) can take advantage of ESSs to present positive suggestions during these moments, or at the very least, negate harmful suggestions.

I have hundreds of stories of spontaneous influence from students and clients, and I've also collected many from celebrity chronicles. I use my daughter's event below because unlike those who come and go in my office, I was able to follow her over several critical hours and days, providing healing conditions and counteracting negative ones. In the healing professions, we stand to lose much of our positive influence once someone leaves the office. This story demonstrates the importance of emotional guidance during prolonged elevated suggestibility.

My teenage daughter Kary suffered from Planter's warts for months. The warts multiplied until clusters of them covered her right foot. Several trips to a specialist for painful freezing treatments proved unsuccessful. Each monthly trip included a ruined school day, tense waiting in the office, a painful treatment, several days of hobbling about, and my daughter's resolve to discontinue the excruciating treatment. Kary described these treatments as unbearably painful. Her only other option was to have the offending warts removed surgically. Her doctor warned her that the surgery would produce protracted pain for up to six weeks as the wound healed.

Writhing in pain in a living-room chair after one of her freezing treatments, Kary was eager to try anything. Hypnosis is most effective when people feel receptive. I suggested she try hypnosis to diminish her pain, and she agreed. I decided to teach her self-hypnosis to manage the pain when it interfered with her sleep, and also as a distraction strategy during subsequent freezing treatments. Several hypnosis treatments created only moderate success at blocking pain. I felt discouraged because I thought I had employed the wrong method with her.

I went with her to the next few treatments. I used a traditional hypnotic induction with her, but experienced only mild success. However, she was able to distract herself during the freezing treatment by using intense visual imagery of pleasant memories. She and the specialist concluded that the pain appeared to be substantially less than previous visits. It proved to be only a shallow victory though. The wart-freezing treatments produced only slight success and surgery appeared imminent.

My hypnosis treatment worked marginally at best, so I decided to wait for her suggestibility to rise naturally. The day of the operation would inevitably generate such an ESS. Anxiety and confusion on that day would provide me with a momentous window of opportunity to steer her thoughts. Then, I would saturate her with suggestions for pain-free healing.

One serious obstacle remained. A physician's prognosis has an enormous effect on treatment outcomes. Predictions from powerful authority figures can act like compelling suggestions, particularly during ESSs. How would I counteract the doctor's predictions of persistent pain over an extended period? Knowing her vulnerability to suggestion would rise during the operation, I garnered permission to attend, determined to guide her through this ESS.

The physician politely listened to my plan, but claimed it was his responsibility to describe to the patient, the almost certain probability of a long and painful recovery. Subsequently, he addressed my daughter and apologetically made his prediction: "I'm sorry, but you will experience intense periods of pain for the next several weeks. It will probably be six weeks before you feel comfortable again. I will prescribe some pain-killers." I had my work cut out for me as the operation began.

The surgical assistant sensed my frustration and provided me with a window of opportunity to negate and counter the physician's prognosis of pain. During the procedure, the assistant described a previous patient who had undergone similar surgery. This patient had experienced no pain and hadn't used any pain killers. Here lay the opportunity I had hoped for. I quickly jumped in and monopolized the rest of the conversation with this assistant. I asked several questions about the nature of this other patient's painlessness. With the help of my subtle direction, Kary's attention shifted toward details of the assistant's story. I gathered as much information as I could about this other person and her pain-free healing. This information would become a potent vehicle in my drive to activate Kary's mirror neuron system to create a pain-free healing experience.

For the remaining time in surgery, I delivered continuous healthy suggestions to Kary, stressing my goals: a high pain threshold and a natural ability to heal quickly. I reminded her of times in her past when she had displayed characteristics of pain-free behavior. We have all experienced times in life when we were apparently oblivious to pain, particularly athletes who often find scratches, cuts, or bruises on their bodies after a game. Recalling these times initiates the same mental framework that in turn generates that same capacity again.

Immediately after Kary's operation I began bombarding her with comparisons between her experience and that of the other person who had overcome pain. Much of the experience of pain is psychological; focusing on it makes it more intense. The opposite is also true; focusing on something else, anything else, diminishes the experience of pain. I recalled stories about other people who had transcended pain, drawing parallels between their experiences and hers. I reminded her of the many times she had exhibited the very qualities that signify an ability to ignore pain; the common ability to focus on something to the extent that it absorbed her complete attention. I made full use of her ESS. I intended to saturate her mind with the high probability that she would experience little or no pain. My healing stories and pronouncements continued down the hallway, in the elevator, through traffic to another clinic for crutches, and all the way home—and then some. I maintained consistent expectations during the crucial hours as the local anesthetic wore off.

Steering someone's attention during an ESS is quite simple. In essence, you lead from the person's experience to a created goal. For example: "Your ability to move carefully (she was hobbling cautiously on her crutches) will speed your healing immensely (goal)." The key is to associate an irrefutable experience with an image of pain-free healing or a speedy recovery. It is critical to note that I could have said anything as long as I associated it with painless healing or a speedy recovery. Every few moments I asked her what she was experiencing and then I carefully linked her experience to a prediction of painlessness or mere minimal discomfort. When she described a tingling warm sensation, I informed her that such a sensation indicated that the pain was retreating. I turned every sensation she had into a sign that she was bypassing the experience of pain. I even framed flashes of her pain experience as certain signs of success: "That throbbing sensation means your pain is subsiding and your healing is accelerating."

She had little choice but to respond to my constant barrage of images of painless and speedy healing. Everything I said was true, honest, and part of her experience. She had no basis for disqualifying anything I claimed. I simply constructed creative associations between her current experience and pain-free healing: "Your fitness level from dancing tuned your muscles for pain-free healing," "Your ability to focus is typical of people who can diminish pain." If she hadn't been a dancer I could have said, "Your relaxed muscles help create a pain-free healing experience."

The result proved magnificent. She experienced little if any intense pain and took only minimum amounts of a painkiller as a precaution. She attended school the next day and only experienced pain once, when she accidentally bumped her foot. Intense, protracted pain never materialized and she discarded her medicine. Healing occurred quickly and completely over the next two weeks. Her thoughts and images fostered painless and rapid healing.

HYPNOSIS OR SPONTANEOUS INFLUENCE

Hypnosis usually includes an explicit contract between the hypnotist and the hypnotized subject, an agreement to be hypnotized for a designated time, and for a designated purpose. Spontaneous influence takes place without an explicit contract; therefore, these conditions don't apply. Although the dynamics look similar the rules governing time, purpose, and explicit awareness dissolve. One more critical difference also exists. In SIEs, suggestions are much more powerful because they are accepted *as* real, not *as if* they were real.

Clearly, one need not be a hypnotist to deliver a powerful suggestion. The elements of spontaneous influence occur regularly, making each of us potential architects of vulnerable psyches. I acted as an emotional guide during Kary's wart treatment. The goal of an emotional guide is to present constructive thoughts and images during the ESS. Because thoughts and images elicit *actual* reactions through the mirror neuron system, the likelihood of controlling a positive SIE increases exponentially. In Kary's situation, my constructions fuelled a genuine experience, moving her in a fruitful direction.

Is the story of Kary's wart recovery one of hypnosis or spontaneous influence? The emphatic answer: It is a clear illustration of spontaneous influence. If you were to ask her, "Were you hypnotized?" she'd say no. She didn't suspend her reality and participate in an *as if* construction. She found herself engrossed in an experience during elevated suggestibility with me as her guide. She'd been hypnotized before and she knows the difference, and now, to a large degree, so do you.

ARE YOU HYPNOTIZED?

Surely, you may think, if someone tried to hypnotize me I would know it and defend myself against it. Yes and no. You would probably identify it if the person designated as hypnotist was using what you would recognize as a traditional hypnotic induction: "As you begin to relax, you sense a heaviness in your body . . . and with each passing breath . . . " However, *hypnotic* effects might not enter your awareness if you were experiencing a naturally elevated suggestibility state. What if a potent authority figure (e.g., a parent, teacher, doctor, therapist, or any other commanding presence) presented powerful suggestions, in the form of commands, during an ESS? Or, what if the person delivering the suggestions was doing so indirectly or inadvertently? The following illustration provides just such a scenario. If you were the adult present, what would you do to turn this into a positive event?

Imagine a nine-year-old male child who is feeling sheepish about his sudden out-of-character outburst. An adult responds with, "You certainly have an explosive nature when things don't go your way." This seems like a relatively simple, common, and harmless exchange, but it bears all the elements of a SIE. The child's anxiety elevates his suggestibility. The imposing adult inadvertently delivers a powerful suggestion: "You have an explosive temper." Such an event may produce a dramatic effect, changing how the child feels about himself or how he sees the world. Such a phrase could easily induce a child into seeing himself as someone with an explosive temper.

The next time things don't turn out the way he hopes, he may exhibit another violent outburst, confirming the earlier pronouncement. If he doesn't explode, he'll just think he's a ticking time bomb waiting for the next inevitable uncontrolled episode. With his increased anxiety regarding his volatile temper, it is only a matter of time before he pops. When he does, as most young people do, he won't dismiss it, but rather, it will further embed itself in his neurological tracks as part of his identity.

Remember that ideas perpetuate themselves once they become lodged in a person's mind. What would you say in the same situation? The prudent adult, one who is aware of ESSs, acts carefully during such circumstances and responds with a neutral or constructive suggestion: "I'm glad you got that little outburst out of the way. Now you're better able to control such expressions in the future." This simple statement by an authority figure during an ESS engages the child in a belief that better control is inevitable in the future. It orients the child's mind toward creating a more appropriate means of managing outbursts.

You may be thinking that this last scenario is too contrived and over-simplified. Unfortunately it is not. This kind of event happens frequently. Consider these next two stories of actual events. Both events, although strikingly similar, generated dramatically different outcomes. Both illustrate powerful emotional reactions by children experiencing difficulty during a public speaking performance. Each episode depicts hypnotic-like elevated suggestibility followed by an implicit suggestion. The first one comes from one of my graduate students and reveals a negative SIE that occurred during High School, producing a dramatic effect on her life.[10]

Many years ago I had an English teacher who made a lasting impression on me. I can't remember her name but I remember the class very well. She was very prim and proper, and she saw herself as an exemplary role model for the students. This leads me to my most embarrassing moment.

One day we were to recite a poem to our classmates. I loved to talk in class and I never had a problem with public speaking. I had even run for class elections and given lots of speeches. I was not at all anxious about the recitation. During my turn I recited the first few lines perfectly, and then I said, ". . . to rape the drapes." (I should have said, ". . . to wrap the drapes.")

As soon as I uttered the words, I heard tumultuous laughter. It was coming from this prim and proper teacher. She said, "I knew someone would say that, but I never expected it to be you." I will never forget that feeling. In fact, since then I developed a fear of public speaking.

The teacher's response surprised and confused this student. The student's anxiety rose dramatically because of the embarrassing circumstances, triggering an ESS. Even though the teacher didn't provide a direct suggestion, this poorly managed episode left the student in a precarious and vulnerable situation. The student interpreted the event from a self-defeating perspective: "I am a poor public speaker, and speaking in groups causes embarrassment."

How might the student's sense of self-image have been different if the teacher had recognized the ESS and given a healthy healing suggestion? The teacher might have suggested something like the following: "All speakers make slips-of-the-tongue. You handled that situation like a seasoned veteran. You are an excellent speaker." Would the student have developed a phobia for public speaking? Probably not. To the contrary, the student may have developed a penchant for public speaking.

Contrast Jimmy's experience with the previous anecdote. Jimmy prepared a magnificent oratorical presentation for his scout troop's Parent Night.[11] He proudly delivered the first half flawlessly, beaming with confidence. The second half proved disastrous. He began to falter, lost confidence, fumbled with several words, and had to be prompted by the scoutmaster several times. Somehow he managed to finish, in spite of overwhelming embarrassment (an ESS). Humiliated, he made his way to his seat as the scoutmaster climbed to the podium. The scoutmaster beamed with pride as he described Jimmy's courage for making a glorious victory out of what could have turned to failure. He lauded Jimmy for continuing to the end, exemplifying the spirit of bravery and steadfast commitment. He painted Jimmy as a leader of the highest merit. A humble Jimmy accepted the obvious truth as the scoutmaster's description embedded itself in Jimmy's psyche.

In hypnosis, we can combat deliberate hypnotic suggestions because of their conspicuous nature. Because of their obvious nature, we can test, dismiss, or counter them. The inadvertent and subtle nature of SIEs makes them devastatingly more powerful precisely because they typically slip past our screening unnoticed.

SUBTLETY IS HARD TO DEFEND AGAINST

Subtle, inadvertent suggestions, absorbed during ESSs take hold unnoticed, making them deceptively powerful. Recall the stories of Cathy and Stephen in Chapter 1. Cathy changed from a discouraged student to an eager learner when her uncle commented, "Someone [like you] who struggles so hard with school will make a great teacher." Stephen changed from an intimated and uncertain student to one with confidence when he overheard his teacher tell his nurse, "He's not learning disabled, he's eccentric." Stephen credited that event as a turning point in his life.

Most of us remain unaware of the powerful effects inadvertent comments can make during ESSs. Few of us know what SIEs are and how to become consciously aware enough to spot them; hence, the opportunity to make the critical interventions necessary to remedy potentially negative suggestions remains elusive. If you think you'd simply recognize it when your behavior changes in response to a subtle command, think again. We all exhibit a human tendency to rationalize our behavior no matter what its origin.

OUR RATIONALIZATIONS KEEP US IN THE DARK

Through clever experiments, famed neuroscientist Michael Gazzaniga demonstrated how we instinctively create rational explanations to explain our unconscious behaviors. Gazzaniga worked with patients who had their cerebral hemispheres surgically separated as a treatment for severe epileptic seizures. Surgeons disconnect the side of the brain with language circuitry from the side that carries out simple commands.

Through ingenious manipulation of experimental conditions, Gazzaniga was able to give a simple command to one part of the brain without the response part knowing. He found that by giving the command "get up and walk" the patient would do so. But when asked why he was up and where he was going, the subject replied creatively, "I'm thirsty. I thought I'd get a Coke." When one hemisphere of the subject's brain was commanded to laugh, he did. When asked why he was laughing, he responded, "You guys crack me up" not, "Because you told me to."

After repeated trials, Gazzaniga concluded that many of our explanations about our behaviors are actually driven by the behavior itself. He believes that all of us do all sorts of things for reasons outside conscious awareness and that one of the main jobs of consciousness is to keep our lives tied together in an understandable and consistent package. We do this by generating explanations that best fit our self-image. We instinctively invent reasons to explain our behavior, but remain unaware that these are creations because they fit seamlessly into a self-perpetuating self-image.[12]

The question as to whether or not you've experienced a SIE is not an informed one. It reflects our naiveté on the subject of influence and development. Once you understand how SIEs work, you see them everywhere in your own life. Then you ask the more informed question "How can I manage them?" not, "Did I have one?"

✳✳✳

You are probably thinking, "I'm a rational person, interested in self-discovery. If spontaneous influence is so powerful and prominent, how could I miss such dramatic influence?" Spontaneous influence takes place at an emotional level and our emotions prefer to direct us without slowing the process through rational reflection. Besides, our innate process of rationalization gives us the false impression that we are in full control. The truth is we are actually manipulated by emotional triggers in our social and physical environment that affect our mood and attention, ultimately affecting our behavior.

The next chapter takes a brief departure from spontaneous influence to examine the nature of how emotions rule our behavior. This ultimately leads us to the conclusion that SIEs create emotional response systems that trigger a cascade of behaviors that unfold automatically.

Chapter 5

Emotion is the Rule: Rationality is the Tool

Spontaneous Influence Events (SIEs) occur at an emotional level, changing rational processes and behavior patterns outside awareness. Before you can appreciate how SIEs capture emotions and then reorient them, you must first understand emotions themselves, how they work, and why we have them. The following story illustrates how emotions rule our thoughts and behavior. Notice how emotions not only urge us to behave a certain way, they also dismiss logical prompts that dispute our emotional prodding. Strong emotions also command our reasoning apparatus to rationalize our behavior. (Note that the bulk of this chapter discusses our current scientific understanding of emotions. This information aids us in learning about spontaneous influence.)

One morning, our family noticed that our cat hadn't returned home the previous evening. Mildly concerned, we set out some of his favorite treats, hoping to find him sitting on our deck when we arrived home from work later that day. Sadly, our cat didn't return that day, or for many days thereafter.

Emotions of sadness prompted us to act. Previously, our cat had not traveled far from home. Nonetheless, we spent countless hours searching and placed posters at every store and on every light post within a 4 mile radius. We worried that he might have strayed far away and become lost. Several weeks later we received a report of a cat, similar to the description of ours, scavenging nightly for food in someone's backyard. Elated, we spent time and money to rent a cat-trap and placed it in this back yard. Rationally, we thought it a long shot. After all, this home was a few miles from ours; a very unlikely place for our cat to wander. Here, emotions overruled reason, prompted frivolous expenditures of resources, and triggered flimsy justifications like, "I know it's improbable, but what if . . . "

The next evening, we received a call. A cat had entered the trap. Our emotions soared with eager anticipation. Off we went with tears of relief and excitement in our eyes, anticipating a happy reunion. Unfortunately, it wasn't our pet. We experienced the rapid swing of emotions, peaked excitement to dismal disappointment. These powerful reactions not only prompted further action, they became associated with that location.

Where do you think we started searching during the next few days, and intermittently, over the next few weeks? You're right if you guessed that same neighborhood where the false sighting occurred. As I write this story, I can vividly recall the home, more than seven years ago, and I still look for an orange cat whenever I'm in that neighborhood. Rationally, the cat disappeared long ago and it is extremely unlikely that it strayed that far away. Emotionally, that location signifies where we felt most hopeful. Here again, emotional urging continues to win over reasonable behavior.[1] To this day, it is the only part of the city that reminds me of our lost pet, and I instinctively take a quick scan whenever I pass through that neighborhood.

I don't want to be reminded of our lost cat every time I go there, but I can't rationally will those thoughts away. Nonconscious, automatic mechanisms control these thoughts. That was the area where our emotional spotlight was shining, where we felt most optimistic. Emotions are the metaphorical carrots on sticks that lead us. They don't always lead us fruitfully, but they always garner our attention.

WHY HAVE EMOTIONS?

Emotions play a gatekeeper role in cognition. The allocation of attention and working memory do not happen by miracle. We attempt to solve problems that are only emotionally important to us. Think of emotions as a biological thermostat that activates attention, which then activates a rich set of problem-solving and response systems. When danger or opportunity arises, information from our senses triggers an emotional reaction that informs the rest of the brain that something requires further attention and maybe even some problem solving. Emotions operate unconsciously constantly evaluating sensory information from our total environment, even while we're asleep or attending to other things. When our emotions enter awareness, we call it a feeling, and then we can begin to consciously deal with the challenge using our reasoning abilities.

Humans survived for as long as we have in large part because we evolved a decision-making apparatus that is capable of making very quick judgments based on very little information. Malcolm Gladwell refers to this innate process as "thin slicing."[2] Psychologist Timothy D. Wilson draws an analogy of the mind to a jet liner's autopilot whereby the mind operates most efficiently by relegating a good deal of high-level, sophisticated thinking to the unconscious. "Emotions do an excellent job of sizing up the world, warning people of danger, setting goals, and initiating action in a sophisticated and efficient manner."[3]

Emotions evolved to guide us into productive behavior. Emotions are at the heart of an unconscious arousal system that triggers all sorts of conscious cognitive activity.[4] They urge us to flee this, seek that, mate with this, and eat that. Emotions don't take direction from our rational mechanism. They simply do most of their prodding beneath our conscious awareness. Our rational processes, located principally in our neocortex, actually evolved *from* our emotional brain, as emotion's tool, to do its bidding. The term "neo" means new. Renowned neuroscientist Antonio Damasio's research shows how emotions occur before cognitive awareness. Hence, emotions constitute a frame of reference for the cognition that follows, having a say in how cognition goes about its business.[5]

Emotions direct us in what to approach or avoid, consciously and unconsciously, and then turn these directives over to the planning department. If we were governments, our emotions would be the legislative branch, creating policy and determining direction. Our rational apparatus would be the executive branch, budgeting, allocating resources, and planning programs to implement the legislation.

Unless we make it our business to discern our true motives (a deceptively difficult job), emotions usually do their work behind the scenes. We don't command our brains to process data as much as we simply become aware of that which our brain has already processed, and subsequently activated. We typically believe that our intellect is in charge, but it is only an illusion. Think about the following scenario. Joe walks into the room. Your reaction depends on whether Joe is a fond friend, estranged brother, dangerous criminal, previous lover, or magnetic celebrity. Your emotional reaction erupts automatically, determining your behavior and thought processes. You aren't aware of your processing, nor did you will it. You can't even stop it once it starts. Your emotional response determined where your thoughts should go, and how you should behave. If Joe is a known criminal, a spontaneous fear response might trigger an urge to escape. Our rational mind will analyze the situation and decide how to get away, but the emotional response occurred first prompting a rational plan of escape.[6]

Reason evolved as a tool for our emotions, giving us the ability to shift from reaction to action.[7] The ability to learn, anticipate, and plan in the form of mental rehearsal gave us a huge evolutionary advantage, but we must continue to remember that our primitive emotions drive this advantage. This is why, in spite of incredible technological innovations, we continue to behave socially the same way we did millennia ago in the

African savanna. Yes, we can send a human to the moon, but wars, violence, crime, and sexual misconduct still distinguish our collective existence.

Emotions happen to us, an automatic reaction lying outside conscious control. We don't create our emotions after deliberations. Although we may be able to curb emotional expression and modify feelings once they become conscious, we cannot stop emotions nor directly determine which ones they will be. To some degree, we can anticipate, plan for, and manage events that may elicit anticipated emotional responses. For example, we can consciously plan events or situations that we hope will trigger positive emotions (like planning a festive occasion). We can also consciously avoid events we fear may trigger negative emotions (like refusing to go to a party your ex-partner will be attending). Yet, the actual emotions themselves lie outside our direct control.

In her book, *Molecules of Emotion*, Medical researcher Candice Pert shows how emotions don't just prompt you to behave a certain way willfully; emotions prod you to do something and actually begin the process.[8] Emotional signals act as emotional drives, propelling you in a direction without making their reasons clear. If the urge is strong enough, it enters consciousness and you recognize it as a feeling. Restraining an urge takes much more effort than fulfilling it, because fulfilling it is automatic while restraining it takes deliberate conscious effort. For example, a friend calls with news of a fantastic fare sale on an exotic holiday excursion. A moment of excitement flashes, followed instantly by rational thoughts racing through your mind: Where will I find the money? How can I get the time off work? Who will watch the kids? What conflicting plans do I need to cancel? All this happens in a mere moment. Note that the emotions initiate a cascade of rational thinking, moving toward fulfilling the goal. Emotions induce you to go; saying no requires a conscious intervention to dispute initial reactions.

The opposite is also true; emotions can urge you to *not* do something. Your emotional system creates feelings of stress, anxiety, or fear when it senses danger. For example, you may feel emotional prodding to *not* approach the boss for that raise you deserve, because of a fear of rejection. It often takes a concerted effort to approach an employer even when we are certain we deserve it. The *concerted effort* is a battle of your cognitive mind trying to dispute your emotional fear of rejection. Many of us give in to our emotional fear and never approach the boss, hoping that the boss sees, recognizes, and then rewards our superior contributions. At least that's what many of the timid among us hope for.

EMOTIONS ARE STRONGER THAN REASON

The brain forges many more neural connections from the amygdala (emotional) to the cortical areas (rational) than the reverse path.[9] This asymmetry gives emotions two advantages over thinking: priority in sequence and greater influence. This helps explain why emotional information captures our conscious thoughts so easily, yet the reverse, conscious control over our emotions, remains difficult at best. That makes evolutionary sense. After all, our emotional apparatus evolved over thousands of years, helping us survive as a species. On the other hand, our conscious reasoning processes are only as old as our life time, and only as sound as our personal lessons in life. Emotions govern us in important situations because of their superior survivability.

Highly charged events not only capture attentional mechanisms and organize our rational systems, they also keep them vigilant for a considerable length of time. This partly explains why it is so hard to concentrate and work efficiently when highly aroused. Maintaining vigilance serves a purpose when facing real danger but results in a prolonged distraction after a false alarm. The following relatively common incident illustrates this quite well.

A dangerous motorist boldly cuts you off: Pow! You experience a full sympathetic nervous system response of elevated heart rate, increased adrenaline flow, increased blood flow to skeletal muscles, and rapid breathing for increased oxygen intake. Mentally too, images of the driver consume your thoughts: "What a dangerous fool. He could kill somebody. I hope the highway patrol locks him up and throws away the key." You'll watch the offending car darting in and out of traffic until it's out of view. Finally it's gone, but you can't remember what you were talking about before the interruption. While it may take less than a second for rage to erupt, it will take much longer for your nervous system to return to its previously calm, homeostatic condition.

EMOTIONS VALIDATE THEMSELVES

Your emotional tone sets your attentional agenda and then demands that your logical processes explain and validate your response. Consider the following scenario. Two colleagues at work give presentations. One colleague is a friend and the other is an insufferable co-worker. You focus on the strengths of your friend's presentation, dismissing any apparent weaknesses. At the same time, you focus on weaknesses in your rival's presentation, disregarding the strengths. You can't help it, although you might rationally think you can. It takes an enormous amount of conscious energy, awareness, and vigilance to suspend this natural predisposition.

Emotions instinctively collect supportive evidence while simultaneously discounting contrary evidence. This is what makes it so hard to reason with someone who is emotionally upset. Your argument, no matter how logical and sound, carries no authority if it is out of sync with the emotional tone of the moment. Feelings are self-justifying, generating their own beliefs and support. Professor Leslie Brothers, in the Department of Psychiatry and Behavioral Sciences at the UCLA School of Medicine, illustrates this point by describing the sense of being ostracized. "Once the amygdala sets certain patterns into motion, these may feed back to the sensory cortex to create a bias on the information being received. On a behavioral level, once someone begins to feel left out, benign social gestures may be perceived as unfriendly and one starts to feel disparaged. The cycle continues."[10]

Many times our feelings are so vague and subtle that we don't even notice our emotional response, even though it discreetly influences our thoughts and actions.[11] Imagine you haven't seen your old high-school classmate in 15 years, but you remember him as a charming manipulator, smooth and cunning, always with an ulterior motive. Cindy, another classmate remembers him fondly as a helpful friend, always looking out for his buddies. You introduce him to your new friends and he makes a grand impression of sincere selflessness, leaving a business card for his budding computer service. You discourage your friends from using his computer service, cautioning them that he is really just a selfish scoundrel, charming yes, but self-serving. Cindy recommends him, suggesting he "does that little extra" that makes him approachable and reliable. Each of you thinks you know him better than the other. Cindy thinks you're jealous and bitter. You think Cindy is naive and seduced by his empty charm. Our feelings lead, generating explanations from our rational processes to justify themselves. In essence, our innate proclivity to rationalize and justify our emotions leads us to a conviction that we know *exactly* what's going on. At such moments the emotional mind has entrained the rational mind to its own use.

Even though our emotional tone sets our attentional agenda, we typically explain our emotional responses as if the rational thoughts occurred first, putting the cart before the horse. We do this because subtle emotional prompting typically occurs outside awareness, while deliberation is a purely conscious act. Consequently, lacking awareness of our emotions, we believe our thinking occurred first.[12] Even if emotions reach the threshold of consciousness to become noticeable feelings, we understand them rationally, once again giving our thoughts apparent priority.

EMOTIONAL STAMPING

By now, you are probably wondering just how emotions guide behavior in a seemingly rational way. Emotions do their prodding by stamping events with simple values. Examining a simple form of such stamping will help illustrate how this works.

Unconscious dispositions lie at the core of decision making in many species. Automatic mechanisms build biases into the organism's action devices, prompting them to behave in a particular way, which may appear to the casual observer as a choice. This is, in all likelihood, how worker bumblebees *choose* which flowers they should light upon to obtain the nectar they need to bring back to the hive. Studying how simpler organisms perform seemingly complicated tasks with modest neural machinery can teach us how mechanisms of a similar nature may operate in us too.

Worker bees are equipped with a visual apparatus that allows them to distinguish the colors of flowers. As recent investigations have demonstrated, worker bees learn, after a few visits to flowers of different colors, which are more likely to contain nectar. They do not land on every possible flower to discover whether nectar is available. After sampling several differently colored flowers, they are able to successfully predict which flowers are more likely to have nectar and land on flowers of that color more frequently. Bees *appear* to formulate probabilities. How can bees, with their modest nervous systems, produce behavior that looks so rational, indicating the use of knowledge, probability theory, and a goal-oriented strategy?

Bees have a neurotransmitter system similar to the dopamine system in mammals. When the reward (nectar) is detected, the system alters basic behavior. As a result, during subsequent passes, the bee is prone to land on the flower of a specific color, and the bee is more likely to find nectar. The bee is, in fact, making a choice, not consciously nor deliberately, but rather using an automated framework that incorporates a preference.[13] Unconscious emotions also drive human behaviors in a similar manner.

Like the bees, we also have a preference-making system (reward) that shapes behavior, dependent on acquired experiences. This is the essence of learning. Our experiences and our responses to events, if they are to be adaptive, must be evaluated and shaped to serve the organism's survival. Evaluation and shaping are vital for success. Neurotransmitters simply stamp every element of our experience as good or bad. The *goodness* or *badness* of situations then shapes subsequent behavior. SIEs are stamped with the proverbial sledge hammer, leaving an indelible impression by initiating a cascade of dramatic changes that profoundly affect the person's outlook and self-image.

Bear in mind that these values are contextual to some degree, and can therefore be manipulated (a tiger in a zoo is valued differently than a tiger in your tent). Having pliable values are the main reason it is important to have a positive emotional guide during, or immediately after, a SIE. The information content provided by arousal systems is weak.[14] Arousal systems simply say that something important is going on. When arousal occurs, for whatever reason, the environment is scanned for cognitive assessment. Weak content means that someone present at the time, or shortly thereafter, can put a positive spin on dramatic events, shaping subsequent values. The unpredictable profile of encounters each individual experiences, and the personal reactions to their contexts ultimately shape the individual's subsequent inclinations. These inclinations are called *response dispositions*[15] because they compel you to respond a certain way.

Events can remodel some response dispositions over and over throughout our life span, according to changes we experience. Others remain mostly stable and form the backbone of the notions we have constructed about our self-image and outlook.

A NEUROLOGICAL DIARY

Emotions alert our mind/body to pay attention and remember: "Something significant is happening here." It does this by stamping the event with a neurological prompt.[16] Some reaction from our emotional apparatus accompanies virtually every object or situation in our experience, real or remembered. These neural cues connect events with a body state, pleasant or unpleasant. Dramatic, subtle, or unconscious urges then direct us to behave in what our prompts read as our *best interest.*[17]

Antonio Damasio, noted neurologist, refers to these prompts as *somatic markers* because they have to do with the body (soma) and they leave their mark. These somatic markers (SM) automatically guide future behavior. We often refer to these quite appropriately as "gut feelings." SIEs can radically and instantly shift a whole constellation of somatic markers, dramatically affecting subsequent behavior.

Somatic markers focus attention on outcomes of behavior, functioning as warning alarms or enticement beacons. These markers eliminate some behavior alternatives automatically while highlighting others that look promising.[18] These urges protect you from future losses while maximizing the possibility for success. These signals can work entirely outside conscious awareness by altering working memory, attention, and reasoning. By controlling these functions, they bias the decision making toward selecting actions from past experience that were most productive. Think of somatic markers as your subliminal survival investment counselor.

This counselor is extremely conservative; it's your life at stake here, not just a portfolio. The counselor's conservative underpinnings come from thousands of years of education (evolution) but are tempered with a keen eye on current market conditions (learned responses). The role of this internal counselor is to instantly eliminate any choices that may ruin you, while simultaneously recommending those that will undoubtedly bring the best yield. If only stock markets were so clear, we'd all be rich. Alas, the market choices (behavior alternatives) are usually cloudy, and the best the counselor can do is make recommendations. There are numerous choices available, so our counselor trims the list, sifting for us, deleting options we would never consider anyway by not even bringing them to our attention. Ultimately we decide according to our comfort level. Of course the information our counselor gives us influences our comfort level. While we like to call our portfolio rational, it is ultimately run by a powerful, underground, emotional lobby that works hard to promote its interest. Like all effective investment counselors, this one works behind the scenes and only calls when something big is going on in the market place. This keeps you from being continually distracted, allowing you to get your routine work done.

BEHIND-THE-SCENES OF A SOMATIC MARKER

Emotions lead us. We can't get away from that. Men in particular like to think they are rational creatures, forgetting that their emotions, in the form of drives and urges, actually set their direction. Once our emotions determine the direction of our behavior, we may make hosts of rational decisions about how to achieve our goal, but our emotions determine the goal.

The depiction below gives a metaphorical representation of how your somatic markers prompt attention. The abbreviated list itemizes "Things to Do On a Saturday Night." Both lists are identical. The first list is what Carmen symbolically sees, while the second list shows what Jamil figuratively views.

<u>Carmen</u>

Dancing, cruise local pubs, ***piano Bar***, poker with friends, ***walk in the woods***, monster truck rally, ***romantic movie with partner***, shooting range, ***symphony***, wrestlemania, ***music festival***, car show, ***home show***, work on car, ***read new novel***, suspense thriller flick,

<u>Jamil</u>

Dancing, ***cruise local pubs***, piano Bar, ***poker with friends***, walk in the woods, ***monster truck rally***, romantic movie with partner, ***shooting range***, symphony, ***wrestlemania***, music festival, ***car show***, home show, ***work on car***, read new novel, ***suspense thriller flick***.

Completing the following exercise will help illustrate this important point. Examine the list below and choose an ideal vacation from this list. Do it quickly before reading further. Imagine that you won this prize in a game show and that you must pick a vacation but you only have 30 seconds to decide. Set your watch for 30 seconds before you begin. Use a pencil or highlighter if you like. You would probably do reasonably well in 10 seconds if that was all you were allotted.[19]

Water skiing	Scuba diving	Spelunking
Shopping in New York	Mecca	Hunting Big Game
Fishing in Alaska	Disneyland	Gambling in Monaco
Plays on Broadway	The Holy Land	Caribbean cruise
Quiet beach in Hawaii	Las Vegas	Taj Mahal
Golf in Scotland	Rock climbing	Hiking Everest
Club Med	Trek in the Antarctic	China
African Photo Safari	Greece	Skiing in Banff

You made a choice based on your emotions, what appealed to you (approach) and what didn't (avoid). Asking you to make a rational choice from the list above would be fruitless. Imagine that I presented this list to a group of thirty adults and instructed them to choose the most rational vacation. The debate could conceivably last forever without resolution. No rational best choice exists. No one vacation is rationally better than another.

However, once you make your emotionally driven choice (which vacation *feels* right), your rational processes now work toward your emotionally determined goal. You shop around for best departure dates, arrange time off from work, pick hotels, select from competing airlines, and so on. Once the emotional compass is set, the rational mechanism executes without question.

Let's go back and examine how you picked your preference. Most people scan the list quickly, checking those that appeal to you most, ignoring those you'd never consider. Now, with a smaller list, you scan them again, reducing them further, and so on. Somatic markers operate by reducing the playing field to a manageable size so that your deliberation process can begin. Even if you read slowly and examined each vacation separately, your emotions still led you. If a vacation appealed to you (emotional) you probably rationalized with a positive thought (e.g., "A quiet beach sounds great. I could catch up on my reading and soak up the sun."). If a choice didn't appeal to you (emotional) you instinctively dismissed it with a rational explanation. We respond, "Shopping—Yech! I don't like crowds." (Emotional to rational). We do not respond, "Shopping? I don't like crowds; therefore, Yech!" (Rational to emotional).

This process goes on 24/7, usually outside conscious awareness. Humans did not evolve to respond rationally first. Each choice stimulated an emotional tag (approach or avoid) that automatically triggered a rational explanation that validates itself.

Let's examine this whole process with a more common scenario. Remember, this takes place faster than the time it will take to read the next paragraph.

Your spouse says, "Let's get away for the weekend." You might be drawn to the ocean, and your spouse to the mountains. You might be drawn toward excitement and your spouse might be drawn toward relaxation.

You might be drawn toward roughing it in a tent and your spouse drawn toward a pampering hotel. Like many couples, my wife and I have polar opposite ideas on how to take a weekend off. Regardless, it is our somatic markers that prompt our first response, promoting an instantaneous reaction, followed by such rational considerations as sorting out costs, arrangements, and accommodations for our partner's preferences. Still, our initial response predisposes us to debate the merits of our first choice strongly, seeing the strong points of our preferences while simultaneously diminishing opposing choices. It's as if the initial suggestion, "Let's get away for a weekend," cued the automatic logical defense of our instinctual (emotional) first choice, including supporting evidence, initial planning, and convincing arguments to fend off opposing points of view.

Ultimately, we perform this same process on a smaller scale whenever we order a donut from a display counter containing a variety of twenty choices. Which is the rational best choice? We do the same when we order dinner from a menu. Rationality (fat content, MSG, high sodium) may help narrow the field, but eventually we pick because of an emotionally driven preference, what we *feel* like.

PURE REASON ISN'T ENOUGH

We often appeal to each other, "Be reasonable," promoting reason as a common-sense approach that puts us at our decision-making best. This point of view suggests that emotions must be kept out of sound decision making. But if reasoning is the only strategy we use, expedient decisions aren't going to take place. At the very least, the decision making will take an inordinate amount of time because we have so many factors to consider.

The pure reason process advocated by Plato and Descartes is really more like the strategy patients with cortical prefrontal damage use to make decisions.[20] Several forms of dementia plagued my father before he passed away. He had lost considerable access to his value system. Before advanced dementia, he always chose an O'Henry chocolate bar as a sweet treat. In the latter years, when I took him to a candy counter, he would scan the display for several minutes, reaching, hesitating, and finally choosing. He never chose an O'Henry bar, and the process seemed to take an eternity. I'm sure his final choice was based on giving up and taking the most appealing package within reach. It appeared that he lost the ability to make value-based decisions. When faced with a value-based choice between several competing selections, his decision-making landscape appeared hopelessly flat.

From an expedient point of view, it is much more adaptive to have some form of neurological device that automatically stamps a subjective value onto our experiences. Without a value system, what would we do about hair style, choice of fashion, shoes, color of shirt, or music preference?

How would your friends respond if you told them they were your most rational choice for relationships? Don't even think about this for your spouse.

CONTINUAL EMOTIONAL VIGILANCE IS EXHAUSTING

It would be disruptive, let alone mentally exhausting, to feel the continual tug of emotions all the time. It's more adaptive to let somatic markers guide our behavior subconsciously and only take notice of critical events, when big opportunities or obstacles stimulate us.

Imagine walking into the lunch room at work where someone has prepared a selection of donuts for a coffee break. You approach the platter, licking your lips, feeling a glimmer of pleasure as you see your favorite is still available. Just as you begin to reach for it, someone ahead of you takes it. You experience a tinge of disappointment. Just then another platter of donuts arrives and you get your selection after all. Now you feel a hint of satisfaction. The event I described here is hardly a roller coaster ride of emotions, yet most of us identify with this common scenario. It would seem strange to experience the feelings in this scenario as dramatic mood swings. As most of our emotions never make it to the threshold of consciousness the vast majority of us remain unaware that they even happen at all.

We spend most of our days in relatively low arousal situations. Chronic arousal just wears us out mentally and physically. Part of the Desert Storm strategy was to bombard Saddam's troops twenty-four hours a day for several days. Bomb blasts produced few casualties, but the blasts continually aroused the troops' fight-flight responses continually for extended periods. Disoriented troops surrendered by the thousands. A state of continual emotional arousal exhausts us physiologically and cognitively. Our rational apparatus works best during relatively calm periods of low stimulation.

Even in highly arousing environments, our biological regulatory devices try to habituate to our surroundings by finding predictability. Hence the saying, "The devil you know is better than the devil you don't know." The devil you know is at least predictable, providing some sort of regulatory comfort.

Most of us spend the bulk of our days in low arousal situations, with only minor disruptions to our homeostasis (physiological "all systems okay"). During these low arousal times, when our emotions are not firing alarm bells or lighting incentive beacons, our emotions are working nonetheless. When not called on to make sudden critical decisions, our emotions work beneath consciousness, allocating attention and evaluating everything we do or think as pleasant or unpleasant. Our emotions, at a subliminal level, set the tone of our thinking, neurologically prompting behavior through our response dispositions. These response dispositions become vulnerable during Elevated Suggestibility States (ESSs) triggered by extreme emotional arousal.

FAST TRACKS TO CHANGE

Spontaneous Influence Events shift our response dispositions. While these influence events are themselves momentous, we may hardly notice the cascade of changes that occur or we may not even notice them at all. During SIEs, the brain makes these indelible neural connections with emphasis because the brain is expedient and efficient. It's as if the brain realizes, "This is too important to think about. Bypass the conscious mechanisms so that they can't interfere, and lock in a new response disposition. Right now!"

Scientists now know we have two response systems when it comes to regulating our impulsiveness. The *fast reflexive* system earned its name because it acts swiftly, bypassing cortical systems, proceeding without conscious consideration. This system evolved to deal with dangers and opportunities that were immediate: act quickly or die or lose a fleeting opportunity for resources (food, mating, status, etc.). The *slow reflective* system solves challenges that permit a rational reflection. The slower system evolved to make considerations among alternatives during low-stress, less demanding periods of time. But even this reasoning is influenced by emotional associations that we're not aware of.

In an interview, prolific cognitive research author Dr. Robert Sylwester, briefly described the fast system: "The reflexive system is triggered by a strong emotional impulse, and it proceeds hell-bent without checking things out with the rational reflective cortical system." Later in the interview, he commented, "The fast reflexive system is obviously the default system because it keeps us alive and well fed, whereas the reflective system may only help us decide which necktie to purchase."[21]

SIEs add new repertoires of response dispositions. When moments similar to the original SIE occur, the response from that event (now a response disposition) takes over automatically. Our cognitive system follows with planning to further execute, maintain, and then rationalize this emotionally driven response. As Antonio Damasio states, "Nature is not that inventive when it comes to successful solutions. Once it works, it tries it again and again."[22] While this system is fast and efficient, it can, and often does create folly and even worse.

SOMATIC MARKERS CAN ALSO SABOTAGE OUR BEST INTEREST

Even though we need somatic markers (SMs), they can easily interfere with our best interests by creating self-defeating behavior that ultimately sabotages our quality of life. Sometimes we know rationally what is best, but feel emotionally compelled to do something else. Our emotional compulsions typically win even when we often know they are wrong for us. The following anecdotes help illustrate this point.

As a psychological intern in forensic psychology, I once worked with an unemployed client on probation. The client's wife of five years had left him, taking their only daughter with her, leaving him bitter and spiteful. Although employable, he continued to sabotage all efforts to find work. When he got jobs, he would inevitably show up late, fight with the boss, or miss days without calling in sick. Regular employment would have certainly eased his dreary subsistence and improved his standing with the probation officer. Throughout the process of therapy, his pathetic twisted logic became clear. As long as he was unemployed, he wouldn't have to pay support to the family who had abandoned him. His anger, indignation, and humiliation at being abandoned severely disabled his rational capacity. Our biological drives and emotional proddings are essential for our survival and guidance in rational planning and decision making. However, they can debilitate our rational thought in some circumstances by creating an overriding bias against seemingly intelligent choices.

We are all guilty of similar behaviors, yet discovering them remains difficult due to our inherent predisposition to rationalize our perceptions. I once worked with a reprehensible colleague whose lack of moral and ethical behavior alienated me. He recently spoke at a convention I attended. During the presentation, I found myself mentally disputing his evidence and attacking his position without even rationally considering it. His shady character and lack of integrity offended me to such a degree that I found refuge in taking the opposite position to the one he espoused. It's as if I instinctively concluded that his position was wrong before he had even started, assuming that the opposite position must consequently have merit. My emotions ruled my choice, disarming my ability to rationally examine his presentation.

Irrational acts don't just sabotage us. They can also make us heroes, lovers, and benevolent benefactors. The qualities we admire most in others are their emotional ones, not their intellectual ones. Rarely does intellect alone inspire romantic acts or heroic deeds. The television mini-series *Lonesome Dove* was a big hit in the 1980s. Two rugged Texas Rangers shared a life together that eventually led them from Texas to Montana where they made their fortune from a cattle drive. One partner died and the other promised to personally return the body to Texas; an incredible sacrifice. From a rational point of view, the dead partner wouldn't know where he was buried; he was already dead. The surviving partner's friends thought his promise was foolish. They pressured him to ship the body to Texas by train. No rational argument would ever win this battle, and if it had, the movie would have lost its charm.

Any altruistic behavior is hardly utilitarian for the person performing the act. If it is utilitarian, then the act is self-serving and not altruistic. Those who perform truly altruistic acts do so because it produces a gratifying feeling. Why? Most parents praised us in our youth: "You're a good girl/boy." That approval, praise, and sense of belonging felt pleasant and embedded itself in our reward system. Our somatic markers, in the form of a gratifying feeling, continue to urge us toward altruistic behavior. When we help or support others now, we re-experience the satisfaction of following those prompts.

※※※

As instinctive spin-doctors of our beliefs and experiences, we make the unbiased discovery of our own personalized world view immensely difficult. We typically use our reasoning ability to justify our behavior, rather than examine it. We are emotional creatures who use rational tools. Emotion is the rule—rationality is the tool. Now that we see how emotions and SIEs shape our lives, we can examine the elements of spontaneous influence to manage them. Chapter 6 uncovers each of these powerful components.

We all hope that those we love, particularly our children, will be lucky enough to experience many powerfully positive influence events, moments that create a positive and self-fulfilling mind-set. At the same time we shiver in horror at the thought of our loved ones experiencing a dramatically negative influence event, one that robs them of vitality, spinning them into a destructive self-perpetuating cycle. Identifying the critical elements of spontaneous influence shows us how to manage these powerful shaping events.

Chapter 6

Elements of Spontaneous Influence

I begin this chapter with a personal anecdote that contains all of the elements of spontaneous influence. While all the elements occur in this singular episode, SIEs may still occur when only some of them are present. Think of a particular baseball game that doesn't include some of the following aspects: a triple, grand slam, or perfect game. Even without these hallmarks of baseball, the match is still a legitimate contest nonetheless. In the same way, spontaneous influence may take place without all the elements being present.

This personal event took place shortly after my formal training in hypnosis 25 years ago. During those early years, I participated in a variety of classes, seminars, and workshops that promoted a wide variety of healing arts. Dr. Rudy Lynn, an internationally acclaimed chiropractor, was coming to town for a workshop. Even though I was not a chiropractor, through connections, I garnered an invitation to the exclusive three-day affair.

I started the workshop bubbling with eager anticipation, excited to be included in this prominent audience of forty health care workers. During the three-day clinic, I sat amazed with his electrifying delivery, hearty laughter, and heartwarming tales. He captivated our imagination with compelling tales from his extraordinary practice. A bearded gentleman with more than 30 years of experience, his imposing, yet paternal presence provided a feeling of intimacy, like a Santa Claus figure.

He opened the workshop with a promise to give all the participants a quick chiropractic neck adjustment at the end of the workshop. At the end of the three days, as the workshop came to a close, the time for the adjustments arrived. The host invited us one at a time to seat ourselves on a chair at the front of the room. As Dr. Lynn slowly manipulated the participant's head from side to side, he continued to describe procedures, tell stories, and laugh enthusiastically. Then suddenly he would stop, sometimes mid-sentence, as if he'd discovered some critical feature in the participant's body. Fascinated, we all awaited his diagnostic pronouncement. Instead, he would make a declaration about that person's character and what positive lot he or she would inevitably find in life: "I can tell by the alignment in C5 that this person finds it easy to work well with difficult patients, and in fact thrives on these challenges—Ha ha!" He always delivered these declarations just as he gave the head a sudden twist; an action that always produced eerie snapping and popping sounds. Whack! He'd clap his hands loudly. The wide-eyed participant would then blink a few times, arise and thank Dr. Lynn.

I was one of the last to be called. When the attendant called my name, I felt the adrenaline surge through my body; the cracking sounds from previous attendants made me apprehensive to say the very least. I pushed my anxiety aside and joined Dr. Lynn in the front of the room. As I sat there, listening intently, he continued in the same fashion he'd done with the others. Slowly my resistance diminished. I began to relax and allow him to move my head freely, loosening the muscles for the inevitable cracking to come. Shortly after letting go, he stopped and concentrated on a small muscle on the side of my neck. He said, "Now this is interesting. This man will always achieve more than simple appearances indicate. Ha ha!"[1] A sudden twist of my neck—Snap!—Whack!—a loud clap, and I was escorted back to my seat. That was 25 years ago and I still remember it like it happened yesterday.

My Elevated Suggestibility State (ESS) and his carefully crafted pronouncement created a SIE. Some readers may be wondering what effect it had. Do I indeed achieve much more than my appearances indicate? Herein lies a critical point; I don't know, and it doesn't matter. It isn't important what others think, and I'll never know with any certainty. *I* believe I have. I've already surpassed my grandest plans in almost every aspect of my life. Even if I didn't, my belief that I have makes all the difference. Note also the intentional vagueness of his shrewd comment. Was Dr. Lynn referring to my intellectual, academic, financial, physical, creative accomplishments, or all of them? He created a perception in me that became self-perpetuating. I describe and teach these important tools and strategies in the final chapters.

That workshop also launched another important journey. I enrolled in the workshop to learn about chiropractic medicine. Instead, that captivating influence event thrust me in a new direction. Shortly thereafter, I began the academic, experimental, and anecdotal quest to uncover the critical elements of spontaneous influence. The culmination of that quest is this book.

Dr. Lynn was truly a magnificent influence agent with a unique style for inducing soaring susceptibility that in turn enabled him to initiate life-changing affirmations. While Dr. Lynn was certainly aware of his influence, he was probably unaware of the separate elements that played a role in his marvelous ability.[2] I discuss each of those elements in this chapter: psychological transference (authority), rapport, absorption in imagery (intense focus), dependence, and emotional arousal. Before I address each of these elements separately, this next section briefly illustrates how I experienced them collectively in the context of the workshop.

THE TOTAL PACKAGE

Authority: Before I even met the man, I heard about his brilliant presentations. Many associates considered him a leader in his field. My registration for the workshop signified a willing eagerness to accept him as an authority. His appearance, age, gestures, and storytelling expertise further enhanced his presence as a powerful authority figure (psychological transference).

Rapport: He kept us enthralled in his presentation by telling compelling stories on topics we collectively came to learn about. His warm receptive manner generated a sense of shared confidence and understanding. As the time passed, feelings of rapport deepened.

Absorption: His vivid storytelling absorbed the audience in imagery. Story, after gripping story heightened interest, keeping us fixated while anticipating the next stimulating anecdote. As a highly animated and gifted storyteller, Dr. Lynn kept our imagination engaged throughout the workshop.

Dependence: The audience came to hear him because he had knowledge and experience that we lacked. That dynamic itself bears a degree of intellectual dependence. We also experienced physical dependence during the head manipulations when we surrendered the muscular control of our necks, allowing him to manipulate our heads without any resistance.

Emotional Arousal: Watching workshop participants receive chiropractic neck adjustments with the inevitable eerie cracking sounds certainly arouses one's anxiety. Imagine that your turn arrives. With your anxiety already activated, it now deepens as you make your way to the front of an eager audience. You now have eighty sets of eyes trained on you with rapt attention. You can feel your anxiety, excitement, and anticipation growing. Even the stage hardy veteran would surely feel the flutter of butterflies in his stomach. Emotional arousal sufficiently entrenched—Crack!—Seed firmly planted.

Previous illustrations of spontaneous influence in this text emphasized their inadvertent nature, without the agent or recipient aware of the momentous change about to take hold. Dr. Lynn used a myriad of strategies to generate conditions to raise susceptibility, boost it further, and then implant a suggestion during a brief window of opportunity. He knew exactly *what* he was doing, although the *how* of it was unlikely. Unlike Dr. Lynn, you don't need an entire weekend with a captivated audience to initiate spontaneous influence, nor do you need all the factors that were present during his workshop. Chapters 8 and 9 describe in detail how to create and manage spontaneous influence. For now, this chapter continues with a deeper examination of the principal elements that Dr. Lynn manipulated artfully.

TRANSFERENCE: LIKE YOUR PARENTS DID

Before reaching success with her own clothing line, high fashion designer Vera Wang worked as a design director for Ralph Lauren. At age 42, she decided to leave Ralph and start on her own. When she told Ralph of her decision, he listened patiently before he responded. She remembers his words clearly, but nothing else. Shocked by his response, she can't even remember how she responded, if at all. He said, "I never say this to anybody so you'd better take it seriously. Although I don't want you to go, I understand. So hear these words and take them to heart. If anyone ever doubts you, if you're discouraged or frightened, always remember that you have talent. Never forget that." Reflecting back on that moment Vera says, "To hear that kind of encouragement at such a crucial moment was nothing short of overwhelming."[3]

No doubt others hailed her talent long before Ralph. Friends, relatives, and colleagues most certainly commended her ability and vision many times before that fateful day with Ralph. It wasn't the words themselves that bolstered her confidence; rather, it was who said them, a potent authority figure whom she looked up to.

Psychologists use the term "psychological transference" to describe the process whereby we respond to someone as an important and powerful parental figure in the same way that we related to our own parents when we were very young. (The rumbling you just felt in the ground is Freud rolling over in his grave as I oversimplify a concept on which he wrote volumes.) When we were very young, our parents appeared commanding and godlike. We were small, ignorant and powerless; they were large, possessors of all knowledge, and powerful beyond our imaginings. During those early years we developed an automatic attitude that mythically perceived our parents as omniscient. This set of instinctive attitudes stays with us and operates spontaneously, usually outside our awareness. Transference refers to how, in later life, we often unconsciously project this attitude onto other people, usually authority figures.

Freud described this process as a fundamental feature of the therapeutic relationship. Those of you not trained in psychoanalytic theory will likely remember the feelings you had toward your early teachers. After all, parents spend much of their time teaching and teachers spend much of their time parenting. For most of us, teachers were our first transference recipients. Before we got to school we looked to our parents to nurture, guide, discipline, and educate us. They were our models for interpreting and responding to adult authority figures. When schooling began, we looked to our early teachers the same way, projecting this dynamic onto our new relationship.[4] Teachers in the early grades reflect this projected role, accepting their role as transference figure and in turn treating their students as their children (Freud called this counter-transference).[5]

Many of us reared in Western civilization might experience Santa Claus as a collective transference figure. Other frequent transference recipients include physicians, therapists, experts in a field, scientists, religious leaders, your 6 o'clock news anchor, and in many cases your boss. Many of us want to please our bosses, looking to them for approval, feeling shame if we disappoint them, trying to get into their favor. Walking into the boss's office to request a raise may still stir anxiety akin to the way we felt when we tentatively asked our parents for an unlikely privilege: "Please, please! This is really, really important. I promise I'll be responsible and get home on time."

When we were very young, our parents made a statement and we accepted it uncritically. Many of us still respond to physicians' pronouncements in that same way. Extreme examples make these phenomena more visible, but similar accounts occur regularly along a continuum from minor to sensational.

Eminent pediatric surgeon and author Bernie S. Siegel illustrates the following two medical episodes in his book *Peace, Love, and Healing*.[6] In the first episode, Dr. Lown was taking his interns on rounds. Arriving beside a critically ill patient's bedside he pointed to the patient describing his conditions as "a wholesome, very loud third-sound gallop" in his heart. Medically, this means the heart is failing because of a badly damaged cardiac muscle. However, the patient made an amazing return to health, explaining to Dr. Lown at a three-month check up: He knew he'd recover when he heard his heart had a strong kick, like a horse. The second example is not as positive. Once again, in this illustration, Dr. Lown was making rounds with his students. Lown referred to one particular patient's condition by the initials TS (tricuspid stenosis). He stated authoritatively, "This is a classic case of TS." Just before leaving, Lown and his interns noticed severe distress in the patient; her pulse had elevated and her previously clear lungs started filling with fluids. Upon inquiry, Lown discovered that the patient thought he had stated definitively that she had a, "Terminal Situation." Her condition was minor, but all reassurances proved futile; by nightfall the patient had gone into acute heart failure and died.

Emotional arousal usually escalates as a physician approaches with a pronouncement. Will it be good news or bad? These moments in movies are always filled with dramatic music, building a sense of anticipation. Couple elevated suggestibility with weighty words from a significant transference figure and the elements of spontaneous influence emerge. Medical literature is replete with such examples. Less dramatic but more common examples of influence from other authority figures occur frequently.

Transference figures such as teachers may also produce devastating or inspiring effects on children. In the following illustration, the teacher described the event and even commented on the student's receptive demeanor.[7] The teacher described the student as "at-risk, attentive, with great insights into literature, but failing due to poor work habits and a lack of effort." On one occasion the teacher approached the young man and asked if he'd ever been tested for learning disabilities. When he said no, she replied adamantly with, "I'm going to do something about this. There is no reason for you to be failing English. You are very bright!" The teacher then described his reaction: "His face took on an astonished look. The words seem to hang in the air as I spoke them." Although the testing revealed no learning disability, he became a different student in class and began to steadily improve. She credited the student's improvement to the influence of her weighty words and her caring manner. The look on his face indicated emotional arousal of some form, elevating his suggestibility.

The previous story was told from the teacher's point of view. The following destructive episode was recalled from the student's perspective. It also illustrates how words from an authority figure can carry inordinate sway. Notice too, an imposing tone from the authority figure may initiate elevated suggestibility by profoundly arousing emotions in the recipient.

Mary adored her teacher. In her own words, "Teachers were as close to God as I'd ever gotten." One day it all changed. The teacher accepted an assignment from Mary and then started to yell at her. "In front of the whole class, she said my clothes were awful, my hair was a mess, my handwriting was bad, my papers were generally horrible, and I smelled."

When Mary reported this story to me, she was a middle-aged mother in graduate school. When asked to express how this episode influenced her life, she wrote the following.

> I have given this much thought through the years and come up with the following probable effects:
>
> - I have a terrible fear of elementary teachers. During teacher conferences for my children, I do not actively participate. I just listen.
> - Since that time I rarely turned in a paper in cursive. I always printed or typed assignments. My mother claims I don't write as much as I draw each letter carefully.

- I've become an overachiever. According to my husband, I give 110% to everything I do. I'm always trying to please, looking for a shred of positive recognition.

- My self-esteem is low. I long for the feeling of total success which I never find, in spite of inordinate effort. I always strive for perfection. Accordingly, I always note my shortcomings before others can.

This experience was especially significant in my life. I try to leave it behind and move on, but somehow it always stays with me.

I've used the term transference recipient and authority figure interchangeably so far. I'll clarify this in Chapter 7 when I examine authority in greater depth. For now, I will progress to the second element of successful influence agents: rapport.

RAPPORT: FEELING CONNECTED

Think of rapport as the harmonious agreement and positive regard in a relationship. Rapport exists both at the conscious and unconscious level. Conscious rapport relates to a positive feeling of understanding and mutual regard. Recall those times you spent with your friend in a pub or coffee shop, solving the world's problems, nodding as each other spoke. Unconscious rapport refers to a state of harmony in which awareness and attention are focused on the other person. For example, your boss, who you don't particularly care for, explains the details of an interesting proposition. Even though you don't feel any positive regard for this person, you find yourself riveted to her presentation. You may even feel a slight metaphorical sense of "being on the same page." At the same time, your boss may not even know your full name, so it's hardly mutual regard.

The conscious mutual regard we feel with friends and family is typically authentic. However, good sales personnel often try to artificially generate rapport to get you to purchase their products. They try to engage us in warm friendly laughter, using good listening skills. Many skillfully ask questions to get the customer into a state of concentration and agreement. Rapport building increases sales significantly. Therapists use rapport building strategies regularly too. They often mirror their client's posture, breathing patterns, hand gestures, and the like to garner unconscious rapport to put the client at ease and awaken the possibility of change.[8] Observe this mirroring phenomenon at work yourself the next time you see two friends having an animated conversation. Usually both sit back, lean in, cross legs, unconsciously at the same time. Simply put, rapport works in the influence business.

The story below, recalled by a doctoral student of mine in educational psychology, illustrates the effect rapport can have on a receptive mind.

At the same time, it also shows what typically transpires without rapport: significantly less influence.

> I was ten years old when I made my first trip to Bible Camp. The minimum age was ten, so most of the other girls were older than me. At that time, there was an evangelical element in the church ministry and I remember hearing visiting ministers shout and roar about hell and damnation, creating a lot of emotional upheaval in the congregation.
>
> One evening, after an electrifying speaker, a group of girls went down to the river bank to sit and talk with one of the counselors. Most of the other girls admired this counselor because she was five years older, pretty, had breasts, and was in charge of the dorm. I personally didn't care for her that much.
>
> We started to talk about God and Jesus, about being loved, and that we just needed to open our hearts to let Him in. I wasn't very involved in the conversation and I remember not feeling like a part of the group. Suddenly one of the girls started to cry and said she wanted to take the Lord as her savior. Then most of the rest of us started to cry, including myself. A box of tissue suddenly appeared.
>
> For the next while, the counselor talked quietly and convincingly about letting Jesus into our hearts. Suddenly, one girl said she felt Jesus enter her heart right there and then, and she instantly felt at peace. Soon, another girl said the same thing, and then another, and so on. I didn't feel anything but claimed I did just to feel like part of the group. It really upset me. I thought something was terribly wrong with me. I must have been a horrible sinner if Jesus wouldn't enter my heart.
>
> Looking at this incident in a new light, I see the many elements of influence that were present at the time. The other girls had rapport with the counselor and treated her as an authority figure in the absence of their own parents. Most of us were away from home for the first time, away from our parents, feeling quite dependent, and looking for guidance. The visiting evangelist boosted our susceptibility to suggestion priming us for sudden influence. The first girl's mystical experience became an indirect suggestion for the others to follow.
>
> I don't think I experienced the same degree of influence as the other girls because the same conditions didn't exist for me. I didn't feel rapport with the counselor. I also didn't accept her as an authority figure; I just thought she was bossy and full of bluster.

The girls who felt connected to the counselor, experienced some degree of rapture. Although many of the elements of influence existed in this episode, rapport proved instrumental. Rapport is not an essential element of influence, spontaneous or otherwise. You don't need it, but it greases the machinery.

A VIVID IMAGINATION: INTENSE FOCUS

We evolved the cognitive hardware to mentally rehearse. Adaptively, this makes great sense. Mental rehearsal allows us to plan ahead. A vivid imagination of being attacked in dangerous circumstances creates anxiety that keeps us away from those situations. Envisioning a great opportunity boosts serotonin, nudging us along that path to success. The price we pay is that we can also visualize ourselves into a depression by focusing on everything that is going wrong, expecting it to continue, and feeling hopeless in the process. What is vividly and energetically imagined, the brain responds to as if real. Remember though, that connections from the amygdala to the cortex are stronger than the reverse, so vivid imaginings are usually less emotionally intense than the actual events themselves. Even so, vividly imagining the loss of a loved one can produce tears; lustfully picturing a love object can generate sexual arousal; and thinking of an imagined transgression can spawn anger. Who hasn't lost themselves in the gratifying daydream of spending their lottery winnings on luxuries for their family and friends?

Where the mind goes, the body usually follows. Ask any golfer. If they think about going into the sand, water, or rough, they've already increased the probability exponentially. Race car drivers know to keep their eyes on the track if they start to lose control; rookies that go into a spin often hit the wall simply because they look at it.

Henry Ford used to say, "Whether you think you can or whether you think you can't, you're right."[9] Jonathan Livingston Seagull stated, "Argue for your limitations, and sure enough they're yours."[10] Visionaries, philosophers, and bumper stickers have always reminded us that what you envision becomes your reality. Of course these pithy sayings generally refer to the big picture, but the day-to-day workings are every bit as illuminating. Consider the following story of temporary amnesia by a university student in his final year of study.[11]

Take special note of the italicized sentence in the first paragraph. (I used the italics for emphasis. The original author did not italicize this part of the story.) When the students tried to imagine what it would be like to experience a blank mind, they performed a mental rehearsal and created a mindset. The friend's comments then triggered its expression.

It was my last year of undergraduate university and I was about to write my final exam in physiology. Just before entering the exam, I talked with a friend about the phenomenon of minds going blank. I had never experienced it, but shivered in horror at the thought. *We both tried to imagine what it would be like.* The time for the exam arrived. I knew the material well and entered the exam confidently. As I sat down at my desk, my friend walked by to wish me luck. I can still recall his final words, ". . . and don't blank out!"

Well you can probably guess what happened. When I received the test I couldn't remember the answer to the first question even though I knew it was easy. The same with the next, and the next, and the next and so on. Panic set in which made things even worse. The more I tried to concentrate, the harder it became. After two hours (it seemed like an eternity) I had only written my name. Frustration gave way to resignation as I realized I failed the test miserably.

Upon resigning myself to failure, a funny thing happened. Now that I had given up, the forgotten information flooded back. I accumulated 39% during the last half hour—a classic case of too little, too late.

The discussion I had with my friend before the exam stayed fresh in my mind and I think his remark triggered a block in my brain. By not thinking of a mental block, it became the only thing I could think about.

If you think this story is farfetched, try this simple exercise: Try as hard as you can to NOT think of a unicorn, those mythical horse-like creatures with a single swirling horn, usually white or cream in color, regal in appearance, and elegant in posture. How did you do? To NOT think of something, you have to think of it first.[12] You undoubtedly imagined one. The object/subject of your imagination creates mental effects that are similar to the real thing, or some proximity thereof. Part of your mind accepts your imaginings as real. The mind must understand it before dismissing it. If it doesn't get dismissed, it stays real. This is most visible in young children because they haven't yet made the black and white distinction between *real* and imaginary.

During a classroom observation while doing my doctoral studies, I watched an amazing teacher weave her magic with a kindergarten class. Laura, a child development specialist, was teaching a lesson on "self talk" to a circle of captivated students. Students warm up to Laura quickly because she typically makes her lessons creative and fun, often delivering them through Pumbsy the Dragon. She started the lesson by saying, through Pumbsy, "I'm doing my self talk now. Can anybody hear me?" The children collectively shook their heads. Laura, forever playful, had Pumbsy caution the students about his slight cough, warning them to be careful because he coughs fire. Suddenly Pumbsy turned to an unsuspecting student and let out a little cough. The student jumped back, eyes aglow, face reddened, and snapped at Pumbsy, "Hey! Watch out!" Other students also reared back. Pumbsy apologized for his careless indiscretion and the class continued. Also entranced with Laura's delivery, I could have sworn I saw a light puff of smoke rise from the corner of Pumbsy's mouth.

DEPENDENCE

Any time someone has something that we need, we become dependent on that person to provide it. Newborns, entirely dependent on their caregivers, would soon perish without them. Dependence diminishes as we mature, but never entirely disappears. The richest and most powerful men in the world quickly become dependent on hospitals and physicians when tragedy or ailments strike.

Dependence comes in many forms: emotional, psychological, and informational competence.[13] Infants without an *emotional* attachment often perish with failure-to-thrive syndrome. This need continues through the life span. While infants without emotional attachment may perish, older humans may become depressed, anxious, or suicidal. Few of us can survive with our mental health intact without regular human contact.

When an event occurs that startles or confuses us, we become anxious. We instantly develop a burning need to solve this *psychological* uneasiness and become dependent on someone or something to relieve this mental discomfort. We've all experienced a time when we were sleeping soundly in our own home, and were suddenly awakened by a loud bang. Your heart rate jumps and breathing quickens as adrenaline rushes through your body. Falling back to sleep is nearly impossible until you solve this riddle. Now in alert mode you hear another bang and two people talking calmly. It is your neighbors, arriving home late after the wedding, slamming the car doors. Uncertainty resolved, your parasympathetic system starts to calm you down, and soon you fall back asleep.

Informational competence also creates dependence. Out golfing, you find you have a downhill lie in a fairway bunker. You don't know which club to use or how to approach the shot. At home, a colorful bug munches away on your rosebush. You don't know how to rescue your roses. Later, while working on your computer, you lose important data by accidentally deleting a file. You don't know how to recover it. All of these problems are easily solved with the right information. We listen intently to those who know how to solve them (even if they don't know the answer, but speak with conviction). I call this form of dependence informational competence, because know-how solves the problem. Dependence in any form (emotional, psychological, or informational) creates a desire to escape or solve the confusion; hence, it increases receptiveness to any information that satisfies that yearning.

Agents of influence enhance their effects through transference or presenting themselves in an authoritative presence. They can further augment their influence capacity by establishing rapport. The recipients of influence heighten their accessibility through vividly picturing or absorbing themselves in the results of suggestions. Their receptiveness also rises if they are in a dependent state of mind. While each of these elements amplifies the likelihood of influence taking place, none of them are essential elements for SIEs. Spontaneous influence occurs only during intense emotional arousal. We already know how extreme emotional arousal triggers elevated suggestibility, creating a readiness for spontaneous influence. In the next section, I will show how confusion also sparks a readiness to instantly accept information, without conscious consideration.

A LITTLE CONFUSION GOES A LONG WAY

Confusion is a state of bewilderment. The hallmark of confusion, disorientation, creates psychological discomfort that creates a drive to quell this cognitive distress. If the confusion is extreme, mental chaos may erupt because your model of the world doesn't work anymore. In this situation any information is eagerly accepted if it restores a sense of equilibrium, a psychological all-systems-okay.

Let me clarify what I mean by the term confusion. I use the term in this text to refer to those moments when we are startled or shocked into a state of disorder, not knowing what to do, think, or feel. This is quite different than those lesser moments of confusion such as when we don't understand an ambiguous statement: "Joe hit Jack before he went to the store?" Do you know who went to the store? (Did Joe go to the store after he hit Jack, or did Jack go to the store after getting hit by Joe? You simply can't tell from this intentionally ambiguous statement.) The examples that follow illustrate how intense forms of confusion can momentarily disorient a person's sense of self and the world.

News anchor Tom Brokaw remembers his early years as a student at the University of South Dakota. He referred to himself as a "total screw off," drinking every night, chasing girls, what he believed to be the good life. One night, in his sophomore year, his favorite professor asked him for dinner. Feeling self satisfied with the professor's interest, he hung on the professor's every word. After dinner, the professor suggested that he drop out. Brokaw remembers feeling stunned and confused. The professor dismissed him, telling him he didn't want to see him until he got all the wine, women, and song out of his system and was willing to settle down to do good work. Brokaw refers to that moment as a "hammer blow." He left school, struggled with menial jobs, mulled over the professor's words, and returned. He credits that incident as a life-changing event.[14]

Brokaw's personal anecdote illustrates all of the elements of spontaneous influence. This wasn't just any professor (authority figure), it was Brokaw's favorite, one who invited him to dine (rapport). Hanging on the professor's every word illustrates intense focus (absorption). Brokaw's status as a student placed him in a subservient posture with the professor (dependence). The surprise statement created a momentary window of susceptibility caused by Brokaw's confusion: "What is he saying? Where is this coming from?" The words that filled that brief window changed him. The surprise and confusion triggered a brief ESS and the professor's words embedded themselves in Brokaw's psyche to produce spontaneous influence.

I describe the window of influence above as brief because disorientation only lasts a short while before the automatic process of rationalization begins. The professor's statement, "I think you should drop out," shocked him. If the professor had not quickly filled that subsequent window of opportunity with profound words, Brokaw's instinctive defense mechanisms would have jumped in: The professor is just an old fool. What does he know? He's forgotten how to grab life and live it to the fullest.

The more potent the authority figures, the more likely we will accept their pronouncements uncritically. In Brokaw's story, the words had a powerful effect, creating a flashbulb memory, but he was able to mull them over consciously during subsequent years before giving into their potent meaning. Young children, during moments of confusion, are much less capable of consciously considering compelling pronouncements from omnipotent authority figures. Children are relatively good at dismissing comments said out of anger because they're used to being called names by peers. Parents teach children to ignore name-calling. But children are ill equipped to deflect pronouncements made matter-of-factly because the tone doesn't trigger a defensive posture.

In the following story, 13-year-old Clarice experienced a flash of intense confusion that created a brief window of momentous suggestibility. During her fleeting vulnerability, the teacher, a potent authority figure expressed a matter-of-fact comment that Clarice accepted uncritically, because it solved her confusion. Note that even though the message was undoubtedly incorrect, Clarice accepted it eagerly because her psychological discomfort made almost any comment irresistible if it eliminated that distress.

Clarice's struggles with school didn't match her psycho-educational test scores. Her teachers expected her to do better and were continually surprised when she fell short. Now that she was in grade eight, they asked me, a school psychologist at the time, to find out why. I examined Clarice's records. Until grade four, she excelled in every subject. In grade four, her grades plummeted and never recovered. During an interview with Clarice I focused on the time between grades three and four. I couldn't uncover any difficulties: head injuries, disease, family or emotional chaos. Unable to find any physical, emotional, or psychological trauma to explain her academic decline, I addressed the concern directly. I told her about the recorded discrepancies between her grade three and four achievement scores. Without hesitation she responded, "The same thing happened with my sister." (Clarice is a member of a visible minority that frequently suffers from discrimination.) Her sister found grade four extremely difficult. The parents went to school often, to speak with the teacher. The parents thought the teacher was a major factor in the sister's academic struggles, but felt unable to do anything about it. Throughout the turmoil her sister became depressed, her grades dropped, and her academic performance never recovered. When Clarice entered grade four two years later, she ended up with the same teacher. Clarice described this teacher as tough, but not mean. Clarice couldn't remember any specific negative comment the teacher said about her. The only episode she could recall was a time, early in the school year, when she was confused with some school work. She asked the teacher for assistance, but rather than answer Clarice's question, the teacher, in Clarice's words "looked disappointed and told me I was just like my sister."

In this particular incident, Clarice, already academically confused, became further disoriented with the teacher's response. It created a flash-bulb memory for her, a potential indicator of spontaneous influence. She learned from this encounter that she too was dumb like her sister. After all, this explained her confusion. "No wonder I don't understand this. I'm dumb." We all know that people who think they're dumb tend to give up easily and do poorly. The subconscious is like an emotionless hard drive of stored programs in which our life experiences are down-loaded. Its function is strictly concerned in engaging in behavior routines. Unfortunately Clarice's program became, "Produce modicums of effort and give up early if it looks hard; you'll never get it anyway."

This chapter started with a master craftsman of influence weaving his magic. I then discussed each of these elements separately. I'll now put them all back together in a form with which you're much more familiar.

THE TOTAL PACKAGE AGAIN, BUT WEAKER

Advertising executives know what works in the influence game. Most TV commercials contain all the elements I discussed in this chapter. Watch them closely some time and see if you can identify each of them. As you read this typical example, ask yourself why commercials don't usually produce the same degree of influence that Dr. Lynn achieved.

Through market analysis, sponsors know who is watching which pro-grams. I was watching a situational comedy of middle-aged actors when I saw this one. The demographics were probably baby-boomers averaging 35–50 years of age.

The commercial: A middle-aged man, in obvious pain, walks the isles of a pharmacy. An acquaintance greets him, asking why he is walking so gingerly, experiencing so much discomfort. The ailing man replies that he feels sore due to his aching joints. The friend asks him what he's done to make himself so miserable. Just then, the pained man reaches for a bottle of relief tablets. The camera zooms in on the popular brand-name label and then scans back to the now smiling man. Clearly relieved now that he's found the medicine to cure his ailment, he replies, "I'm forty, ya know."

Of course the implicit suggestion is that forty-year-olds are plagued with soreness in their muscles and joints simply due to the aging process. Those so afflicted can get easy and safe relief from brand "X" pain relief tablets. This kind of suggestion is insidiously powerful and at the same time an unconscionable self-serving hustle.

Transference (authority): This commercial uses the medical field as an authority. Medicine is strongly governed and typically well researched. Characteristically, this society projects enormous authority onto the medical community and medicine in general.

Rapport: Advertisers use a nondescript character to represent the common man. As *one of us* we're more likely to associate with him. Therefore, his obvious discomfort triggers our empathy and deepens our feelings of rapport. Who hasn't felt the aches and pains due to muscle and joint soreness?

Absorption: The vivid portrayal of such a common scenario, looking for relief from pain, activates our imagination. We sympathize with his distress and may recall the last time we felt that way. Some of us may even experience a sudden slight soreness while watching such a commercial. Have you ever noticed how you instinctively rub your nose or eyes when you talk to someone experiencing the symptoms of a raging cold? A great deal of our learning takes place through these implicit learning channels, our mirror neurons at work. Watch a movie audience the next time you see a fight scene. Many in the audience reel and grimace in their seats as punches find their marks.

Dependence: Reliance on our health system runs rampant in our society. Yes, we have other approaches to deal with soreness (yoga, stretching, regular exercise, relaxation training, massage, etc.), but the pharmaceutical community continues to foster this self-serving reliance.

Confusion: Who is this man? Why is he so sore? How will he deal with it? Why is he suddenly smiling in relief? All these questions generate an urgency to unravel the mystery. Humans hate not knowing answers. Clever writers bait us with implicit inquiries, then hook us with their answer. By the time we see the pain relief tablets, we're cognitively screaming for the answer.

The indirect, insidious nature of this advertisement diminishes the chance for a rational evaluation of the premises of such a suggestion. After all, the commercial didn't come right out and say, "All people at or near forty will experience regular pain in their muscles and joints as a normal result of the aging process. This pain can be quickly and easily remedied by taking brand 'X' pain relief tablets." Had the commercial been so blatant, the sponsors would likely be charged with misleading advertising. Cleverly, although deceptively, the commercial only implies that the message above is true. The alert and informed consumer can easily dismiss this propaganda and put it in its proper place: self-serving commercial hype intended to swindle the audience. But how many of us are attentively cautious during commercials. Advertisements go to great lengths to avoid activating our defenses, hoping to slide their messages into our collective psyches without us even knowing. Market studies continue to affirm our gullibility in this regard. Now that you know the separate elements of influence, take heed. Watch for implicit messages and subtle manipulation. They're rampant.

THE SAME, BUT DIFFERENT

This chapter concludes by comparing the television commercial with the chiropractic workshop that started this chapter. You probably noticed immediately that the hallmark of spontaneous influence, an ESS due to intense emotional arousal, wasn't present during the advertisement. Although the commercial did generate mild confusion, with a corresponding yearning for information, it was not nearly intense enough to trigger an ESS. I doubt anybody in the viewing audience experienced a SIE.

The commercial produced a much milder punch because all the elements in it lacked the personal, intimate touch. I shared my workshop experience with a small group, face-to-face. I met the transference figure and he called me by name. He manipulated my neck with his own hands until I relaxed, signaling avid rapport and dependence. I watched, absorbed in the vivid, visual stimulation of authentic people: cracking necks, surprised looks, and surrender. Emotions soared. To use a well-worn cliché, "the place was electric." Everything was authentic, in the present, spontaneous, and personal. While advertisements lack Dr. Lynn's degree of influence and its spontaneous nature, through repetition and subtlety they enjoy a milder form of reliable persuasion.

✳✳✳

I'm sure Dr. Lynn probably doesn't remember any of the events I experienced in his three-day workshop. He may not even remember me or his trip to Edmonton in 1982. Other participants may not have experienced the degree of influence I did. Influence events are deeply personal and typically unpredictable. Now that you know the elements of influence, Chapters 8 and 9 show you how to recognize ESSs, incorporate these elements, and weave some of your own magic. Preparing and passing on positive comments doesn't always have a dramatic effect. If elevated suggestibility isn't present when you give someone a positive or liberating suggestion, at the very least, you've produced an encouraging moment.

This chapter introduced the separate elements of influence, discussing them individually. I then compared a Spontaneous Influence Event with a more mundane attempt at influence: television commercials. One of these elements, authority, deserves much more consideration. Therefore, I've devoted the next chapter to discuss it in much greater detail.

Chapter 7

Aspects of Authority

Most human development takes place after birth. As such, children exhibit extreme susceptibility to environmental conditioning. From an evolutionary perspective, those who learned quickly from parents and elders increased their rate of survival. Accordingly, parents, and other authority figures, hold a powerful position as influence agent due to the child's genetic predisposition to soak up information. Additionally, as we now know, emotionally charged information often makes the learning process spontaneous.

When we are very small, our parents sustain us in every way. Human infants can't survive on their own. As we grow, we learn that they have the final word on everything because they are smarter, stronger, capable, and always right. However, by the time we get to grade school we learn that parents aren't perfect. Yes, they are powerful figures, but they aren't perfect.

Once we get to school, we rediscover perfect: the teacher. Robert Wright, acclaimed author of *The Moral Animal*, believes that our awe for role models has the same neurobiological origins as those we have for our parents.[1] I remember my first teacher. Everything about her was flawless. She dressed immaculately, moved effortlessly, managed each of us while we struggled to get her attention and approval, spoke exquisitely, and her demeanor was flawless. My first teacher, like most of us, was our first archetypal, omniscient parent figure.

As students, we hold a collective stake in believing in the omnipotence of the teacher. Our parents, now flawed, pale in comparison to this new authority figure manifest before us in all her glory (I use the feminine pronoun because the vast majority of primary teachers are female.). She has all the answers to our questions, teaches us how to read, write, and learn about the world. She soothes us when frightened, inspires us with encouragement, nurtures our every need, commands our attention, and to a large extent defines our identity (good, bad, invisible, special, etc.). She is calm, collected, and impenetrable: our hero. We students all collectively project this omniscience onto this awesome creature. That's partly what inspires the adoration; we are a cult of thirty, swept away by this goddess.

When I arrived home from school, the teacher still remained the supreme authority and was frequently cited as the current "expert." I remember rebutting my parents with, "My teacher said one shouldn't eat when they are not hungry." I would say this when I had eaten everything on my plate except the kidney beans. Kids don't just cite their teachers as experts to get out of eating yucky food. These challenges actually testify to the replacement of the parent by the teacher as superior authority. If your parents love you but your teacher doesn't, your self-esteem will take a dramatic turn, particularly in the early years. Your parents have to love you; they're your parents. Your first teacher is a true judge because she has no genetic investment. The teacher's evaluation reflects the big picture, how you fit into the world; accordingly, her opinion reflects the truth.

I remember the tremendous influence my grade school teachers produced. I also remember how it diminished as I got older, except for the occasional teacher who inspired admiration. Times that I reverted to that idyllic phase occurred less often as I matured, but I must admit that even as a doctoral student I occasionally had those same feelings of awe and attributed uncommon greatness to a mortal professor or advisor. At these times, I regressed to early childhood feelings and patterns, accepting information uncritically, fearing censure, seeking approval, and generally yielding hastily to influence.

TRANSFERENCE: COMMON INSTANCES

Transference is a phenomenon that stays with us eternally, just as our parent's influence is part and parcel of our identity, values, beliefs, and behaviors. We experience transference anxiety when we drive down the highway and see a police patrol car in the rearview mirror. We quickly check our speedometer and do a nervous mental check of our driving behavior: "Did I signal correctly, go through a school zone without slowing, or change lanes inappropriately?" This anxious feeling is not much different than the one we had when a parent caught us sneaking a snack.

Going through a foreign custom's agent checkpoint can also produce transference anxiety. This official determines your acceptance or rejection. The powerlessness you felt as a youngster returns. The following story illustrates the common experience of a foreign student.[2]

> For some reason, authority figures have a way of intimidating me, especially if they are wearing a uniform. Perhaps because my father was a police officer and he was very intimidating to me.

When I arrived at the U.S. border, the officer asked where I was going, how long I planned to be, and several other details. I felt calm because I had all the necessary documentation. I expected the officer to wave me through. Instead, the officer told me to park my vehicle, come into the building, and bring my papers. That unexpected response quickly reduced my calm deportment to moronic mumblings. I was shocked.

I'm glad my friend accompanied me. It was as if I couldn't understand the officer's questions. He asked for my papers, but I couldn't find them in my purse. My friend found them for me. I could hear my friend and the officer talking, but I couldn't understand anything. He intimidated me so much I froze, afraid I might say something that would deny my entry. My heart pounded, my face flushed, and I felt my hands shake. Finally the officer stamped my paper and we left.

This anecdote, although extreme to many of us, illustrates how susceptible we are to influence from authority figures when their presence produces anxiety. She instantly regressed emotionally to a state of "moronic mumblings" similar to the emotional response she experienced in childhood with her father.[3] In this case, her soaring anxiety stayed with her as a conditioned response. A frequent traveler, she now gets butterflies in her stomach every time she crosses a border.

Transference anxiety, if extreme, can also create elevated suggestibility, the precursor to spontaneous influence. I met the student below when she was a proud veteran teacher, completing her doctoral program in education. She almost quit the teaching profession but the following Spontaneous Influence Event (SIE) catapulted her into a long and rewarding career.

I have always wanted to be a teacher. Maybe at the beginning it was for the wrong reason. I had overheard my mother talking to her sister. She said she knew my sister would be a good teacher but she wasn't sure about me.

Nothing got in my way until my senior year in college: Student Teaching! During the first term, four students are assigned to a master teacher for half days. At first you observe, and then you teach just one reading group for 20 minutes. The master teacher observes and criticizes, and criticizes, and criticizes.

I cried every night. We had to write scripts. "The teacher says . . . The student responds . . ." For six very long weeks I could do nothing right. Not one single positive comment could I squeeze from the master. To show how tense it was: during one reading group, fearful of not receiving the scripted answer, I put my hand on a little boy's knee and looked deep in his eyes and asked my question. Instead of answering the question, he leaned over to the boy next to him and said, "Watch out. She pinches."

We had to go to the master teacher's home for one final evaluation. With only one term left, I had decided to quit. I had my speech all ready. I would just have to find something else to do.

I don't honestly remember all of the points we went over that afternoon. Just as we finished, the master held out her hand and took mine. She said,

"In spite of what you thought was a dreadful experience, I believe you are
going to make a cracker-jack teacher. You're one of the best I've ever had."
    I turned, took two steps toward the door and fainted dead away. When I
came to, I saw true, sincere concern on her face for the first time.

Her mother's comment to the aunt set the stage for self-doubt as a teacher.
Crying every night, squeezing a young boy's knee a little too hard, and
cringing at frequent criticisms illustrated her on-going anxiety. The final
evaluation, delivered by the omnipotent transference figure of the master
teacher, the root of her anxiety, put her near the edge. The shock and
surprise of the unexpected comment triggered a SIE.

THE ROLE OF AUTHORITY

Authority plays a critical role in the effectiveness of a suggestion.
Note though, the recipient does not have to like the authority or respect
the authority. You may not like your boss, but you still yield to her
position of authority. Similarly, you may not like your coach, but respect
her expertise and listen intently.

We earnestly accept authority in our adult lives, similar to our childhood. Many positions in our culture enjoy considerable status as authority
figures (medical experts, scientists, technical experts in diverse fields
including sports, and even celebrities). Some forms of information also
enjoy authoritative status (newscasts, prominent magazines, and scientific
journals). A medical specialist, speaking with conviction, suggesting
a treatment and predicting an outcome, is rarely challenged robustly by a
patient. Celebrity endorsements by athletes, popular figures, and entertainers reliably increase sales. Reports in popular investment periodicals
or other investment media may instantly change the financial landscape.

Although the delivery of a suggestion by an authority figure is usually
more powerful than by a peer or subordinate, exceptions certainly exist.
During moments of high susceptibility, we instinctively ascribe authority
to any agent that produces a suggestion with some conviction. It is the
conviction itself that is the key. For instance, we often ascribe honesty and
transparency to young children because they haven't yet learned social
graces and political correctness. A friend of mine teaches grade four. She
recently changed her hairstyle from conventional to bold, spending an
inordinate amount for the special treatment. When she walked into her
classroom, one of her astonished students asked, "What did you do to
your hair?" According to her report, other students just looked at her hair
in stunned silence. All her polite and supportive colleagues told her the
new hair style looked marvelous. The next day she arrived with a more
conservative cut. Conviction, regardless of your status, born of honesty,
carries its own authority.

The following story recalled by one of my graduate students, illustrates how authority figures, speaking with conviction, can create devastating results even when the suggestion is obviously false. In this particular circumstance, the victimized student was surrounded by supportive students who vigorously disagreed with the teacher's pronouncement. Experiments show that once a belief is accepted, it can support itself even when the supporting evidence is disproved.[4] The teacher's ultimate status as authority figure, together with the Elevated Suggestibility State (ESS), trumped any contradictory support for the mistreated child.

> We started fifth grade with a teacher we thought to be wonderful. As the year progressed, we learned otherwise. Bobby was popular with his classmates because like many jolly class clowns he brought comic relief to our mundane existence. On one fateful day, Bobby was unusually energetic, full of light-hearted humor. Nobody knew it, but it would be his last day like that.
>
> Our teacher snapped, "Move your desk to the front of the room and stop your disruptions!" He complied with half the request. He moved his desk to the front but continued joking. The teacher worked silently and devilishly at her desk. Shortly thereafter she jumped up and moved swiftly to Bobby's desk. She had fashioned a dunce cap and elephant ears (Bobby had abnormally large and protruding ears.). As she fitted Bobby with the ornaments of ridicule he went strangely still. The teacher proclaimed to him, for all to hear, "You're not so clever. The students laugh at you because you're a FOOL, not because you're funny!" Bobby remained motionless until the lunch bell sounded and then he dashed from the room.
>
> Bobby was never the same after that. He was never the class clown again. In spite of continuous and sincere efforts to counter the teacher's wicked statement, he withdrew from the rest of us. We all hated the teacher for what she'd done. Bobby never recovered. Several years later I met Bobby in the mall. He stuttered and seemed nervous. He spoke briefly and left abruptly. I couldn't help but remember the episode from the classroom.

This episode not only changed Bobby dramatically, it also had a profound effect on Angeline; it continues as a flashbulb memory for her after 25 years. Angeline eventually became a teacher and enrolled in a doctoral program in educational psychology. She wants to rescue students.[5]

Bobby's elevated suggestibility, activated by embarrassment, coupled with the severe pronouncement by a powerful authority figure, produced a dramatically negative spontaneous influence. Testaments to the contrary by his classmates: "She's just mean," "We think you're funny," "You're hilarious," fell ineffectively. (Chapters 8 and 9 teach how to intervene, counter, and spin these events into positive or neutral events.)

Endowing a figure with an inordinate amount of authority creates an arena for amazing events. The most commonly documented of these events is the placebo effect. Placebos are sham procedures or artificial medicines (like a sugar pill) that have no inherent therapeutic value, but inexplicably heal the sufferer. Many times, the mere words or attitude of a physician, or any other medical authority, may induce such an effect. The treatment in and off itself has no therapeutic value without the suggestion by the doctor, or elicited expectations by the patient. The following story of Ken, a five-year-old boy I treated for bed-wetting, illustrates the hallmarks of spontaneous influence, and incidentally, placebo responding.

Ken's parents took him to a physician regarding his bed-wetting but they didn't discover any physical problem or infection. The parents exhausted all the traditional remedies but remained stymied. As a last ditch effort, they asked me to use hypnosis. I agreed, but unbeknownst to them, I decided to generate an ESS indirectly through emotional arousal, and then use my authoritative status to administer a healing suggestion.

The parents didn't allow Ken any drinks in the evening before bed. Ken wore pull-ups, in a bed with a rubber liner, and was awakened at midnight to go to the toilet. Clearly the situation provided many non-verbal messages that Ken was a "bed-wetter."

To establish rapport, Ken and I read a story together from his favorite book. Abruptly, I asked Ken if I could examine his throat. I did this to surprise and mystify him, thereby enhancing my authoritative status. (Why would someone look in a throat to treat bed-wetting?) I went through an arbitrary routine, looking around, having him move his head from side to side, then suddenly exclaimed, "I see it! There it is! That's why you wet your bed!" I now informed a very excited Ken that the problem could be easily, effectively, and immediately resolved. Ken's excitement with the diagnosis, confusion with my approach, together with his eager anticipation of relief, created the required elevated suggestibility. The stage was set.

In front of Ken, I told the parents that they should eliminate all the bed-wetting precautions and treat Ken as a dry-sleeper. I then gave Ken ten dry-night pills (Children's chewable vitamin C). I informed them that he should take one before bedtime every night for five consecutive nights, and then take half of the remaining five tablets for the next ten nights. I told Ken that these pills would inform his bladder to wake him up when it was full, and that he would then go to the toilet for relief. I explained how he would only need half doses after the first five days because the tablets were training his bladder, just like when he learned to ride a bike after a few days and learned to feel comfortable on his bike. I firmly expressed that the bladder would be fully trained in 15 days or less, but to continue to take the tablets until they were gone. He was to celebrate his imminent success with a toast of orange juice before he went to bed.

Ken phoned the next morning to tell me about his first dry sleep. On the sixth day, Ken had a little trickle. I told him that a trickle was expected on the sixth day and that it indicated a successful treatment. Ken triumphantly finished the 15-day treatment and continued with dry nights.[6]

I wanted to incorporate all the elements of spontaneous influence to assure my success. I arrived as a healer. That and the fact that Ken was very young placed me in a position as a powerful authority figure. I started the procedure by reading his favorite book with him to establish rapport. His youth, and status as my patient, created a dependent dynamic for him. I used touch and a surprising therapeutic ritual (looking in his mouth and rotating his head) to absorb him in the process and elevate his suggestibility. I then increased his already elevated suggestibility by surprising him with a sudden proclamation: "I see it! There it is! That's why you wet your bed!" While the placebo effect is never guaranteed, I used every tool in my spontaneous influence kit to enhance the likelihood of success. (The latter part of this chapter addresses placebos in greater detail.)

Environmental conditions are also important. Signals in Ken's environment conveyed implicit suggestions to him that he was a bed-wetter. Take special notice of the precautions the parents took to deal with the bed-wetting. Did the precautions to treat the problem actually maintain it? If they created it, we have a classic case of a self-fulfilling prophecy, whereby the means taken to avoid an event actually create it.

Parents' expectations of their children play a dramatic role in child development. Bear in mind though that a child's interpretation of parental expectations is more significant than the parents' verbally stated ones. What you do usually sends a stronger message than what you say. For example, parents may state verbally, "You're very bright and talented." In the meantime, the parents may only focus on mistakes and become disappointed while supervising the child's tasks. The parents' intention is to improve the child's performance, but the child's experience may not match the parents' expectation. The child may perceive the parents' behavior as an expectation of failure.

Suggestions work best in an environment that supports them. In many cases, the environment can be strictly internal: self-image and world outlook. External conditions that support the suggestions will also increase its effect. That's why we celebrated with a glass of juice before bedtime and took the rubber sheet off the bed. I removed any doubt by removing the implicit counter-suggestions. Psychologists sometimes call this the Pygmalion effect: When we treat other people in ways that are consistent with the image we hold of them, they tend to behave and become like the image.

THE PYGMALION EFFECT

Educators and psychologists study this phenomenon extensively. The seminal research was titled "Pygmalion In the Classroom" by Robert Rosenthal of Harvard University and Leonore Jacobson.[7] This frequently cited research studied 18 women teachers and over 600 students.

The entire group of 600 students received intelligence tests. Researchers told teachers that the students' intelligence scores would help them form a superior class. Researchers then deceived the teachers by enrolling a random sample of students into the "superior" class. Thus, the only difference between the elite group of students and the others resided solely in the minds of the teachers. Additionally, testers told the teachers that students in the "superior" class should make rapid and above average intellectual progress in the coming year.

Researchers administered the same intelligence test to all the students at the end of the school year. The randomly selected students in the "superior" class showed authentic above average increases in achievement *and* intellect. Additionally, the teachers of this class reported that the "superior" students had distinguished themselves through academic industry and intellectual curiosity. For ethical reasons, the researchers decided not to establish a "dull" class; if teachers' behavior and expectations can dramatically enhance achievement, the opposite is undoubtedly true of the converse.[8]

If the "superior" students in the Pygmalion experiment really improved their test scores, how did this happen? Did they begin the school year by acting more intelligent? Probably not. They probably acted in the same manner as their peers in other classrooms. As we instinctively notice behavior that fits neatly into our perceived notions, these teachers showed a predisposition to interpret ambiguous or benign behavior as intelligent behavior in the "superior" students. What is deemed intelligent and not intelligent behavior is often subjective, more due to the teachers' perceptions than the students' behaviors. In other words, much of a student's behavior is neither intelligent nor unintelligent: it's just behavior.

Teachers typically expect intelligent behavior from those they deem intelligent; conversely, they expect less intelligent behavior from those whom they think are less intellectually endowed. Accordingly they may interpret an "intelligent" student's gaze as one of intellectual curiosity, admiring the spinning wheels of a superior mind at work. The same gaze by an "unintelligent" student might be perceived as an inability to concentrate. Like everyone else, teachers are predisposed to notice behaviors that validate their perspectives. What they observed was more a product of what they believed than the way things really were. Teachers perceived intelligent behavior because that is what their expectations directed them to notice. This explains how the teachers responded, but how did these expectations create authentic results in the students?

THE POWER OF EXPECTANCIES

Once the teachers accepted the invented reality of a superior class they then acted congruently. The convincing display of expectations by authority figures, imposed upon susceptible and dependent minds, created a corresponding reality for the students. The students modified their implicit model of themselves to reflect the positive expectations of their teachers. Thus, a complementary self-perpetuating cycle ensued. The students thought of themselves as intelligent and responded accordingly.[9]

Firmly held expectations by students don't just affect academic performance, they can save a life. The esteemed British medical journal *Lancet* reported that a study of women diagnosed with breast cancer revealed that recurrence-free survival was significantly more common among patients who reacted with denial or with a "fighting spirit" than among patients who responded with stoic acceptance or feelings of hopelessness. This cancer research suggested that the mortality rate was higher in those patients who prepared themselves for death, or fell victim to negative self-fulfilling prophecies. After 10 years, 70 percent of the "fighting spirit" patients were still alive versus 50 percent of deniers, 25 percent of stoic acceptors, and 20 percent of the hopeless/helpless group. Patients who expected to survive or those who clung to life in a seemingly irrational manner, had a considerably more favorable prognosis. Simple expectancies alone can produce dramatically significant results.[10]

Supportive environmental conditions can also dramatically affect breast-cancer patients even after the cancer has metastasized. In a now classic study conducted at Stanford during the 1980s, psychiatrist David Spiegel showed that breast-cancer patients assigned to a support group lived an average of 18 months longer than those receiving standard care. Group members listened to each other, cared for each other, and worked together to understand and manage their symptoms. These activities enhanced their survival expectations.[11]

The power of expectations can occasionally take a life as well as give it. Curses, spells, and voodoo deaths operate through imposed negative expectations by a cultural authority figure. Holocaust survivor, psychiatrist Viktor Frankl tells of a fellow concentration camp inmate who dreamt he would be liberated from his suffering on March thirtieth. He fervently believed it would happen. As the date came closer it became clear that the Allied forces were still far from the camp. On the twenty-ninth he suddenly became ill, and on the thirtieth he dropped into a coma. He died of typhus on the next day. His expectation actually prophesied his end to suffering.[12]

I witnessed a similar event with my grandmother when I was a teen. She lived thousands of miles away from my parents. They worried about her declining ability to manage her affairs. My parents invited her to come and live with them. She thanked them for their offer but respectfully declined it; she wanted to spend her final days in her own home. After considerable prodding, she acquiesced and we made arrangements. My parents flew out to help her prepare and pack. The night before her departure, in apparently good health, she bid my parents goodnight and went to bed. That night, she slipped inexplicably into a coma and died in her own home a few days later. Like Frankl's prison camp inmate, her expectations prophesized her death.

EXPECTATIONS GENERATE SELF-FULFILLING PROPHESIES

Expectations may not only create self-perpetuating cycles, they may initiate self-fulfilling prophecies. A clear distinction lies between the two. A self-perpetuating cycle occurs when information is interpreted in such a manner as to confirm the preconceived perception. For example, if Charles expects woman in positions of authority to act cold and arbitrary, he will interpret their behavior as such. If a woman in authority acts warm and sincere, he will interpret her behavior as phony and manipulative. His interpretations perpetuate his predisposing belief. Notice though that he did not create any behavior, but only interpreted that which was already present. Self-fulfilling prophecies are different in that the expected event occurs directly as a result of the expectation. For example, Californians expected a gas shortage during a crisis in the mid-seventies. Motorists stormed to the filling stations to top up their cars and whatever extra tanks they had available, thereby depleting the reserves. The California allotment of gas had not changed, but the motorists' behavior caused the shortage. Herein lays the critical difference: the expectation of the event actually caused the event itself. Cause and effect become reversed. In California, what was supposed to be a reaction (effect) turned out to be an action (cause); the very steps taken to avoid the event actually created it.

We clearly see self-fulfilling prophecies at work in the antiquated art of matchmaking. Matchmakers in former patriarchal societies took on the task of awakening a mutual desire in two people, characteristically to appease their families for political, financial, or social reasons. The matchmaker typically talked separately to each person, asking if they had noticed the other person secretly watching them longingly. This prophecy, disguised as fact, often fulfilled itself.

The result of spontaneous influence is a new set of expectancies that occur as the result of the shift in self-image or world outlook. These expectancies set up the behavioral machinery to fulfill themselves. Those of us, who try to produce spontaneous influence deliberately, try to generate all the conditions discussed in Chapter 6, or take advantage of ESSs when they occur naturally. Placebos are a form of spontaneous influence whereby physicians (or other healing agents) embed their expectations into the patients' models of themselves and their worlds. Examining placebos—the conditions in which they operate, the conditions that minimize them, and the conditions that enhance them—helps prepare you to produce your own SIEs. The next section describes the current scientific and medical understanding of placebos.

Caution: I don't endorse the lay use of placebo cures. By all means, share your positive expectations and support for those in need, but avoid the untrained deliberate use of such a strong tool.

PLACEBOS AND SPONTANEOUS INFLUENCE

In medicine, placebos are chemically inert substances that resemble certain medicines in shape, size, or color but which have no pharmaceutical effect. Placebos can also be medical procedures, such as fake acupuncture and sham surgery. Many cures in previous centuries were almost certainly placebos. Regardless, these powdered toads, crabs' eyes, and ground horns created many reliable cures. Despite the extensive use of many bizarre substances as curative agents, healers in those days continued to hold respected and honored status in their societies because they themselves (physicians, medicine men, healers, witchdoctors) were the healing agents. Note this important point: The physicians of those days believed in those cures *and* the people believed in their physicians. When physicians ceased to believe in the cure's effectiveness, their curative power vanished.

The most robust of these "medicines" survived as home remedies. In the last century our healing arts improved considerably. Sophisticated empirical testing can often determine the exact nature of a medicinal effect/procedure. Still today though, many medical treatments produce an effect we can't explain. As recently as 2005, the US office of Technical Assessment estimated that ". . . only one fifth of modern medical treatments in common use have been proved effective. Modern placebo effects include prescribing antibiotics for colds and flu, evidence that placebo use still has a place in modern medicine."[13] Current beliefs about megavitamins, diets de jour, organic foods, stress reduction, cardiovascular exercise, and many holistic medicinal treatments may be examples of recent popular placebos.

While controversy continues to rage regarding the placebo effect, the disagreement addresses *how and why* it works, not *if* it works. Virtually all medical practitioners, clinicians, and medical scientists agree that placebos exist, occur regularly, and can produce dramatic effects. Although its specific mechanisms of action are something of a mystery, its efficacy in thousands of studies is hard to deny. So much so that the medical field requires that all new drugs be tested in double-blind placebo-controlled situations.[14]

After considerable experimentation, scientists have been unable to locate a consistent "placebo responder." More and more the medical profession and scientists are beginning to emphasize the greater importance of immediate situational and interpersonal factors, and that even the role of the physician itself may be a potent placebo in its own right.[15]

I believe placebos and their counterpart nocebos (when the effect is negative, bringing on discomfort or illness) are a form of spontaneous influence. If I am right, that partly explains why the search for a single placebo effect continues to be fruitless. No particular placebo gene or identifiable mechanism exists. Placebos occur because of the conditions present at the time of the placebo suggestion. Many of these suggestions, explicit or implicit, take place during moments of elevated suggestibility, given by authority figures. In many cases, the mere presence of a medical authority during times of distress will generate emotional arousal that elevates suggestibility. Dr. Howard L. Fields, esteemed professor of Neurobiology and Physiology at the University of California, San Francisco, expresses the following about a physician's suggestions and emotional arousal.[16]

> What I would predict is that if you had an experiment where you gave a person a pill, and said, "This is a very powerful pain reliever, take it," and so on, and then you compare the person to an untreated group, you will see a placebo effect. However, if you were to take a third group and say, "Look, this is a very powerful pain killer, but it is a dangerous drug, and I don't give it out lightly. Here is a list of potential things that could happen to you if you take it." My prediction is that the pill that is described as dangerous might be a more effective placebo. In other words, part of what we do as physicians is to scare people, and that adds to our own placebo effectiveness.

Patients may not always feel fearful, but visiting a physician for most of us is an event charged with emotions and expectations. Harvard medical professor Herbert Benson, author of *Timeless Healing: The Power of Biology and Belief*,[17] writes how he first developed an interest in placebos. After his junior year at college he obtained a summer job as a merchant seaman. "Knowing that I planned to be a doctor, my suffering shipmates would come to me for relief. But all I had to offer them were vitamins, which I promptly dispensed. Though the vitamins should have had little or no effect, my shipmates' symptoms—and foul moods—improved rapidly and dramatically after taking the pills."

While the episode above hardly rings authoritative with scientific scrutiny, it does reflect a question posed by many: Does the expectation of a change in experience produce a perceptual bias, so that patients or research participants mistakenly perceive a change that has not in fact occurred? In other words, is the placebo effect purely subjective? Indeed, expectations play a role in placebo cures, but the body definitely undergoes authentic biological changes.

MORE THAN SUBJECTIVE EXPERIENCE ALONE

In Western culture, medicine distinguishes between symptoms, which are subjective feelings reported by the patient, and signs, which are objective indications of disease detectable by the physician. For example, pain is a symptom because it cannot be measured by any physical test; redness or swelling is a sign.

Numerous scientific studies show that placebos can generate signs, not just symptom relief. In the following study, researchers looked at the effect of ultrasound on postoperative dental pain and determined that objective signs were also affected by the placebo response. "Not only did those who received the fake ultrasound (while the machine was switched off) experience a reduction in pain, but in one of the studies trismus was also significantly reduced compared to the no-treatment control group. Trismus is an involuntary contraction of the jaw muscles which keeps the jaw tightly closed-and can be measured objectively. Furthermore, in both of the studies there was also a significant decrease in swelling in those receiving the fake ultrasound."[18]

Benson reported a study whereby experimenters found that belief in toxic contact with a poisonous tree was slightly stronger than actual contact. "Boys were blindfolded and one arm was brushed with toxic lacquer tree leaves and the other arm with a chestnut tree branch. They were told the opposite. Many developed no reactions to the toxic leaves when they believed they were chestnut, while many developed toxic reactions to the chestnut leaves when they believed them to be toxic. In 51% of the cases the suggestions were a more powerful force than the actual brushing of the toxic tree." In this experiment, skin reactions indistinguishable from actual allergic reactions were induced by believing contact with a poison had occurred.[19]

Discover Magazine reported recent research where two placebo cures were examined side by side. Researchers compared sham acupuncture procedures to fake medication for the treatment of chronic arm pain. Twenty-five percent of the acupuncture group experienced side effects from nonexistent needle pricks including pain or redness and swelling.[20]

Some placebo responses are so strong that they actually show greater effects than known pharmaceuticals. For example, in studies of placebo alcohol, instead of effects being specific to the pharmacological properties of alcohol, the effects are specific to beliefs that vary from one culture to another. Studies of placebo caffeine show the same phenomenon; the effects of placebo caffeine on motor performance vary as a function of the person's beliefs. The placebo caffeine effects impede motor performance in people who expect that effect and enhance performance in people expecting improvement.[21]

In the following study, the placebo not only reversed the known property of a pharmaceutical, it also produced an objective sign. The subjects in this study were pregnant women who experienced greater than normal morning sickness. "The women were told that they would be given a powerful drug to cure the nausea, but the drug they actually received was, in fact, known to produce nausea rather than relieve it.

Not only did the women feel less sick after the injection, but their stomachs showed an objective decrease in the type of movement associated with nausea."[22]

Some critics of placebo research suggest that placebos may simply be the result of hope and optimism. But how then does one explain the frequently unwanted side effects produced by placebos? According to Dr. Raymond C. Pogge, "drowsiness, headaches, nervousness and insomnia, nausea, and constipation are among the most commonly reported side effects of placebo treatment." Benson suggests that, "reading the informed consent document one has to sign before participating in a double-blind study is undoubtedly the culprit in some of these cases. Knowing a long list of potential undesirable and toxic effects may bring them on."[23] For example, in the research that compared sham acupuncture with fake pain-relief pills, 31 percent of the pill group experienced side effects including dry mouth, fatigue, dizziness, restlessness, rashes, headaches, nausea, and nightmares. The side effects exactly matched those described by the physicians at the beginning of the study.[24] Side effects such as these are hardly what one hopes for or is optimistic toward.

HOW PLACEBOS WORK

We know they are not simply subjective responses to experimental or clinical demands. We know they are more than hope and optimism at work. Somehow, the placebo stimulus, whether it is the physician's behavior, some procedure, or a pill appears to trigger the internal pharmacopoeia that all humans possess. Dr. Bernie Siegel believes, when there's a strong belief in the value of the therapy, the power of suggestion can go to work, causing a fundamental change in the internal environment of the body. He believes that feelings are chemical messengers, and as such can initiate a cascade of neurobiological and physiological changes. "Placebo responses are neither mystical nor inconsequential, and that ultimately psychological and psychophysiological processes operate through common anatomic pathways. What is in your mind is often quite literally, or 'anatomically,' what is in your body: Peptide messenger molecules manufactured by the brain and the immune system are the link."[25] Research professor Candice B. Pert, Ph.D., strongly agrees. Pert does AIDS research in the Department of Physiology and Biophysics at Georgetown University Medical Center in Washington, D.C. She states, "Beliefs effect emotions, which effect neuropeptides, which direct energy, chemicals, and neurotransmitters." She cites the following research as a landmark study.

Howard Hall at Case Western Reserve University of Ohio demonstrated in 1990 that the immune system could be consciously controlled. In his research, he instructed his human subjects to use several self-regulatory strategies (self-hypnosis, relaxation training, guided imagery, and biofeedback) to consciously increase the stickiness of their white blood cells, as measured by saliva and blood tests. Hall was the first to show that psychological factors could directly affect cellular function in the immune system.[26]

Pediatric surgeon, Bernie Siegel of New Haven Connecticut, tells the following story of how a young boy's visualization directly affects the cellular function in his immune system and successfully eliminated his cancer.[27] Garrett Porter, then nine years old, was diagnosed with an inoperable and supposedly incurable brain tumor. He enrolled in the Menninger Foundation's Voluntary Controls Program to learn visualization skills. He created a Star Wars scenario whereby he visualized his brain as the solar system, his tumor as an evil invading planet, and himself as the leader of a space squadron fighting a successful battle against the tumor. The tumor disappeared within five months without any other therapy. Many years later, he continued to live in good health.

Research and clinical anecdotes such as those discussed above provide strong evidence that placebos somehow activate the neurobiological circuits required for healing effects. Placebos are not magic; they work through natural mechanisms. So what then are these natural mechanisms?

WHY PLACEBOS WORK

Even after thousands of studies on placebos and experiments with placebo control groups, we still don't know who in particular will or won't benefit from these effects. By manipulating clinical conditions, we can increase the number of people who profit from placebos and we can even increase the potency of some placebo effects, but researchers still can't reliably predict which particular person(s) will exhibit the placebo response. I believe this is due in part because they don't yet look to elevated suggestibility as a factor.

We can look at groups of people who have benefited from placebo therapy and offer overall rates of success. But at this time, experimental tests and measures are not sensitive or sophisticated enough to gauge the individual preferences and life experiences that are at play in each placebo study. Think of it this way. Imagine that you are a restaurateur. Statistically you know how many burgers you are likely to sell in any evening but you don't know to whom you are going to sell them. While you expect your clientele to order approximately eighty burgers on Wednesdays, you can't tell by looking at the customers which eighty will order them and which will order fish, chicken, or pizza, and so on. You can increase sales by having burger specials, but you still don't know which particular person will order them. What then are the conditions under which placebos operate?

Benson believes placebo effectiveness, which he refers to as "remembered wellness" is due to three components: (1) Belief and expectancy on the part of the patient, (2) Belief and expectancy on the part of the caregiver, and (3) Belief and expectancies generated by a relationship between the patient and the caregiver. After years of reviewing studies he cautions that the widespread acceptance that one-third of all patients are placebo responders is a myth. He believes that placebo effectiveness ranges from 1 percent to 100 depending on the conditions of the trial.[28]

Numerous studies reflect his point of view. In a review of treatments for angina, later found out to be placebos, the initial treatment worked 70–90 percent of the time when both the patient and doctor believed in the treatment. The effectiveness quickly dropped to 30–40 percent when physicians started doubting the procedures.[29] This study supports Benson's components one and two above.

Those who study placebo literature claim that placebo effects are enhanced by more believable and more technically convincing agents. This supports Benson's third component. For example, placebo injections are more effective than placebo pills and that placebo morphine is more effective than placebo aspirin.[30] A $1,614,605 National Institutes of Health research study comparing placebo treatments agrees. In the study comparing placebo acupuncture with placebo pills, both groups showed significant gain in pain relief, although the pain relief was considerably higher in the fake acupuncture group. The researchers suggested the difference in the two groups was due to medical rituals: performing acupuncture is more elaborate than prescribing medicine.[31]

A Newsweek article "Pondering the Placebo Effect" written by three prominent doctors at Harvard Medical School states, "The placebo effect is the healing that occurs not because of a particular drug or treatment but because of the expectations, beliefs, or hopes embedded in the encounter between a patient and a clinician." The doctors also support Benson's three-component theory.

> Studies suggest that trial participants are more likely to experience a placebo effect if they believe strongly in the treatment they are helping researchers evaluate. Doctors' attitudes may also affect outcomes. Studies suggest that when physicians are hopeful and enthusiastic about the active treatment in a study, their patients are more responsive to the placebo.
>
> The usual placebo is an inert pill that has no direct physical effects. In some studies, however, patients receive an "active placebo"—a drug that causes noticeable symptoms (rapid heartbeat, for example) but has no therapeutic effect. Not surprisingly, patients receiving that kind of placebo are more likely to believe they are being treated with the active medicine—and more likely to experience relief.[32]

Authority, rapport, intense imagery, dependence, beliefs, and emotions appear to play a considerable role in placebo responses. The mechanisms of spontaneous influence factor prominently. Is the placebo response a SIE?

PLACEBOS AS SPONTANEOUS INFLUENCE

We know that placebos are powerful; we know how to increase their potency; we know how to broaden the circle of those who experience their effects; we know placebos can release endorphins;[33] we know they can reduce inflammation; we know they can counteract known pharmaceuticals; and we know they can trigger the autoimmune response. We also know that the hunt to locate a specific placebo effect is doomed to failure. We don't have a placebo trigger; we have a genetic predisposition to trigger our powerful self-healing ability and internal pharmacy. Under the right conditions, this happens spontaneously, regularly, and naturally. The conditions vary widely, but they all share elevated suggestibility as a fundamental feature. Essentially, placebos are suggestions, implicit or explicit, during moments of elevated suggestibility, by powerful authority figures or authoritative contexts. Placebos tap into our propensity for spontaneous influence.

Recall the elements of spontaneous influence discussed in Chapter 6: authority, rapport, absorption in imagery, and dependence along with a catalyst for an ESS. Recall also that the first four elements are not necessary precursors to spontaneous influence but only enhance its likelihood. The only critical component of spontaneous influence is an ESS.

Authority: Physicians, medicine men, or healers that go by any other label have always received esteemed status in their communities as authoritative leaders. Benson and other placebo researchers show consistently that the placebo effect is increased when these authorities strongly believe in the cure. This explains why placebo effect percentages are lowest in double-blind studies, higher in single-blind studies, and highest in uncontrolled clinical reports of a treatment believed to be effective but subsequently shown to be ineffective or a placebo. The highest percentages occur in uncontrolled clinical reports because the physicians believe in their treatment and hence give their prognoses with conviction.[34]

Rapport: Patients rarely share mutual regard with their physicians for two reasons: the imbalance of power in the relationship and doctors don't usually have the time to build a friendly connection. However, the unconscious aspect of rapport, a state of harmony in which awareness and attention are focused on the other person, clearly plays a considerable role. Most patients give their doctor avid attention, listening carefully with eye contact and a furrowed forehead steeped in concentration. Studies show indirectly that increasing the rapport increases the placebo effect. This explains why some alternative therapies typically produce higher placebo responses. Doctors who practice alternative therapies often spend more time with the patient, show more enthusiasm, touch the patient more often, and also produce more ritual in their procedures.[35] They do this because alternative therapists are usually great believers in their therapies. All their procedures enhance rapport; subsequently, placebo effects increase.

Absorbed in Imagery: When a representation (pictorial or ideational) is vividly and energetically imagined, the brain responds to it as if it were real. When doctors speak, and our health is on the line, we listen. We wonder what will happen next, how the treatment will affect us, what the final prognosis will be, and how long it will take. These questions prime our imaginations as we await the doctor's pronouncement. The intensity of our focus virtually assures a greater degree of imagery. Once again, a greater degree of imagery also helps explain why alternative therapists tend to produce more placebo effects. Alternative therapists often surround the administration of the remedies with a certain degree of ritual. These healing rituals usually absorb the patient.

Dependence: The patient–doctor dynamic itself commands a dependence posture from the patient. We go to doctors for help because we are unable to cure ourselves. We depend on them for healing and guidance in matters of health. Our society is also dependent on medicines and therapies, not just the physicians themselves. Rituals in standard practice may also enhance dependence: distinctive white coats or surgical greens, stethoscopes hanging from necks, degrees on the wall, long waits, permission forms, and admission procedures.

Extreme Emotional Arousal: As Siegel stated earlier, "In other words, part of what we do as physicians is to scare people, and that adds to our own placebo effectiveness." Even those of us who aren't scared, when we're ill and in need of a treatment of some sort, usually approach the doctor with a degree of apprehension. For some, the emotional arousal can be so high that it triggers an ESS. During that momentary window of influence, a prognosis by the physician can be accepted uncritically whether it's an effective therapy or placebo. Remember also that confusion creates psychological discomfort that creates a drive to quell this cognitive distress. If it's profound enough, confusion alone can trigger an ESS. I think this helps explain why researchers are unable to predict which person in particular will respond favorably to placebos; it's hard to judge a patient's suggestibility.

SIEs are those times when we instantly accept or change a belief. Placebos only work to the extent that patients believe they work. Ultimately, it is the belief in the treatment that sets off the placebo response. And belief is something that lies inside the patient's mind. All the other ingredients of the ideal placebo—the external trappings, such as technology and the paraphernalia of medical authority—only work by increasing the patient's belief in the efficacy of the treatment. Anything that enhances the credibility of a particular kind of treatment will boost the capacity of that treatment to evoke the placebo response.

✳✳✳

We now know how and why spontaneous influence works. The next stage of this journey moves us toward practical applications of this vast and untapped resource. Chapter 8 teaches you how to become a powerful emotional guide, one who structures events so that they maximize potential benefits while actively negating or neutralizing harmful effects. You'll learn about fundamental assumptions to integrate into your world view that inevitably generate positive moments for everyone around you. You'll also discover how to mine core strengths and deliberately structure your language to take advantage of our natural human proclivity to personal growth and fulfillment.

Chapter 8

Creating a World of Possibilities

An informed emotional guide present during an emotionally critical event can constructively manage the tone, context, and interpretation in a positive manner.[1] Emotional events, given a positive spin, produce constructive self-perpetuating streams of events. Isn't that what all of us deserve? Isn't that what we want for our children? I designed this chapter to teach parents, teachers, counselors, and all those who work with children how to use powerful communication patterns effectively to foster successes for those in their care. These elements also work well with adults, but the wording and emphasis for much of this chapter is aimed toward children. This chapter presents the artful basics of becoming an informed emotional guide.

Carol, now a successful author, told an attentive talk-show audience her story of an abusive childhood. As a child, she found her only comfort by writing in her journal. The journal became her confidante. Tearfully, Carol named her fifth grade teacher as the inspiration for her writing. This particular teacher sat secretively backstage, listening to the account. At the appointed cue, the teacher walked on stage and surprised Carol. Carol walked up to the teacher and hugged her intensely. The teacher hugged back hesitantly, shrugging her shoulders, still unable to recognize Carol. Carol then told more of the story.

One Friday, many years ago, Carol arrived home realizing that her journal still sat on her desk at school. Frantically, she raced back to find the school locked. Unnerved all weekend, she rushed to school early Monday morning. Bursting into her classroom, she froze in panic. Her desktop was empty. The journal sat on the teacher's desk with the teacher sitting stoically behind it. Carol fought the urge to run. Mustering all her courage, she approached the desk. The teacher returned the journal to Carol with the following words, "Some day you'll be a great writer." Clearly, the teacher's words, intentional or not, produced a profound impact on Carol.

Carol's extreme emotional arousal catapulted her into an ESS. The teacher's surprising pronouncement further deepened her soaring suggestibility exponentially. Now, almost three decades later, she recalls this event tearfully as if it happened yesterday (hypermnesia). At the time of that event, Carol herself, her friends, family, and teachers probably didn't notice an immediate change in her behavior. Carol credits that moment as a monumental event that changed her life: a Spontaneous Influence Event (SIE).

The event itself passed unceremoniously; her teacher couldn't remember Carol or the event. Events like this appear serendipitous. Carol's teacher didn't plan such an intervention to maximize Carol's elevated suggestibility. Carol was simply the lucky recipient of an empowering comment, said with conviction, by a positive authority figure. This chapter, and the next, teaches the reader how to structure interventions and language to maximize positive effects during ESSs. At the very least, you will learn how to generate empowering pronouncements, like Carol's teacher did, making you a powerful emotional guide for those around you, adults as well as children.

Carol's teacher created a magnificently productive influence event without even knowing how. Positive agents of influence like her just seem to say the right words at the right time, intuitively. The power of knowing what to do is not magically parceled out to a fortunate few. This ability resides in all of us, awaiting its cultivation through knowledge. Learning the timing, skills, and attitudes at a conscious level can make you a similar influence agent.

LEARN ABOUT THE POTENTIAL POWER YOU WIELD

When I teach workshops on spontaneous influence, many participants feel paralyzed by the sudden realization of the personal responsibility this concept reveals. Most reflect back on some past events with sadness and remorse, horrified by the potential trauma they may have caused. If you find yourself experiencing feelings of guilt, forgive yourself unconditionally. After all, you were doing the best you could with the knowledge you had at the time. Make a conscious plan to use your new wisdom to correct any past unintentional misdeeds. Move forward confidently by practicing the constructive tools in these next chapters. Use them indiscriminately, whenever you can, and the balance of constructive results you inspire will soon tip the scale favorably.

We've all met extraordinarily positive people who inspire us. We feel warm and comfortable around them, beaming with confidence, ready to tackle our next challenge in life. They radiate a manner and fundamental belief system that invigorates us. We don't know how they do it, but we clearly feel the results of their encouraging interactions. These next chapters teach you the inherent components that help make these masters the constructive influences they are. These are not skills many of us possess naturally. When it comes to the use of specific language patterns, many of you will feel clumsy, tongue-tied at the prospect of saying the wrong thing. Stay with it. Like riding a bike, while daunting at first, the awkwardness soon diminishes as confidence and grace emerges. As this new behavior and attitude becomes ingrained, you will find yourself much like these masters you admire. You may find this the most fulfilling skill you ever learned. I did.

BECOMING AN INFORMED EMOTIONAL GUIDE

As adults, we typically hesitate at direct attempts to influence other adults. Two reasons for this exist. First, we shy away from attempts to change others because of an instinctive respect for their individuality. They are who they are and we question our right to meddle. Second, many of us don't believe people are capable of change, so we wonder why we would waste time trying. Additionally, we balk at other's bald-faced attempts to change us, expecting them to also react defensively to our efforts at influencing them.

We feel differently about influence with children. In fact, most of us feel duty bound to do what we can for the young. It's also safer to try and change them because they don't typically snap back with indignation. Discussing influence, with children as the recipient, seems much more palatable. Although the strategies discussed in this chapter work equally well with all ages, I prefer using anecdotes from childhood for the reasons listed above. I sprinkle anecdotes of adult SIEs lightly, to remind you of the breadth of applications available. These strategies make good medicine for the child in all of us.

While the techniques presented herein may appear simple, fruitful applications require as much artistry as methodology. Linguistic knowhow, exquisite timing, and the ability to elicit rapt attention are all crucial components of effective, artful intervention.

The applications considered in this chapter relate to communication patterns that maximize the effects of a suggestion. Some critics might say, "What ethical or moral right do we have to influence each other directly in this manner?" I address this concern emphatically: We do it anyway, even if naively. Everything we do influences others. By learning the tools in this chapter we make ourselves more responsible and deliberate in our methods, taking advantage of windows of opportunity by maximizing the teachable moment.

Ultimately, we are not trying to change people through influence events. Whenever I use these tools, I try to highlight some resource to help that person optimize his or her potential for success and happiness.

MAXIMIZE THE TEACHABLE MOMENT

As each of us drop in and out of ESSs regularly, we should take advantage of this and act in such a way as to maximize these teachable moments. Creating a world of possibilities, rather than one of obstacles, assures us that those we care for will always receive optimal benefits. At the very least, the procedures I discuss in this chapter make powerful tools, easily enlisted to build strengths in everyone.

We never know with certainty when a person's suggestibility rises to the threshold of spontaneous influence. Therefore, we should practice vigilance with all of our interactions, ensuring that they yield empowering mindsets. This doesn't mean we can't express honest anger or disappointment. It does mean that we should avoid the use of attributive statements, those that label or assign personality features, such as, "You're an idiot," which asserts the person's character as stupid. Attributive statements such as these plant the seed of pessimism and depression because *being stupid* is permanent, pervasive, and personal.[2] (Attributive statements work well when they're positive, planting an energized seed of optimism—"You're brilliant!")

Psychologists believe that attributive statements make a deep impression, particularly with children (e.g., "You're a troublemaker"; "You're a loser"). Attributions define for us *what* and *who* we are as individuals. They become perceptual filters that screen out contradictory evidence and accept validating information, creating a self-perpetuating cycle. Wounds delivered in words can create far more permanent damage than physical injuries. Words possess the power to program awareness and can be enlisted as tools or weapons. Therefore, we must exercise extreme caution regarding attributive statements.

Rather, we should practice more descriptive comments such as, "Playing recklessly and breaking the lamp sure got you into lots of trouble." This criticism identifies the problem as temporary and specific, something correctable. The statement focuses on the bad decision by the child, not the child's character. To do this we must ensure that our fundamental assumptions about development and learning yield maximum benefits for the developmental nature of the child. Children benefit most when adults caring for them work from positive fundamental assumptions. Holding these assumptions benefits adults too, serving all of us.

SEVEN POSITIVE FUNDAMENTAL ASSUMPTIONS

Positive people do more good by accident than negative people do by design. People like Carol's teacher from the previous anecdote, who unwittingly inspire others, literally nurture potential greatness in everyone. These human catalysts of empowerment typically embrace the following fundamental assumptions about humanity.

1. What we often refer to as failure is really just feedback. Bill Marriott of the immensely successful Marriott Hotel Chain said, "Failure? I never encountered it. All I ever met were temporary setbacks." Successful people usually view any current lack of success as critical information about how to improve. Success develops by learning from setbacks. The only true failure comes from quitting. Losers will say, "I can't do it" and not try, while winners will often qualify by adding, "I can't do it YET" and keep trying. The powerful word *yet* orients the mind to continue to search for solutions rather than dwell on obstacles and excuses. Remember that every failure provides a lesson on improvement or change. Every successful person has a long list of failures that taught important lessons. High achievers exude confidence in their ability to learn. This does not mean that they do not feel discouraged from time to time. All learners suffer frustration, and the great ones probably more so. When you see a successful person, you also see someone who likely survived an inordinate amount of failures. Failures do not incapacitate achievers because they believe that failure provides a critical step in the process of learning.

2. We all possess the capacity to wield tremendous influence. We need to acknowledge this capacity to appreciate the gravity of our messages. A careless comment ascribed to a child's character may create a lifelong result. An attributive comment made during a moment of weakness requires immediate attention. The astute emotional guide (1) addresses the correction immediately, (2) disqualifies the earlier statement, (3) reframes the negative interpretation to positive, and (4) models responsibility for owning behavior. The portrayal below illustrates these components.

> I'd like to talk with you for a moment, Wade. Earlier today I said, "You never pay attention when I'm talking to you. All you ever do is goof around." [1. Addressed the same day or as soon as possible.] I'm sorry for saying that. Clearly I was wrong. [2. Disqualify the earlier statement.] Obviously you pay attention to things that interest you. I see you are paying close attention to me now. Thank you. [3. Not paying attention is reframed to "paying attention."] I snapped at you because I was frustrated. [4. Modeling responsibility for your own behavior.]

3. The person is not the problem. Children who exhibit recurring patterns of problematic behaviors usually hold an unfavorable interpretation of themselves or the world in general. Attempts by adults to correct the behavior may generate resistance from the child because each views the behavior differently. For example, adults may view aggressive behavior as a problem while the child may experience it as a solution.

Teachers told Jordan's parents that Jordan had difficulty with anger management. Jordan got angry easily, produced violent outbursts, and frightened other children who feared for their safety. Jordan lived a relatively unhappy life. He suffered abuse from alcoholic parents and classmates frequently picked on him because of his unkempt appearance. Those close to him had produced most of his suffering, and Jordan's anger effectively kept others from getting close enough to hurt him again.

The teacher and the other children saw Jordan's anger as the problem. Jordan regarded his anger as the solution to his problem. His anger worked as a barrier to keep potentially painful people away. Attempts to correct his "anger" resulted in resistance (consciously or unconsciously) because Jordan experienced his anger as his ally. Effective change must focus on the child's understanding of his or her world, not the adult's.

4. *We hold all the personal resources we need to solve our own problems.* Changes in behavior, self-esteem, motivation, attitude, or the development of a skill result from changes in the child's model of the world. What one child sees as a stumbling block, another sees as a developmental opportunity. What one child experiences as insurmountable odds, another experiences as the ultimate challenge. One child may perceive a high degree of difficulty as discouraging, while another child may perceive a high degree of difficulty as motivating.

Consider the humorous story of the little boy overheard talking to himself as he practiced his baseball swing. "I am the greatest batter in the world," he would say proudly while throwing the ball in the air. Time after time he swung and missed with the bat, all the time repeating his claim, "I'm the greatest batter in the world." After countless missed swings he appeared frustrated, paused, then smiled as he proclaimed, "Wow! What a great pitcher!" He found a way to constructively name a personal resource to build upon.

Children possess immense potential. Our job is to note their resources and enlist them to help in restructuring a constructive model of the world. Change that comes from within, a change in our models, is fundamentally more influential than external changes. We take our models of the world with us wherever we go and we apply them indiscriminately.

Changing a destructive self-affirming model of the world typically requires the shattering of that current model. There are two ways to change them. SIEs are the only device powerful enough to do it instantly. However, we can't always manufacture spontaneous influence, so how then do we change a negative model? This chapter and the next one teach you the precise mechanisms to renovate harmful models over extended periods of time. In addition, Chapter 9 shows you how to initiate elevated suggestibility to produce a SIE.

5. *The core of all behavior yields a useful resource.* To lead others, you must start where they are and guide them gently using their own resources and

strengths. Challenge yourself to find something positive at the core of even the most disagreeable behaviors.

Genes give us the foundation of our models. Experiences give us individual identities. Behaviors express our individual needs, desires, urges, attitudes, beliefs, and so on. In this way, all behaviors are purposeful. It is our job as supportive adults to find a constructive purpose. This does not mean that we should view violent behavior as resourceful; rather, we can enlist the core of violent behavior as a positive resource (e.g., Violent behavior may exemplify an eagerness to take control, an ability to respond authoritatively, or a refusal to be victimized). Ask yourself in what context or situation would the core of a particular behavior signify value? For example, "Your refusal to be victimized will help you grow more tolerant with people as you mature." This comment orients the child toward a more fulfilling future because it validates the child's world view and enlists the core of the behavior as a positive resource.

6. *We build from our strengths, not our weaknesses.* Focusing on children's strengths helps them cultivate their personal resources, empowers them to take responsibility for their actions, and channels their behaviors in constructive directions. Focusing on weaknesses orients the child toward failure, fosters anxiety and discouragement, and promotes feelings of helplessness. Discouraged children find it all too easy to *not* do something and they evolve into masters at avoidance or compulsive perfectionists. Emphasizing strengths keeps children solution-focused, not problem-centered.

7. *Children may easily or spontaneously excel in the most extraordinary ways.* Our culture promotes a rather narrow perception of intelligence. Once we abandon our restricted way of seeing intelligence, we soon discover that children know a great deal more than we typically give them credit for. Because children typically learn faster and behave more creatively than many adults, we find it easier to see that they are indeed bright with great potential. Celebrate these moments to create positive SIEs; many exist for those who look.

We now know that emotional intelligence, and the ability to manage your emotions, is a better predictor of happiness and success. Excelling in these areas pays off with remarkably productive results. Signs of emotional or intellectual genius may erupt at any time. Ready yourself and eagerly anticipate pleasant surprises. Charles Darwin, Thomas Edison, Louis Pasteur, and Leo Tolstoy received poor to average evaluations from their early teachers. Nurture successes, however small. It's easy to imagine children as imminently successful if you rid yourself of narrow beliefs about intelligence, success, and happiness. Excellence, intelligence, and success come in many forms (e.g., altruistically, athletically, artistically, dramatically, emotionally, intellectually, mathematically, mechanically, musically, organizationally, passionately, rhythmically, socially, tenaciously, verbally, etc., ad infinitum). Celebrate them all.

Those who operate from the fundamental assumptions mentioned above can't help but encourage the children in their care. Think of those who forged the most positive influences in your life. Fundamental assumptions like the ones described here create high expectations of the self-perpetuating variety.

HOW GENUINE EXPECTATIONS DRIVE BEHAVIOR

We frequently misunderstand the concept of expectations. Parents may *expect* their children to keep their rooms clean at all times, teachers may *expect* that everyone come to class on time, and the boss may *expect* you to take professional development seriously. Expectations such as these are really demands. Demands impose external requirements and serve some authoritative goal of the person in power.

Genuine expectations reflect a self-concept or world view. They direct the expectation holder's energy, attention, and awareness. The following examples of internal, *genuine*, expectations illustrate their dynamic nature.

I expect to get along with my colleagues (an expectation of *my* behavior). An internal expectation such as this focuses my attention on opportunities to make connections and smooth out tensions. My model of *myself* drives this expectation. In this next example, my model of the *world* steers it: I expect my boss to be insensitive (an expectation of the *boss's* behavior). This expectation doesn't just focus my attention on the times the boss is insensitive, it also drives me to instinctively interpret his intentions as insensitive, and dismiss moments of sensitivity as artificial. Note that my expectations of the boss's behavior do not affect his behavior, only *my* interpretation of it is affected. Whether expectations are driven by my model of self or the world, genuine expectations drive *my* behavior and interpretive mechanisms, not someone else's.

If I expect my children to excel, but my children expect themselves to fail, their expectations direct their behavior with considerably more influence than mine. However, expectations we hold for our children, if held with consistent conviction, produce active responses, that eventually generate corresponding expectations within our children. Our goal is to help children generate their own positive expectations.

Holding high expectations of children refers to the process of seeing them as possessors of potential greatness. When you truly see children this way, your expectations manifest themselves in a host of verbal and nonverbal messages. Those that see potential greatness in children take every opportunity to encourage the child and dwell on success, seeing temporary setbacks as masked opportunities. Encouragement is emotional nourishment for the ravenous ego of the young child. Even lower mammals crave emotional nourishment more than physical nourishment. Scientific experiments on rhesus monkeys showed that babies actually preferred furry mother models without milk to wire models with milk.[3] With children, their hypersensitivity to emotional nourishment increases their susceptibility to words of encouragement "You sure learn quickly."

It's important to understand the difference between praise and encouragement. Praise is an external reward that has to be earned; it's usually given when a standard is met: "Good job, Hal." Encouragement isn't contingent on meeting an external goal; it focuses on strengths and assets, not the result. What would you rather hear? "Good job, Madeline," or "Madeline, I see how well things are going and I appreciate how hard you're working at it. Your attention to detail makes my job easier" (shows appreciation, notes assets and effort, and it isn't contingent on success).

In essence, high expectations do not create success in and of themselves. High expectations help eliminate mental blocks to success by elevating motivation and generating a success orientation. While sincere high expectations don't ensure success, they create those conditions most suitable for it to exist, but only if the expectations are reasonable. For example, my expectations to play professional basketball are futile. I'm in my fifties, I'm relatively short (5' 9"), and out of practice. However, holding expectations to flourish at basketball with my peers is perfectly reasonable, but only if I am committed to the effort required to excel. Expectations, if genuine, generate action. The holder of the expectations actively pursues that which is expected as if success is merely a matter of time and opportunity. The person who expects to succeed instinctively pursues that end. The person who only hopes to succeed waits for success to come knocking. Hope, masquerading as an expectation, is easy to identify; a passive component of *wait and see* exists, often exemplified in such language as the hesitant, "I'll try."

Parents and teachers must convince themselves that all children have immense potential. This is easier than you think because it is true. Under the proper conditions, prodigies may quickly develop. If development goes slowly, we can plant fertile seeds of success for future yields. Children do not need to show brilliance now for it to evolve later. A great Chinese proverb states, "To see things in the seed, that is genius." Many famous figures unfolded slowly or later in life: Beethoven initially played the violin poorly, Caruso's teacher claimed he could not sing, Einstein's teacher described him as slow and unable to concentrate, Winston Churchill failed grade six, and Isaac Newton received poor grades in elementary school. While all children may not achieve such greatness, all children possess the basis for success and happiness.

What would you do differently as a parent or teacher if you actively expected that your children were capable of great achievements? Remember that great achievements are not restricted to Olympic gold medals. Great achievements are reachable goals like completing a somersault, making tasty brownies, or forgiving a friend's mistake. How would your children act if they sensed your unconditional faith in their achievements? The answers to these questions are clearly documented in scientific research as well as common sense. We must saturate children with positive suggestions. In this way the likelihood of the anticipated future increases exponentially. Faith (in the form of active expectations) shall move heaven and earth, and most certainly a child. The following anecdote illustrates the critical element of genuine expectations, held by a teacher.

Eric Butterworth tells an inspiring tale of high expectations in *Chicken Soup for the Soul* (1993).[4] A professor sent his sociology class to a school in a slum to record case histories of 200 young boys. The sociology students concluded that each boy appeared doomed to a bleak future. More than two decades later another sociology professor sent his class out to find out what had happened to these 200 boys. Of the 180 still surviving in that neighborhood, all of these men had achieved extraordinary success as doctors, lawyers, and productive members of the community. The professor, determined to find out how these men had beaten seemingly overwhelming odds, followed up with interviews. Each of the men credited the same particular teacher; someone who had seen great potential in each of them. This teacher's expectations, held with conviction, drove her to actively nurture and support imminent success in all her students.

Genuine expectations generate internally driven, automatic behavior. If I expect children to excel in some form, I am prone to notice evidence of excellence everywhere, celebrate it, and ignore or minimize contradictory evidence. Noticing and celebrating behaviors increases their expression. Hence, positive expectations, actively pursued, and held with conviction, foster greatness in children. Make sure your expectations are genuine.

Now that we know how expectations generate affirming behavior, we can focus on learning tools that generate expectations. Building expectations assembles the foundation of self-perpetuating behavior.

PRESUPPOSITIONS: BUILDING EXPECTATIONS

To build expectations, we must create mindsets that generate them. We can dispute or accept direct statements because of their clarity "You will graduate from college." Assumptions, on the other hand, elicit a degree of faith and often pass unchallenged because of their undeclared nature: "What do you think you'll do after you graduate from college?"

Essentially, presuppositions are assumptions embedded in statements. The embedded assumption that this person will graduate from college lies concealed. Presuppositions work effectively because of their subtlety. The opportunity to consciously challenge the statement diminishes considerably because the underlying assumption is never really stated directly. Clinical hypnotists use this strategy regularly to expedite a therapeutic state "Would you like to go into a deep hypnotic state or a mild one?" This statement presumes the person currently exhibits a readiness to go into a hypnotic state. The subject feels compelled to answer the question and is often too busy paying attention to its literal meaning to unravel the embedded assumption. Gracefully, the therapist implicitly initiates an expectation of a hypnotic state in the subject. When therapists elicit an expectation of a specific result, the manifestation of that result increases considerably.

Expectations generate a way of fulfilling themselves through self-validating perceptions. For example, we usually produce numerous muscle twitches during normal day-to-day living. The vast majority typically pass unnoticed, but a person preparing to enter a hypnotic state will notice the twitch and interpret it as a sign that the hypnotic state is developing. Those who think they can't be hypnotized will interpret the same twitch as a sign of wakefulness. In either instance, the perceived meaning of the normally ignored muscle twitch supports whatever expectation the subject holds.

Presuppositions, if unchallenged, generate their own self-confirming evidence. They ordinarily remain unchallenged because of their subtle, undeclared nature. This makes them powerful seeds of influence. Learning the structure of presuppositions will help you create your own positive seeds for planting.

THE STRUCTURE OF PRESUPPOSITIONS

Examine the presuppositions that follow and determine what assumptions are present.

1. "More effort is required."
2. "You throw that like a girl."
3. "Those questions become easier with practice."
4. "One day, and I don't know when, that will seem easy to you."

You probably noted that the first two statements are discouraging and negative while the last two statements are encouraging and positive. The first statement presumes that this person produces inadequate effort. Comments like this ultimately discourage someone who may already be working hard, leading to feelings of helplessness. The second statement insults the recipient and half the population of the world. The last two statements used presuppositions in a positive way. These statements presuppose intelligence, capability, and perseverance, leading to eventual success (perseverance is a hallmark of optimism). Presuppositions often perpetuate ethnic and gender stereotypes. For example, many adults might ask a young girl playing doctor, "Are you going to be a nurse when you grow up?" This gender-biased question appears to assume that women in medicine should be nurses and men should be doctors.

Presuppositions generate responses because of their hidden meanings. We feel inclined to respond to the literal level of the message and consequently, we often miss or don't consciously acknowledge the deeper assumption. Using the conjunction *but* can produce that effect. Have you ever been complimented but felt criticized at the same time? "You're doing excellent work, *but* you could get even better results if you tried harder." At a social level it appears like a compliment, and the speaker probably intends it that way. However, we typically respond consciously or unconsciously to the presupposition that our effort needs boosting. The conjunction *but* discounts or disqualifies whatever came before it. The result produces the empty feeling of discouragement.

I believe that most of us issue communications of the discouraging variety out of ignorance, not out of malice. Once we gain an awareness of our "big buts" we will prudently replace them with "ands." Notice the difference in the following statement: "You're doing excellent work, *and* you will get even better results as you *continue* to try harder." This language structure acknowledges good work without discounting it, acknowledges the person's effort, and anticipates a continued effort. The statement validates the effort and offers encouragement at the same time. The formula is rather simple but intensely effective. Change *but* to *and*, and place *continue* immediately before the contingency (better results are contingent on continued effort). Here is another example: "Your training is going smoothly, *but* you need to pay more attention to detail. Applying the formula you get: "Your training is going well *and* your success will increase as you *continue* to pay attention to detail."

Use presumptive language whenever you can. In addition to changing *but* to *and*, use *when* instead of *if*. Change "If you improve" to "When you improve." Teach yourself and children to use presumptive language themselves. Learn to say "will" instead of "hope to" or "want to." Correct yourself and children who say, "I want to try harder at _____" and commit to saying, "I *will* try harder at _____."

Presuppositions elicit expectations that orient the person's mental framework and behavior in the direction of fulfilling such expectations. This whole process of seeding and fostering healthy expectations speeds up immensely if we feel that we are already en-route to success. You can do this by interpreting all their current behaviors as aids to inevitable success in the future.

ALL BEHAVIOR IS RESOURCEFUL, IF IDENTIFIED AS SUCH

Almost every aspect of your personality is arguably a resource (or obstacle) for your successful adaptation in life. I addressed several teachers during a presentation on communication structures. I looked at one teacher and said, "Your careful attention to detail *makes* you an excellent leader." This teacher nodded her head in a matter-of-fact motion, indicating that what I had said was self-evident. I then asked the others to comment on my statement. The teachers listed numerous ways that leadership is enhanced by paying attention to detail: "It ensures that everyone gets to be heard," "It helps by avoiding problems in the long run," "It's the little details that makes things run smoothly," and so on. I then asked what would have happened if I had stated the complete opposite: "Your careful attention to detail *interferes* with your leadership abilities." The teachers found it equally easy to list numerous ways leadership could be hindered by paying attention to detail: "Losing sight of the overall picture," "Becoming insensitive to people," "Forgetting long term goals," and so on.

I provided this illustration to show them how my statement had directed their thinking, channeling it into the direction I wanted it to go. Additionally, I demonstrated to these teachers how, upon hearing my message, they automatically set about validating it by generating evidence in its support. Our thinking organizes itself around understanding a message before we agree or disagree. We need to do this to make sense of the communication. How we evaluate a communication comes after we understand it.

Associations between abstract concepts such as *leadership* (something we all display, depending on contexts and motivations) and *paying attention to detail* (something we all do, but in varying degrees) are tenuous at best. It is precisely this tenuous quality that triggers us to automatically go about mentally searching for evidence to support the comment. Making sense of the communication helps us avoid the mental uneasiness associated with not knowing. The mental act of making sense of the comment actually invests us in the statement itself, "It must have merit if we've assembled validating evidence."

Consider the following apparently contradictory comment, "I can see how losing a lot of money could make you a richer person." The obscure nature of this comment demands that the listener work at interpreting its meaning. For example, losing a lot of money may force someone to recognize friends as supportive; accordingly, they may feel richer. Another person may interpret this to mean that losing a lot of money teaches you a great lesson about how to make even more money next time; hence, a richer person through experience. Notice that each interpretation leads in a positive direction. That's because the statement proposes a positive result, ". . . could make you a richer person," guiding you subtly in that direction.

When we hear obscure statements like the one above, we each create our own interpretations, consistent with our models of the world.

Listeners individually determine exactly how the statement best fits for themselves and their models. Obscure statements orient the listener's mind toward a positive outcome that subjectively suits him or her best. In a very real sense, each listener receives a challenge to produce a personalized positive thought.

Read the following two statements and consciously observe yourself going through this usually unconscious process. "Sometimes a speeding ticket can be the best thing," and "Getting sick can really help you put things in perspective." Pause here and make sense of the statements before you continue reading. (Pause) Notice how you instinctively attempt to understand these statements by validating them with supportive statements (e.g., A speeding ticket makes you slow down; hence, a safer driver. Getting sick can be a signal that you are working too hard, thereby putting things in order.).

After all is said and done, is attention to detail beneficial, detrimental, or indifferent to leadership? It depends. Everybody pays attention to some details and not others. Whether it works as an obstacle or a benefit depends on how we think about it. How we think about it stems from our beliefs. For example, if I believe attention to detail enhances leadership, I will pay attention to detail boldly and confidently, incorporating these modes as a conscious part of my leadership style. If I believe attention to detail hinders leadership, I will pay attention to detail hesitantly, anxiously, and privately.

We all pay close attention to detail sometimes; at other times we ignore details and focus on the big picture. Sometimes we look for consensus, and other times we may make dogmatic, unilateral decisions. This list of apparent contradictions is inexhaustible. Who is to say which of these opposing behaviors serves as a resource for which goal, and at which time? If we asked ten different people what qualities make up a first-class leader, we would probably generate ten different lists. Of course some items would overlap, but many would also conflict. Someone might list tenacity as a fundamental quality of leadership while someone else might steadfastly disagree. The point is, we all achieve our goals in different ways by calling upon different resources. We can enlist almost any behavior as a resource if we believe it to be one.

Sadly, we can also enlist almost any behavior as an obstacle too.[5] Delegating authority can enhance or impede leadership; so can its opposite, centralizing decisions. For example, imagine the following scenario. You would like to tell your associate that delegating authority among his staff causes confusion. Which of the following two comments would produce the best result? "Your delegating of authority causes confusion among your staff," or "Your centralizing of decisions fosters clarity among your staff." Both comments address the same issue; one names an obstacle and the other a resource. Be careful not to highlight that which is apparently negative, discouraging the recipient with a careless comment.

While not all behaviors are positive, every behavior encompasses a positive feature at its core. Steer perceptions to a positive focus and you've found a personal resource. In this past section, we used examples of behavior that were already present (e.g., paying attention to detail). Now that we know we can enlist almost any aspect of behavior as a resource, we must practice finding inherent resources in behaviors that may not look all that resourceful.

FINDING RESOURCES

Contrast the following two statements said to students: "Your frequent talking *makes* you a real annoyance in my class," and "Your eagerness to express your thoughts *helps* you come up with all sorts of interesting ideas." "Frequent talking" was reframed to "eagerness to express your thoughts." Finding the inherent resource allows the teacher to move in a positive direction. Consider another common problem that teachers raise. Contrast "Your constant aggressive outbursts make the other children avoid you," with "Your ability to express your emotions will help you learn to get along with people in a more positive way." "Aggressive outburst" was reframed to "ability to express emotions."

Some readers may accuse me of oversimplifying the correction of recurring behaviors. Quite the contrary. Correcting behavior takes time, patience, and a clear goal. I believe that engaging the child and the child's personal resources as an agent of change, speeds up the process dramatically. Outside moments of spontaneous influence, adults need more than a single statement to address patterned disruptive behavior, but statements like the ones above assist children in constructing their own growth. Proposing an explicit goal (to get along with people in a more positive way) accompanied by an identified inherent resource (an ability to express emotions) garners much more support than a direct command ("Stop being aggressive."). Our goal is to name resources to recruit children in their own quests for adaptation. Commands trigger defenses and don't provide coaching for correction.

Identify some feature of the child's behavior as a resource that can be employed to empower the child. Children will then automatically set out to validate this belief and manifest it in their behaviors. Teach yourself to see the underlying assets of all behavior. Take fighting as an example. What purpose does fighting serve? It keeps people away, shows others who is boss, and establishes a sense of power. What inherent resources are present? The ability to size up a situation quickly, form snap judgments, and react quickly are all assets. Always look for the underlying assets in a behavior. If a child exhibits recurring problematic behavior, using the strengths inherent in the child's behavior moves a giant step toward building a constructive future.

Children produce an enormous variety of behaviors throughout the day. Always point out how underlying skills serve a purpose for them. Channel their assets to serve more productive ends. Teachers can describe the class clown as someone with a great sense of timing. Encourage the student to use timing toward a more productive end. Honor the child's skill and encourage him to develop it further. "Your great sense of timing *makes* you an excellent learner. *As* your timing *continues* to mature you'll gain a better sense of when, and when not to be, humorous." Be creative, "Your ability to help everybody see the lighter side makes you a great leader." The following anecdote illustrates just such an episode.

Comedian John Lequizamo loved cracking jokes in school, playing the role of class clown. He recalls a time when his math teacher pulled him aside. He awaited the usual scolding, but this time his teacher said, "Listen, instead of being obnoxious all the time—instead of wasting all that energy in class—why don't you re-channel your hostility and humor into something productive? Have you ever thought about being a comedian?" Stunned, he found himself speechless, without his regular smart-ass retort. He couldn't get that thought out of his head for the rest of the day. Recalling that moment he says, "But that one moment Mr. Zufa collared me was the turning point in my life. Everything kind of converged, you know? The planets aligned."[6] This incident turned into a SIE because the teacher's statement stunned him (elevated suggestibility through emotional arousal).

All the strategies discussed so far work smoothly. As you practice and develop proficiency using these tools, your confidence increases. Confidence carries conviction. Speaking with conviction enhances influence. Authenticity is essential because we all see through contrived statements.

EMPOWERING OTHERS BY SPEAKING WITH CONVICTION

Seeing immense potential and naming it with conviction is the single greatest gift we can give to each other. It bears a lifelong gift of empowerment when delivered during an Elevated Suggestibility State (ESS).

Speaking with conviction gives your expression that essential ring of truth. The key is to speak as if your statement bears its own objective validity: "Your willingness to make errors makes you a good learner." Some may snicker when they hear this because it initially sounds like a contradiction. Invariably though, people are more likely to tackle their next tasks with confidence, failing proudly. Whenever I deliver that sentence, I say it with conviction because I *believe* it. Even if you deliver a positive suggestion awkwardly, it still works. Conviction provides added punch by driving it home with authority.

Sometimes people are uncomfortable giving compliments. If that is you, do it in the third person when the subject of your tribute is present: "I'd like you to meet Jerod. He's absolutely magnificent with numbers." This way it sounds descriptive avoiding the emptiness of flattery or self-serving praise. It also sounds sincere, magnifying itself with the weight of conviction. Affirming people regularly, in the third person, makes you a master builder of self-esteem in others.

If you believe with certainty, as I do, that we can enlist the root of any behavior as a resource, then suggestions you deliver will undoubtedly carry immense weight. We are not trying to dupe each other or our children to control them with veiled influence. That is clearly wrong and it will ultimately fail. We are trying to broaden our models of the world to lay the groundwork for a healthy and positive mind-set. The surest way to do that is to identify and then nurture personal strengths.

NURTURING RESOURCES

We all produce extraordinary amounts of behavior in the regular course of a day. Most of the underlying assets pass unnoticed. Highlight an asset and watch it grow. When you underline a phrase in a sentence it stands out. Noticing a resource makes it stand out too. When people dress up for a party and you tell them how attractive they look, they feel and subsequently act more attractive. They carry themselves more proudly, smile more deeply, and exude more confidence—you underlined them.

Noticing any commonly unnoticed behavior increases its expression, validates you as a keen observer, enhances rapport, and raises the person's susceptibility to subsequent information by reducing his or her resistance. Abrupt salespeople use this same approach awkwardly, "I can tell by the way you examine that car that you're a person who admires the finer things in life." Such comments usually make us suspicious for two reasons. They don't know us well enough to make such observations, and they spew these flattering statements for self-serving reasons. Still though, many of us blush at this heavy-handed overture, agreeing with the obvious "truth" of the salesperson's astute observation.

It isn't necessary to collect strong evidence about a person's behavior before you use it as a resource. Herein lies a critical point. Highlighting previously unnoticed details or making subtle observations about a person's strengths can make the biggest difference in achieving a goal. Uncovering a resource from what appears to be troublesome behavior is particularly powerful. To a withdrawn or shy child "Your ability to examine situations carefully keeps you prepared to work well with others." To the aggressive child "Your ability to sense a person's weaknesses will make you a sensitive friend."

A wonderful teacher from my past once told me, "If you want something, just imagine it, and sure enough, it will appear." We don't even need explicit evidence of a skill or resource if we want to enlist it. I worked with a teacher who continually berated his students, using every opportunity to find fault and criticize. I spoke with him one day and commented that his sensitive and supportive manner really helped the children in his class feel comfortable. Over the next few days, and almost every time we crossed paths for several weeks, he related episodes of his patient and supportive attitude with students. It's important to note that he didn't report these events as if he had successfully tried out a new behavior. He simply related these events to me because he sensed in me someone who appreciated his sensitive and supportive manner. Now the wheel squeaks less often. He eventually developed a reputation as a gruff teddy bear with a big heart. Did my comment make him more considerate? No. However, my highlighting of his sensitive and supportive manner led him to similarly highlight it (evidenced by his comments to me), creating a self-perpetuating cycle.

A CAVEAT REGARDING FAILURE

It is important to let children fail. Parents who overprotect their children from anxiety and frustration often produce the very feelings they are trying to avoid. Without the opportunity to rebound from mistakes, using their own resources, fearfulness takes hold and opens the door to helplessness. It is better to acknowledge failure as temporary, specific, and a reflection of circumstance: You did poorly on that project because you didn't give it enough attention, needed better materials, needed more time, and so on. Treat failure as fleeting. Don't dismiss it. If your child thinks he's lousy at math, don't tell him he's a great athlete. Tell him you understand that he struggles with math and empathize with his frustration. When the time is right, point out that he's good at athletics because he spends more time with it and perseveres through failure. These skills, that he currently possesses, are the same ones that will help him improve in math when he's committed and ready.

This chapter opened with Carol's inspirational story of how her teacher empowered her to become a great writer. Carol's teacher spoke with conviction, making a prophetic pronouncement during Carol's ESS. The teacher performed this profoundly influential act without understanding how it worked its magic. Think how powerfully positive you will be, armed with these tools and a sound understanding of their dynamics.

Now that you've captured the role of emotional guide, your foundation stands secure. The next chapter gives you the tools for refining your technique. These powerful tools equip you to construct positive suggestions and then create conditions that magnify their effects.

Chapter 9

Tools of Influence

When we honestly see others as vessels of immense potential, and when we direct or redirect them constructively, we help them conceive a brighter future. Is anything more rewarding than that? The language patterns described in this chapter are powerful mechanisms of influence for anybody, at any time. The power of these tools increases exponentially during an Elevated Suggestibility State (ESS), making them a Spontaneous Influence Event (SIE). Use them generously whenever you can. The time is always ripe.

These tools may appear magical, but they are not mysterious in any sense of the word. Magic acts work by taking advantage of our brain's natural optical propensities and attentional predispositions. What the magician calls sleight-of-hand and misdirection remains almost entirely invisible to most of us, while the trained eye of an experienced magician sees what we typically miss. In a similar fashion, the subtle tools presented here also take advantage of our mind's natural propensities, also producing effects outside the conscious awareness of an untrained observer. One such natural propensity is our inclination to make crude associations of cause and effect.

ASSUMPTIONS OF CAUSE AND EFFECT

In the absence of obvious contradictory evidence, we automatically associate events when they are closely related in time or space. I recently volunteered to collect door-to-door donations for a heart-fund. I walked up to Mrs. Miller's home and rang the bell. Instantly, the porch light came on. Wow! Connecting the light to the bell seemed like a clever security feature. I asked her how she did it, but she laughed, explaining how she had seen me walking up her steps. By coincidence, she turned the light on at the same time my finger hit the bell. If I hadn't inquired, I would have continued to assume that the bell and light were connected. My hasty assumption is a prime example of how we constantly make connections in our world, interpreting events in a way that makes sense to us. Our minds evolved in such a way that we automatically make associations where none may actually exist. We then go about our lives accepting our interpretation of events as objective reality. This happens in the interpersonal world too.

A short time ago I told a funny story and laughed with my friends. Everybody laughed except one friend who glared with a sullen expression. I wondered how my story had offended her, or if she was privy to some information that would have made my story inappropriate. I immediately associated her scowl with my story. Such associations are often absurd, but we make them automatically nonetheless. Later, when I inquired, I found out she had intended to frown at another acquaintance; the one who began reading while I was talking. I unwittingly caught the glare intended for another and assumed it was directed toward me.

One of the problems with the mind's automatic processes is that we instinctively accept rudimentary associations as correct, rarely checking to confirm them. This makes evolutionary sense. If we challenged the hosts of daily assumptions we make regularly, we'd never get anything done. In our evolutionary past, the immense benefit of making swift decisions outweighed the minor cost of making hasty assumptions.

Our inclination to make rough and thoughtless connections happens linguistically as well. Hypnotists subtly lead their subjects into calculated experiences by taking advantage of the mind's natural proclivity to generate hasty linguistic connections. This linguistic technique is called a *cause–effect language construction*. Cause–effect language constructions make powerful tools when used skillfully during SIEs. Creative use can put a positive spin on even the direst circumstances.

CAUSE–EFFECT LANGUAGE CONSTRUCTIONS

Cause–effect language constructions claim that some behavior, internal state, or external factor affects you in some definitive way: "Closing your eyes *helps* you to relax before a test," "Thinking of past successes *gives* you more energy," or "More light in the room *makes* your concentration improve." These constructions don't need to be true to be accepted.

One of my graduate students told me of a personal incident she experienced in junior college. She had worked diligently on a topic for her public speaking course. The presentation succeeded and the instructor commended her, saying, "Your ability to prepare and present clearly would make you an excellent teacher." That comment prompted her to consider teaching as a career. Soon thereafter she enrolled in an education program, graduated, and began a successful career in teaching. Sincere praise by an authority figure probably elevated her receptiveness to suggestion, and the linked statement oriented her toward finding success in teaching. She recalled this comment as a critical factor in her career choice. The vivid memory of such a mundane statement indicates an ESS.

A cause–effect language construction does not always work as gracefully as it did in this example; still, the effects are often as dramatic. It is important to note that the instructor's comment didn't *make* her become a teacher; rather, it only focused her attention on teaching as a possibility. Her career considerations may have differed if the instructor had commented, "Your ability to prepare and present clearly would make you an excellent advertising executive." Linking statements by using cause–effect constructions orients the mind in the same way that looking through a telescope orients your field of view. Transition words are simple forms of cause–effect constructions that smoothly link ideas.

TRANSITIONAL LANGUAGE

Words such as *as, and, while, because,* and *when* build a relationship between parts of a sentence. These transition words imply a meaningful relationship between ideas. "*As* you wrestle with the first few examples, you will detect a sense of excitement about your ability."

Clinical hypnotists practice this strategy regularly. Imagine that you are listening to someone deliver the following two sets of statements. Contrast these two examples. This first set has no transitions.

> "You are sitting in your chair."
> "You are thinking of your breath."
> "You are waiting."
> "You are relaxing."
> "You are tired."
> "Your eyes are blinking."

This second example incorporates transitions to create flowing language.

> *While* sitting in your chair you notice your breathing ... *and as* you wait ... *and* notice your breath ... you become more relaxed ... *making* you begin to feel tired ... *and* you realize that your eyes are beginning to blink.

Even when ideas aren't related, simply adding transitions connects them. Therapists use these powerful constructions to skillfully guide their clients into highly suggestible mental states.

Using cause–effect language constructions to steer awareness is a simple process. If you want someone to consider an idea, construct links between what is verifiable and what you want to occur. Remember that to lead someone effectively you must start from their current position. For example: "As you read this passage (reading this passage is verifiable), you begin to recall a distinctive teacher from your past (leading)." These two ideas bear nothing in common, but they sound related when presented in this way. The purpose is not one of deception; you want to lead through smooth transitions.

Ideas cultivated and proposed in appropriate ways often bypass conscious screening. The conscious mind, limited by a belief system, continually makes judgments about what is possible and what is not. Linking-statements, such as cause–effect language constructions, can broaden possibilities. Using words that imply a cause–effect relationship between two ideas invites the listener to respond as if one thing did indeed cause the other.

Follow the instructions in the short passage below while paying careful attention to your thoughts and mental images.

> *As* you look closely at each word, individually, while reading this passage slowly and carefully, you begin to wonder what experience it is initiating, *and as* you continue reading, you may begin to notice the blinking of your eyes *because* of the work they are doing. *And while* reading this passage you also discern a sense of the book's size, weight, *and* the texture of its cover, which *makes* you recall the first time you saw this book.

Were you aware of looking closely at each word while reading slowly? Are you now? Were you aware of blinking your eyes (or not blinking)? Were you aware of the size and texture of the text, and your first encounter with it? None of these experiences are necessarily related, but transitions make it easier and more natural for the reader to submit to the process. Go back and read this passage again; deliberately submit to the process.

I used three kinds of transitions in the indented section above: *and*, *as*, and *makes*. They range in strength from mild to strong.

THREE KINDS OF LINKS

Three kinds of linking exist. Think of "X" as the current behavior, and "Y" as the behavior you wish to elicit. The simplest form of link is "X *and* Y."

You are scratching your chin (X) *and* preparing to get to work (Y).

This linking makes use of conjunctions to make a connection. Somewhat stronger is "*As* X, Y."

As you ponder your next question (X), you relax and prepare (Y).

Words such as *as, when, during,* and *while* link statements by constructing a connection in time. They imply a cause–effect relationship. The strongest linking actually states causality, "X *makes* Y."

> Breathing like that (X) *makes* you more relaxed and ready for the next section (Y).

When using links, start with something that already occurs and connect it with something you want to occur. Use weaker linkages when constructing verifiable results: "*As* you start to relax you will notice an ability to concentrate better." The ability to concentrate can be verified to some degree. Verifiable results are those we can detect with our five senses. When constructing unverifiable results or those projected well into the future, use stronger links: "Your ability to see things clearly makes you an effective parent." Effectiveness as a parent is not something you measure with your five senses. For this reason, you can get away with stronger connections because immeasurable results are hard to dispute. Cause–effect language structures produce even greater effects when you add presuppositions: "*As* you *continue* to relax (*continue* presupposes relaxation has already started), it *helps* your concentration improve."

You can link any resource with any positive outcome. The more capabilities you identify, and the more positive outcomes you speculate about, the more possibilities arise for the person who hears them. Make links clear and immediate: "Your deep breathing (clear) makes you relax and concentrate better (immediate)." You can make them vague and distant: "Your ability to make people laugh and enjoy the lighter side (vague) will make you a wonderful parent (distant)." You can also make them obscure and indefinite: "Your ability to look ahead (obscure) makes you a good planner (indefinite)."

Linking becomes part of your natural repertoire of communication very quickly after several deliberate attempts. Even the inevitably clumsy early attempts work quite well. It's not important to know all the technical aspects of preparing or presenting polished links. Just connect whatever is present (real or imagined) to any goal. The simplicity and effectiveness will astound you.

The following anecdote illustrates how sequential use of these types of constructions over a period of only a few days can enhance their effectiveness. I supervised a teacher who experienced unending frustration with a third-grade student. She asked me for some assistance. I observed the student yell out an answer whenever the teacher asked a question. The teacher failed to convince the young student to curb her behavior, and the other children began withdrawing from class participation. I instructed the teacher to say the following statement during subsequent outbursts, "Your ability to answer questions makes you a good learner." I instructed the teacher to make similar statements for the entire day. The next day I showed her how to link the child's *ability to learn quickly* with the child's *obvious* proficiency with teaching, "Your ability to learn quickly makes you a good teacher." The teacher used these types of statements whenever the opportunity arose. After a few days, the teacher had laid the foundation of good learner and proficient teacher in the student. During lunch one day, the teacher asked the child to help prepare a lesson. The teacher coached the child to think of interesting questions, like a *good* teacher does, for the other children to answer. The problem diminished, and then disappeared altogether. In a follow-up, the teacher informed me that the student occasionally falls back into the earlier pattern, but a simple hand gesture by the teacher ends it. In essence, the teacher redirected eager, although annoying, behavior to productive ends. The teacher met her complementary goals of classroom management and the socialization of the child. She structured the intervention in such a way that the teacher and student met their goals.

In the process of directing the student's behavior, the teacher developed rapport with the student. Rapport lubricates relationships and subsequent communication.

BUILDING, THEN USING RAPPORT

If we feel people know us well, we experience a feeling of rapport toward them. Building rapport enhances your credibility by making others more receptive to incoming messages.[ce1] Gathering information about a person's behavior helps develop rapport with that person.[ce2] Noticing obscure behavior, or interpreting common behavior in a new light is especially effective. Seeing what others miss helps you develop rapport[ce3] because it indicates that you care enough to notice small positive details. Being positive enhances your rapport further[ce4] because we generally only find nice things to say to people who appeal to us. Everybody enjoys feeling appreciated. Noticing obscure details about someone also sets you up as an expert authority[ce5] because you see things others usually overlook. For example, "The way you get involved mentally (*mental involvement* is obscure) leads you to creative solutions." (The five superscripts in this last paragraph, ce1–ce5, illustrate cause–effect constructions. It's easier and more fluid than you might first have thought.)

Another sure-fire way to enhance rapport is to say something praiseworthy in a descriptive manner (e.g., "Your ability to size up a situation quickly . . ." or "Your clever way of looking at things . . ."). Everybody likes to think they can "size up a situation quickly" and that they look at things in a "clever/unique way." Acknowledging a personal strength garners their attention, crumbles defenses, and thereby raises suggestibility to a positive statement couched with transitions. Once we fill the spoon with sugar, we can lead the person in the direction of growth and empowerment: "Your clever way of looking at things will help you discover creative ways to solve problems."

In Chapter 8 you learned that all behavior is purposeful and contains underlying assets. Discovering an underlying asset in a behavior not only builds rapport, it also invites that behavior to become prominent. Name an asset and watch it flourish as a personal resource. The next section presents an opportunity to practice these linguistic tools. Taking the time to practice with them, reserves a special place for them in your toolbox.

CAUSE–EFFECT CONSTRUCTION EXERCISE

Knowing your tools intimately makes each of them a reliable resource. Following these simple steps creates a personal comfort level with the process of constructing your own conscious style of maximizing the potential of your family, friends, and colleagues. The simple elegance of such a procedure makes you a potentially positive influence with all those you meet. (Did you notice that the previous three sentences illustrate cause–effect constructions?) The power of cause–effect constructions rises exponentially during ESSs, so practice them now to ensure that they will arise instinctively during emotionally charged events.

The following two steps illustrate how to create a cause–effect construction.

1. Gather information about the person's behavior, hobbies, interests (e.g., talks a lot, loves kites, reads science fiction). Obscure information is also very useful (e.g., observes intensely, taps foot while thinking).

2. Link one of your observations to a positive outcome: "Reading lots of science fiction *gives* you a strong sense of reality," or "Tapping your foot while you think *helps* you keep distractions at bay."

Here's another example. This one is imaginative. I use it to illustrate that your opportunities for creating positive statements are virtually limitless.

1. Identify a skill, ability, or potential that lies inherent in the information you gathered (e.g., talking a lot may infer an ability to think quickly).

2. Link this inherent quality with a positive outcome ("Your ability to think quickly *makes* you a clever problem solver.").

Try this following simple exercise right now. Think of someone you want to influence in a positive way. Stop and proceed only once you've got a picture of that person in your mind (spouse, child, friend, colleague, etc.). Create a goal (e.g., wonderful parent, creative worker, keen observer)? Finish the following three statements below, directed toward that person, by inserting that goal at the end of each sentence.

1.   Your clever way of looking at things makes you a great . . . (listener, parent, comic, mechanic, friend, learner, team player, etc.).
2.   Your interest in (stamp collecting, football, reading, music, computer graphics, etc.) makes you a great . . . (listener, parent, comic, mechanic, friend, learner, team player, etc.).
3.   Your ability to size up a situation quickly makes you a great . . . (listener, parent, comic, mechanic, friend, learner, team player, etc.).

The word "makes" produces a powerful and direct connection. Less powerful verbs (helps, enhances, etc.) also produce compelling connections.

Your ability to think clearly helps you solve problems.
Your strong sense of self enhances your attractiveness.

Many verbs that imply causation exist. Here is a short list: build, create, fashion, establish, form, construct, generate, and produce. Use a thesaurus to find more, but you really only need a couple.

The three statements numbered above are generic enough to fit almost anything. These, and others like them, can be used over and over again. Some readers might think that the recipients of cause–effect constructions might notice such phrases as contrived or unauthentic. Definitely not. I've used these phrases time after time with my family, friends, co-workers, students, and indiscriminately with many people I meet. I haven't received a raised eyebrow yet. The form is always the same; only the content changes. These language constructions work equally well on children and adults.

Which of the following statements would you make to a struggling child, who is working slowly, obviously experiencing difficulty and frustration with the correct use of punctuation? "Good work, but you need to pay more attention to your commas," or "I see you've already started to place some punctuation correctly. Your slow, careful work will help you learn it in good time."

The second statement acknowledges some success, interprets frustration as careful attention to detail, and links them in a way that initiates an expectation of *continued* success. Left unaided, people frequently interpret frustration as inadequacy, and an impediment to success. The beginning of the latter statement acknowledges the child's current behavior and interprets it as a resource by presupposing *careful*: "Your slow, *careful* work . . ." The phrase "will help" links the child's resource to the positive expectation "learn it better." We are all better off if we identify frustration as a seed for achievement: "Your willingness to examine your mistakes makes you a great learner."[1]

These tools amplify results exponentially when used during elevated suggestibility. We can use the element of surprise to start the ball rolling. Surprise not only captures attention, but the subsequent heightened arousal triggers an alert response, creating an eagerness for information.

SURPRISE: TRIGGERING ELEVATED SUGGESTIBILITY

Surprising someone by doing the opposite of what is expected creates an emotionally charged moment. The startled response heightens their susceptibility to suggestion because their regular patterned world of predictable reactions suspends itself, if only for a moment. The confusion that results creates an eagerness to understand what is happening. Not knowing what is going on creates an uncomfortable mental state; subsequently, the person's susceptibility to any suitable interpretation soars.

When we use *the opposite twist* strategy described in the following anecdote, we must carefully plan a positive and beneficial result. Many of us already use this technique intuitively. Greta, a female graduate student of mine recalled the following event from her childhood experience in her fourth grade class.

As I walked past several students toward the exit, I felt a strong sense of relief; I had just successfully completed my geography test, or so I thought.

Uh, oh! Why is Bradley pointing at my desk and looking at me? Oh no! I forgot to wipe off the cheat sheet that lightly covered my desk. The pencil marks that were once my friends have now betrayed me. Mrs. Johnson will catch me for sure. What will I do? She'll think I cheated all the way through her fourth grade class and send me back to grade three.

As the bell rang and the class filed out, I turned and looked at Bradley. He was walking toward the teacher. Oh, no! Numbly, I found my way to the computer lab. The librarian smiled at me the way he always did. I asked if I could use the games on his computer in the office. He smiled and ordered me to have fun. He was the best librarian in the whole world. What if he finds out that I cheated? I worried about that. I worried about my mother, and the teachers, and how I would face everyone tomorrow. A firm hand upon my shoulder interrupted my thoughts. I knew who it was, but it still startled me since only my parents ever touched me like that. I turned around and sat there with a blank expression [stunned into an elevated suggestibility state] as I listened to Mrs. Johnson.

I don't remember many of the details about the conversation but I do remember the enveloping hug that she gave me, and the piles of work I received to make up for cheating on the test.

Still today, I can feel that firm hold on my left shoulder, and the flip-flop feelings of relief and discomfort that I experienced throughout the day [hypermnesia from the extreme emotional arousal]. Most of all, I remember the forgiveness I received, and her confidence in my character.

In this anecdote, Greta initially experienced prolonged anxiety in anticipation of punishment from the teacher. The surprising twist of the teacher's warm and accepting response reeled Greta into a mental state of shock and confusion, an ESS. She interpreted the teacher's response as confidence in her moral character, an ethical person who learns from mistakes. Greta responded accordingly, because the teacher reframed a potentially negative event into a lifetime of positive influence.

If we attempt to elevate someone's suggestibility using surprise, how do we know what is surprising? It depends on your instinctive response. If a child's behavior triggers in you an instinctive response of frustration or an impulse to snap angrily, the child usually senses this and expects your wrath. A warm encouraging response would certainly be the opposite from the child's perspective. For example, imagine that your youngster has just walked into the family-room with muddy shoes. As you look at the trail of mud, your irritation lights up your face. Your child looks up sheepishly in anticipation of your anger and you say, "Your ability to recognize your own mistakes will help you learn to avoid similar ones in the future."

Greta's anecdote illustrated how the element of surprise elevates suggestibility. Luckily, she interpreted the teacher's actions as a positive suggestion (confidence in her character as an ethical and moral person who learns from mistakes). Greta could easily have interpreted the teacher's unstated suggestion as the opposite. Be certain to maximize ESSs by adding a cause–effect construction, eliminating chance from the equation.

Test your grasp of the *surprise* strategy and your ability to construct a cause–effect construction. Teachers and parents find endless opportunities to use this strategy. Imagine you are a teacher. How would you handle the following situation? A student, one who frequently botches instructions, begins marking a worksheet with X's after you carefully described how you wanted it done with check marks only, emphasizing it is not to be done with X's. Like many adults, you find yourself tempted to snap, "I told you to listen carefully! Why don't you listen when I give instructions?" You might wish to pause here and test your own ability to construct a more positive intervention that incorporates a cause–effect construction. Read on only after you've created your own constructive and surprising twist. A teacher I observed said, "I see you are marking the paper with X's and not with check marks." (An expression of fear masked the student's face, as he expected the fury of a frustrated teacher.) This clever teacher proclaimed, "Wow! You're so eager to start working you haven't even taken the time to listen to instructions carefully. These are sure signs of a clever learner, and you'll soon learn to listen carefully because of your eagerness."

Did the opposite twist device and cause–effect language construction in this example work magic? We don't know. However, this technique and language construction definitely oriented the student toward a positive outcome. Where your mind goes, so goes your attention, expectations, and behaviors. What you perceive, you achieve.

Surprise elevates suggestibility in adults too. In the following anecdote, Jo Ann's husband doesn't present a cause–effect construction during the ESS, but his comment contains an embedded suggestion that produces a positive result. Remember, you don't need to see an asset to enlist it.

Jo Ann recalls an apparently simple event from several years ago that surprised her and changed her behavior noticeably. Before this simple event, her husband rarely missed an opportunity to find fault and complain about something. One day, her husband thanked her graciously for recording so many correct entries into their financial ledger. The uncharacteristic comment stunned her momentarily. She dismissed it and went about her business, or so she thought. The next day, writing a check for groceries, she noticed a more conscientious effort on her part to record amounts accurately. Her meticulous effort startled her. It appeared that her behavior spontaneously changed.[2] Did her behavior actually change, or did her attention merely shift to more diligence with her bookkeeping? It doesn't matter. The comment produced a self-perpetuating cycle of conscientious effort. What makes this mundane event extraordinary is that she noticed the change and related it with her husband's earlier comment; a comment made to her while momentarily stunned into an ESS. Because her behavior changed spontaneously during an ESS, it qualifies as a SIE. Not all spontaneous influence is life-changing.

SURPRISE AS A THERAPEUTIC TOOL

I frequently use the "opposite twist" as a therapeutic strategy. Occasionally a parent sends a child to me, claiming the youth has an anger management problem. Typically, I ask the youngster to relate a story to me (e.g., "I told Donny to leave me alone but he kept pestering me. Finally, I'd had enough and I let him have it."). I usually laugh. This response typically surprises them, and then I reframe the issue, "Wow! You really showed exceptional restraint. You obviously have pretty good control. Can you tell me any other times when you show such good restraint?" They all can. I typically say something like the following: "Your ability to show restraint will help you express your anger more appropriately as you mature." This simple cause–effect construction makes them focus on the inevitability of eventual improvement in expressing anger. At the end of these sessions, these young people begin to feel empowered to fine-tune their already existing management. Their focus changes from anger restraint to constructive expression. They now focus on what to do (positive prescription), rather than what not to do (negative prescription).

Examine this following anecdote provided by a resource-teacher I trained. She used this intervention effortlessly to calm an irate student and then foster that student's acceptance into a group of peers.

> Six-year-old Gerardo found himself in trouble regularly. He was frequently sent to the time-out room across the hall from my office. I know him well. Gerardo's day was typically full of restless movements, verbal outbursts, and aggressive behavior. His interactions with teachers were usually unrewarding: demands, warnings, and punishments. (e.g., "Sit still! Go back to your desk! Put that down! Go to the time-out room!")
>
> On this particular day Gerardo was once again sent to the time-out room. I was working with the Friendship Group across the hallway. Gerardo thought he'd like to visit me. We usually get along well and he sees me as his warm and trusting friend. I interrupted him saying, "Gerardo, I'm working with some other children and I can't see you right now." Gerardo erupted; he felt deceived and rejected by another adult whom he thought cared about him. "Shut-up! I don't want to be your f_____ friend anymore!" he roared. His outburst shocked the friendship group. I knelt down and hugged Gerardo while saying, "I know you're upset with me right now and you don't want to be my friend anymore, but I still want to be friends with you. I hope we can talk together later." Gerardo was shocked by this unexpected reaction; he had a look of disbelief on his face. He calmed down immediately and I eventually asked him to join the Friendship Group.

The generalized alert response triggered by a surprise also delivers an opportunity to build rapport. On the other hand, by acting sour or punitive we diminish rapport.

USING SURPRISE TO BUILD RAPPORT

I coach young women's volleyball. I recently began coaching a new team and the young women knew little about me other than I was their coach. I wanted them to accept me. During a drill, I watched from a corner of the court. One player intentionally bumped into me, surprising me with her boldness. Catching my balance, I looked at her with a crooked grin and she returned one just like it. That moment of instant rapport initiated a deeper relationship with the new team. She tested me by doing the opposite of what I'd expect.

Doing the opposite of what is expected helps to build rapport, but only if you sincerely care. When children experience a momentarily elevated suggestibility state, they also gain a heightened awareness of cues in their environment. They become hyper-alert to signals that help them sort out what is going on. If at that time you can show sincere care and concern, it will imprint upon them. Your nonverbal communication is most important here: e.g., voice tone, facial expression, and posture.

This next anecdote illustrates an elementary school counselor's successful use of this approach to develop rapport.

> Psychologists labeled twelve-year-old Katie as moderately handicapped. She grew up in an abusive, violent, and extremely unstable environment. Teachers sent her to me frequently. Teachers described her behavior as aggressive; she tore pages from books, hit other children, threw objects, responded fiercely if touched, and generally frightened other children. Some of her behavior looked bizarre: she talked to her doll, spoke in gibberish, and engaged in other age-inappropriate behaviors. She had worked with many child care workers over the years. The following is what happened the first time we met.
>
> As a counselor, I like to build rapport first. I don't feel I can speak meaningfully with children unless I'm *with* them. After we had talked for some time, I told Katie that I liked to have a special greeting with my students. I explained that some children didn't like hugging, in which case a pinky-shake or high-five would be a fine alternative. I gave Katie a choice; she chose the pinky-shake. We practiced. When our baby fingers separated, I waved my hand wildly, snapping my fingers while saying, "GIRLFRIEND!" in a way that mimicked a popular television character. It startled Katie, and she slowly began to giggle. The two of us connected at a deeper level, right there and then. From that time forward, Katie's self-esteem grew and her objectionable behaviors diminished considerably.

The school counselor's intervention implicitly suggested that Katie was worth the time, effort, and friendship of the counselor. Because the suggestion took place during an ESS, it probably produced a considerable influence. Unfortunately, the profound effects of doing the opposite can go either way. Snapping angrily can harm a vulnerable psyche. If you should catch yourself reacting with a strong negative comment, deal with it positively as quickly as possible. Let the person know that your tirade erupted from your own anger or frustration, and that he or she still remains a good person. By all means, name the problem, but own your response with an "I" statement: "I go off the charts mad when you show up late." Contrast that statement with, "You're so inconsiderate with your constant tardiness." This second statement blames the other person for being inconsiderate; an attribution to their character that usually triggers a defensive posture. Taking responsibility for your angry outbursts by using "I" statements empowers you to see others' problematic behaviors as temporary and changeable. They win too because it also empowers them to view their problem as one they can address. Being "inconsiderate" is much harder to deal with because it is offensive, vague, pervasive, and personal. "I" statements empower both the giver and receiver: a win-win.

Katie suffered regular emotional trauma from an abusive home environment, but even children who grow up in supportive homes can experience emotional traumas. Traumatic events occur regularly in children's lives, playing a critical role in their development.

THE NATURE OF EMOTIONAL TRAUMA IN CHILDREN

Childhood traumatic events happen everywhere: schools, playgrounds, birthday parties, the mall, and even in our backyards. In a control group (supposedly comprised of non-traumatized children) to study kidnap victims from the infamous Chowchilla kidnapping, researchers found that approximately one in three children suffered a serious childhood trauma. Researchers concluded emotional trauma is common in childhood.[3] What often appear as simple events to adults may be experienced as emotionally charged trauma to a child. Consider the following two illustrations. In the first anecdote, Debbie suffers rejection, a common childhood trauma. However, serendipity played a positive role and she recovered well.

By age 13, Debbie had lost all her hair. Doctors failed to find the cause or develop a treatment. Debbie resorted to wearing a wig to avoid the regular barrage of jibes and nicknames. One day, while roller skating with friends, her wig flew off. A cute boy, the object of her affection, acted repulsed and Debbie ran off to the washroom. Horrified and traumatized, she sat crying, curled on the washroom floor. Thirty minutes later the boy walked into the washroom, apologized, and asked her to finish the skating game. Proudly, she held her head high and skated the rest of the night.[4]

The second example recalls Jimmy's drastic failure, another common childhood trauma. This positive result differs from Debbie's in that an emotional guide, present at the time, quickly seized the moment, turning a devastating moment into a positive event. In *Unlock the Genius Within*, Daniel Janik describes how traumatic events become encoded according to associations and interpretations available at the time.[5]

Recall the story of young Jimmy, the Boy Scout who flopped miserably with his presentation during Parent Night. Humiliated, he made his way to his seat as the scoutmaster climbed to the podium. The scoutmaster beamed with pride as he described Jimmy's courage for making a glorious victory out of what could have turned to failure. The scoutmaster lauded Jimmy for continuing to the end, exemplifying the spirit of bravery and steadfast commitment. He painted Jimmy as a leader of the highest merit.

Both stories illustrate traumatic moments turned into events that fortified dignity and self-esteem. All of us should be so lucky to experience moments like that. We all want our children to meet boyfriends like Debbie's and have leaders like Jimmy's. Unfortunately, a positive outcome like that is by no means guaranteed.

Children recover from physical trauma relatively quickly, but emotional trauma may produce devastating and continuing effects in the form of enduring negative influence. Many traumatic events remain distressing with far-reaching consequences, embedding themselves in the child's psyche, appearing later in all sorts of guises and symptoms. Adults hold a broader landscape of life experiences, usually allowing them to place an emotionally traumatic moment in context. Accordingly, adults are better equipped to dismiss a caustic comment as mere venom spewing from a frustrated or vicious person. Children suffer more ill effects because they have not yet graduated from the school of hard knocks. Tune into children's moods, ask about their traumatic moments, and treat them seriously.

TREATING EMOTIONAL TRAUMA IN CHILDREN

The longer you wait to deal with a trauma, the more its effects entrench themselves in the child. The adaptation of neural networks in the brain, that predominates childhood, takes place quickly; accordingly, children's identities may spontaneously organize around these traumas as defining features in their lives. If not dealt with early, traumatized children soon return to daily routines and the symptomatic results can show up much later. Experience literally molds the brain. After the passage of significant time, therapy to correct or manage an ingrained dysfunctional behavior pattern can be effective, but then the old pattern still remains as an underlying predisposition. Deal with trauma immediately and thoroughly.

As children inevitably suffer emotional traumas, what is the best way to manage them? Ideally, we would surround our children with those who recognize emotional danger and know how to reframe it into empowering moments. Clearly such vigilance remains outside the bounds of common supervision. However, all parents can minimize negative effects and vitalize resources by being aware of the effects of spontaneous influence and carefully debriefing the daily events with their children. Next to being present with your child when traumatic events occur, bedtime is the best time to play emotional guide, weaving strengths and personal assets into their daily events. Recent research suggests that once the "fight or flight" process is tripped, the memory of the event is encoded traumatically first, and is saved for cognitive processing until later.[6]

Debrief episodes extensively as opposed to hoping they missed it, or hoping that if you don't talk about it, it will go away. A traumatized child is often unable to formulate a congruent picture of the harrowing experience, yet continues to be haunted by the experience and the emotions it triggered. Helping your child find words to describe the event can start the process of dealing with the terror, moving it from a sensation to a concrete experience that can be tackled. When the fear is identified and can be named, it becomes less terrifying and more manageable.[7]

Try to link the child's personal assets to managing the trauma. Avoid statements like, "You'll get over it," or "The pain will diminish with time." Although these statements may be true, the recipient of such a statement feels trivialized when they need emotional support and validation of their feelings. Some traumas last forever (e.g., loss of a parent at an early age or witnessing domestic violence, to name a couple). However, children are more resilient than adults and can learn to face traumas effectively. It's better to say, "Your ability to experience the pain and confusion now (current and validating) will help you get through this (future goal of adapting)."

Dream researchers generally believe that what we experience during the day, particularly critical moments, synthesize and store themselves in our memories during sleep, while we dream. We dream intermittently through the night. During our several dream periods, our brain constantly activates memory networks. Essentially, dreams work as a testing and updating process for maintaining key survival patterns so that successful patterns will function when we need them. According to medical science and health editor Barbara Strauch, metaphorically speaking, dreaming is probably the way nerve cells sort through our junk mail, keeping the good stuff and throwing out the trash.[8] If we can debrief children's emotional traumas before they go to sleep, we have a much better chance of putting a positive spin on the day's events.

Even if no traumatic episode needs debriefing, take that pre-sleep window of opportunity to name a resource your child exhibited that day and create a cause–effect connection to promote a healthy future. If nothing specific pops up, make it vague: "Your ability to bring happiness to others makes you a cherished friend." Now you and your child can review the day finding evidence of emerging greatness. Do this regularly, as often as you can.

This next passage gives you an opportunity to test your skill at sizing up situations that require interventions. Examine the following anecdote and contemplate what you would do differently with your new wealth of insight and information.

> Claire, a forty-year-old woman, suffered from a dental phobia. During treatment, she recalled a traumatic incident that happened when she was eight years old. She had been sent on her own to the dentist, triggering feelings of abandonment and anxiety. An impatient dentist had strapped her arms to the dental chair and she had a panic attack. At the end of her ordeal she ran home crying to a mother who told her to "grow up." She avoided dentists from that time on and her fears worsened. She started to develop panic attacks frequently after the birth of her first child. She also developed the beginnings of agoraphobia; she feared leaving her home. During treatment, she revealed that the most upsetting part of her trauma was not the dentist, but her mother's reaction.[9]

Before reading on, determine what you would have done differently. Consolidate your new fledgling instincts. Pause here now. Were you able to link some positive attribute of Claire's with some future outcome (e.g., "Your ability to recover quickly [a presumption] will help you deal with life's uncertainty."). As children don't know how long it takes to recover, regardless of how long Claire takes to calm down, she will begin to see herself as a rapid recoverer, building faith in her own coping strategies.

Claire's mother's reaction implied that Claire failed at coping with the day-to-day ordeals of life. By finding a positive resource, Claire's mother could have saved Claire from a great deal of unnecessary suffering. Love and support from a nurturing parent during that traumatic moment, linking Claire's personal resources and strengths to her ability to cope, would have minimized the immediate trauma and eliminated long-term negative effects. For example, after acknowledging her fear and anger, the mother might have said something like, "Your amazing self-control helped you through that terrible ordeal and makes you a stronger person." Notice that I linked *self-control* to her reaction. *Self-control* is what she thought she was losing. Focus your goal on the recovery of the *apparent* loss. Your response probably differs from mine, but if you used any cause–effect construction or presupposition to name a resource for Claire, you succeeded. With practice, your interventions flow smoothly and naturally.

WHEN TRAUMA GOES TEMPORARILY UNNOTICED

Clearly, immediate management works best, but what do you do if significant time has passed since the influence event? Consider the following analogy. Do you know what to do if you see a bear while hiking in the woods?[10] Even if you know what to do, are you confident you would remember to do it during such an extremely charged moment, at the pinnacle of fear? You would if you had rehearsed many times before you hiked. Play therapy for children is analogous to rehearsal. What if children play the game "Bear Attack" wherein they must act out the correct procedure whenever a playmate roars at them? They will probably respond accordingly if they happen upon a real bear. Why? Because the heightened emotions of play (laughter, surprise, etc.) helps build the circuits much better than a chunk of dry information we call instruction.

Play and games are important emotional and attention machines. But how does a brain unconsciously generate the requisite emotional arousal without the presence of real danger or opportunity? Good games simulate problems and arouse emotions, which in turn activate our behavioral-response and problem-solving systems.[11] Because past and present are connected in our emotional systems, positive treatment effects spread and the child can begin to respond in a positive manner to similar situations.

Play therapy, or games that mimic original events with new outcomes, can reshape a child's emotional memory. During play, memories repeat in a context of relatively low arousal, compared to the original traumatic event. This desensitizes the trauma, allowing a new more functional set of responses to emerge and embed itself in the child's emotional circuitry.[12]

Pairing success in play sets up new patterns. From a neurological point of view, the amygdala wants to associate the initial event with the initial response, but continuous play associates it with something less debilitating: the new and more effective outcome. Depending on the degree of emotional trauma, the play sequence may require numerous repetitions. These repetitions eventually compartmentalize the event so that anxiety doesn't creep into every aspect of the child's life. As emotional learning takes place throughout our lives, even the most deeply developed habits benefit from reshaping.

We can change behavior patterns by acting out traumatic scenarios with better outcomes, ones that emphasize our personal resources. In Claire's case, an attentive mother could have reenacted the traumatic event over and over again, noting Claire's strengths and changing the outcome (e.g., "I'm glad you ran home to me. Asking for help in situations where you feel trapped makes you a strong person."). In this way, the memory repeats itself in low anxiety situations, thereby desensitizing it and restructuring the emotional response.

✳✳✳

Do these techniques guarantee success? No. Do they at least improve the chances of success? Absolutely. There are no guarantees with human interactions. However, we do know about probability, and the probability for success increases exponentially when we know and understand what we are doing. A previously mysterious and random process is now considerably more understandable and manageable. The human condition doesn't get any more predictable than that.

Seeing the world through a spontaneous influence lens creates a mental framework that magnifies positive interpretations and outcomes in your own life too. The next chapter challenges readers to critique their own way of seeing the world and themselves in it. Readers learn how to accept positive suggestions and reverse or neutralize negative suggestions. In addition, the final chapter teaches those readers who have suffered devastating SIEs how to address these past ordeals, and move toward a more fulfilling life.

Chapter 10

Becoming Your Own Emotional Guide

We should take care not to make the intellect our god. It has, of course, powerful muscles, but no personality. It cannot lead, it can only serve.

Albert Einstein

The first nine chapters described spontaneous influence, how it works, why it works, and how to manage it. You know how to intervene for others, but how do you become your own emotional guide? What can you do to manage your own emotional wellbeing? The rest of this chapter provides guidelines for building your own emotional wisdom.

First, I should address what to some readers may appear contradictory. This entire book, until now, illustrated how change frequently occurs spontaneously, dramatically, and inadvertently. However, this chapter teaches you how to initiate change and increase your own emotional wisdom by using intentional, methodical, and extended practice. This may sound like a contradiction, but it's not. You now know that emotionally charged moments create instant, one-shot learning opportunities. However, it's extremely tricky to deliberately create conditions of spontaneous influence for yourself so that you can take advantage of the corresponding soaring suggestibility. Trying to create your own spontaneous influence is rather paradoxical: like insomniacs trying desperately hard to *make* themselves go to sleep.

Even though it's difficult to manufacture your own Elevated Suggestibility States (ESSs), unplanned emotional arousal still occurs. For those times that emotions soar unpredictably, it's best to be armed and ready. Manipulating your emotions and taking advantage of naturally occurring high-suggestible states can speed the process of change considerably.[1]

MANAGING YOUR ELEVATED SUGGESTIBILITY STATES

When stressed, we instinctively resort to what we used to do or think. This reinforces the old patterns, embedding them further into our identity. However, these moments of stress, because of their emotional charge, produce windows of opportunity to develop new strategies.

Practicing the strategies in this book so that they become habitual gives you the option of considering them during your own rousing times, when they are most needed. Your ability to use your new strategies during emotional arousal, followed by a firm positive suggestion to your self, goes a long way in dislodging a previously held negative belief and replacing it with your new, productive perspective. If you get upset when your colleague snaps at you, thinking to yourself, "He's a jerk," change your belief to "Some people are miserable and blame others because they're irritable. I feel sorry for him. He must be very unhappy." Convince yourself of that and you'll feel compassion, keeping yourself from getting all wound up. This only works if you can change your emotional tone: "He's a jerk" (anger and indignation) to "I feel sorry for him" (compassion and sympathy). Just saying the words won't work unless you *feel* the corresponding emotion. However, just saying the words will help you move toward building the corresponding belief, which in turn expresses the emotion.

Over time, the need for vigilance and practice will diminish as the new behavior becomes entrenched in your repertoire of automatic responses. We literally rewire our brains when we engage in new behaviors during emotional arousal. Inserting new beliefs and beginning new habits works most effectively during emotional intensity.

Learn to be aware of your emotions before they hijack your ability to cognitively intervene. Learn about your triggers and uncover your underlying beliefs. Read the signs your body sends you.

IMPORTANCE OF UNCOVERING NEGATIVE BELIEFS

What obstacles to fulfillment do you carry? Many of us make choices in our lives based upon emotionally, erroneous information from an outmoded past. We may curb these choices because of limiting beliefs, not what is possible.

Uncover your own self-fulfilling prophecies. Many of them come with physical, respiratory, emotional, and verbal clues. Typically, you'll have one of two responses. Your shoulders may slump as you let out a sigh; you feel helpless and may think something like the following, "Here we go again." That response indicates helplessness. The next one reflects anger. Your shoulders tighten, breathing becomes shallow and quick, you feel tense, and may say or think, "Here we go again." Clues from both responses tell you that you're in a rut, and probably one that is self-fulfilling. Recognize it when it happens, and when you have a moment for reflection, after the emotional arousal subsides, make a plan to intervene with a positive suggestion for the next time that it occurs.

DISPUTING NEGATIVE BELIEFS

Once you've discovered a limiting belief, learn to contest it. The most convincing way of disputing a negative belief is to prove that it is factually incorrect. Much of the time you will have facts on your side, as pessimistic reactions to adversity are typically overreactions. For instance, you may believe, "I'm stupid" because someone once called you that when you were in an ESS, someone close to you continues to say that, or you may have performed poorly at school. Whatever the reason, you continually perceive your mistakes as indicators of your stupidity. To you, mistakes are displays of your character. That's hard to change. Someone with a more optimistic framework who makes the same mistakes interprets their errors as temporary lapses with lessons for learning.

To dispute your own beliefs, scan for all possible contributing causes. Focus on the changeable (not enough time spent studying), the specific ("I forgot to preheat the oven. I'll know better next time.") and the nonpersonal ("Bob says those things because he's a bully."). If you were called "Stupid!" at a critical time, realize that the person who called you stupid did it out of anger, frustration, or malice. It is not a true reflection of you as much as it is a true reflection of that other person's character (ignorant, mean, angry, etc.). Start focusing on those moments when you performed fittingly, the ones you usually gloss over because of your ingrained false belief of being stupid. You've demonstrated thousands of episodes when you were street smart, people smart, intuitive, musical, creative, rhythmic, humorous, and so on.[2] Some may think that this *sounds* like a simple solution, but it's not. When your first inclination is to think, "I'm stupid," it takes considerable conscious effort to defeat it. That's why you must make a constructive plan to intervene when those moments of weakness arise.

In the throes of emotions, your instinctive beliefs play themselves out automatically. While that is the time when change is most effective, it is also a time that change is least likely *unless* you've identified beforehand what you want to change and practiced your intervention. Interestingly, uncovering your self-defeating beliefs is an exercise worth exploring because the act of uncovering them also diminishes them.

Think of this simple example. Frequently your spouse spends money on things you think are ridiculously frivolous. Although it doesn't cause any financial hardship, you frequently explode or silently seethe when this happens. Your underlying belief, "My spouse should be thrifty and forgo irrational and overpriced luxuries" is threatened. If you want to change your reaction to something productive, determine ahead of time what you want your new belief to be. Let's say, for example, you want your new belief to be, "Not everyone sees the world the way I do. My spouse is entitled to those little luxuries without me blowing a fuse. I am more mature and tolerant than a hot-headed bully." The very act of preparing your suggestion so that you can embed it during your next episode already diminishes that inappropriate response. You begin the process of encoding a new core belief from which your emotions and behavior will naturally flow. It takes commitment and constant reminders to stay focused on replacing negative beliefs. Soon though, if practiced during emotionally arousing events, the new belief itself becomes automatic.

Our brains still maintain the ability to sprout fresh connections through-out life. It just takes more effort and energy to learn or replace lessons that would have come rather easily in our early years. That's because these new lessons fight an uphill battle against the ingrained patterns of neural circuitry the brain already has in place. This explains why reading this book and learning the information within isn't nearly as effective as deliberately practicing these skills over an extended period of time. By reading or listening only, you've increased your knowledge base dramat-ically, but only through practice will you use your new skills instinctively in the right situations.

USE MENTAL REHEARSAL TO BUILD NEW HABITS

The director of the Institute of Neuropsychology and Cognitive Performance in New York, Elkhonon Goldberg, states the following, "We are able to form goals, our visions of the future. Then we act according to our goals. But to guide our behavior in sustained fashion, these mental images of the future must become the content of our memory; thus the memories of the future are formed."[3] Whatever is vividly and energetically imagined by the mind, the brain believes and acts as if it were true.

You must have a target, some picture of what you want, so that your sensory system can hone the image. Any time you imagine something vividly and you feel the related emotions, it makes a solid imprint and becomes *reality*. Every time you rehearse it, you reinforce that image. Additionally, you can speed up the process of habit formation by getting excited with each mental success. Your excitement (emotional arousal) triggers adrenaline which increases the neural signal strength.

Consider the following common scenario. You think you work hard and deserve a raise. You imagine approaching the boss with your presentation, feeling somewhat tentative about your success. In your thoughts the boss argues and states you already get fair compensation. You then feel demoralized and undervalued. While your imaginings took place entirely in your head, you still experienced the accompanying emotion of dejection. To avoid re-experiencing it again, during the actual event, you decide not to approach the boss to avoid that sense of discouragement. You just did a mental rehearsal for failure and it gained its power from the emotions it evoked: gloom. Do the opposite. Approach it like confident optimists do. If you mentally rehearse with a positive affirmation and incorporate vivid positive feelings (replace gloom with hope) you may not get the raise, but at least you asked confidently.

Use the following three steps to enhance your mental rehearsal. First, write an affirmation of your goal to trigger your image. Second, picture the anticipated positive image vividly. Third, recall a time when you experienced the emotion you want to feel, and then absorb yourself in that emotion while you picture the image from step two. Experiencing the emotion is critical. It not only accelerates the process, but keeps self-doubt at bay.

Here is the previous scenario as an example. You want to approach your boss confidently, asserting your value to the organization, and ask for a deserved raise. In short, your goal is to act confidently when you are used to feeling intimidated. (1) Affirmation: "I work hard and deserve appropriate recognition through financial compensation." (2) Picture yourself approaching the boss with confidence. (3) Remember a time when you felt confident, absorb yourself in that event, and now implant those feelings into your image of approaching the boss. Run this scenario mentally several times, with the implanted feelings. Get pumped; feel positive and confident. Practice at bedtime or just after awakening in the morning. That's when we're most susceptible. Rehearse several times to build your confidence. If you feel negative expectations or emotions creeping in, dismiss them right away and drop in emotionally positive content. If you do it vividly, with positive feelings inserted, you should feel energized. Now it's time to make your appointment. Do your last rehearsal just before entering the office; get those positive emotions flowing.

While these strategies are simple to understand, they require substantial resolve. Think of weight loss as an analogy: all you need is less caloric intake and increased exercise. Even though the prescription is simple, most people find it immensely difficult to manage. Likewise, it takes hard work to systematically overcome limiting beliefs and emotional interference. You must also expect setbacks; they happen, but if you're prepared, they provide you with golden opportunities to implant new optimistic beliefs (e.g., "Next time I'll tweak my approach a bit and do a better job."). To build resiliency you must first create a positive expectancy and an attitude of taking all setbacks as temporary.

IMPORTANCE OF SETTING GOALS: BUILDING RESILIENCY

By making specific goals with corresponding affirmations, you build resiliency to setbacks. Thomas Edison, the man who invented the filament for electric lights, had over 3000 temporary errors before he got it right. Look at obstacles as challenges and learn from them, just like Edison.

When you set your goal, expect adversity as you move toward it. Prepare yourself and plan an optimistic perspective. (To determine if you are an optimist or pessimist, take an on-line assessment.[4]) If optimism isn't your natural perspective, structuring your self-talk and explanatory style ahead of time will help immensely when setbacks strike. The fundamental difference between optimists and pessimists is how they react to adversity.[5]

When optimists experience life's regular setbacks they tend to believe defeat is temporary, the causes are confined to this particular occurrence, and that their misfortune is not their fault. In other words, circumstances, bad luck or other people brought it about. Optimists typically perceive problems as challenges and try harder. They perceive problems as temporary, specific, and external.

The defining characteristics of pessimists is that they tend to believe bad events will last a long time, will undermine everything they do, and are their own fault. They perceive problems as permanent, pervasive, and internal. Permanence is the most crucial dimension. Those that believe their problem is permanent won't act to change it. This helplessness inevitably leads to depression. Perceiving your predicament as temporary, makes it changeable, and energizes you to act to change it.

By planning your self-talk ahead of time, for those times when you struggle, you'll avoid the predictable despair that pessimists encounter regularly. Planned optimism operates as a sort of cheering section, urging us on during hard times. The accompanying feelings of assurance also work to quiet the feelings of frustration and worry that trigger discouragement.

CAUTIONS WITH OPTIMISM

Our habitual ways of thinking and behaving are not permanent. We can all learn to manage our emotions, build beliefs, and counter destructive habits. While I believe that most of us are better off with a more optimistic point of view, be wary of unbridled optimism. Pessimism has its place in the world. Optimism is not a panacea, but it can protect you against depression, raise your level of achievement, increase your energy, enhance your physical well-being, and it is simply a much more pleasant mental state to enjoy.

Pessimism has its uses. While optimism is more pleasant, we should be cognizant of pessimism's virtues, and use its keen sense of reality. Feeling bad has its important uses. You may need to change why you feel bad in the first place, not just replace it with optimism. Reivich and Shatte, authors of the Resilience Factor, endorse what they term "realistic optimism."

> Realistic optimism is the ability to maintain a positive outlook without denying reality, actively appreciating the positive aspects of a situation without ignoring the negative aspects. It means aspiring and hoping for positive outcomes, and working toward those outcomes, without assuming that those outcomes are a forgone conclusion. Realistic optimism does not assume that good things will happen automatically. It is the belief that good things may happen and are worth pursuing but that effort, problem solving, and planning are necessary to bring them about.[6]

Optimists believe in themselves, even when the world around them is crumbling. Remaining pessimistic in critical situations outside your control only hastens helplessness and depression. It's better to find something you *can* control than to wallow in pity and helplessness. Consider those who suffer from a terminal illness.

We've all met those delightful souls, dying with incurable illnesses, who continue to march on optimistically as if everything is right in the world. Tim McGraw sold millions of records entitled, "Live Like You Were Dying."[7] That mega-hit generated its own cottage industry, a testimony to our appreciation for those who can generate authentic optimism for aspects of their lives that they can still control. We admire those eternal optimists who have a way of finding something positive in the time remaining. That kind of optimism is contagious, allowing those near the sufferer to feel cheerful and optimistic about the remaining time.

In extreme cases like the one above, those among us who fight through and conquer hardship show us what we can achieve emotionally. Exercising your own strengths, helping others, and cultivating a feeling of self-efficacy are the keys to building emotional wisdom.

BUILDING EMOTIONAL WISDOM

Wisdom:

- The ability to discern or judge what is true, right, or lasting; insight.
- A wise outlook, plan, or course of action.[8]

We have considerable research that shows we can increase our level of happiness for considerable periods of time.[9] While eternal happiness is no doubt elusive, habitually experiencing more happiness in your life does more than raise your mood, even though that alone is worth considering.

Many of us wrongfully look for happiness in external trappings such as money, good looks, and notoriety. Lots of people have these but remain unhappy. Wealthy and attractive people, in general, are no happier than their peers. A sense of optimism, gratifying relationships, and finding purpose in life produce a far greater influence on your happiness. Recall some of your happiest and most satisfying moments. Most of us recall laughing with friends or accomplishing a significant task.

The most reliable ways to raise our level of happiness and optimism for extended periods is to emphasize our strengths by using them in new ways, and by doing deeds for others. Studies show that the happiest people are those who devote much of their lives to caring and focusing on others. The flip side is also true: selfish people tend to be unhappy.

Tuesday's Children is a nonprofit service organization founded by family and friends of September 11th victims. This organization made a long-term commitment to safeguard the health, happiness, and future of both individuals and families. One popular activity they regularly engage in is to do acts of kindness. Recently, an entire team of children were sent to Costa Rica to help a poor community. They believe that helping others repairs their own hurt and anger. One child who lost a parent said, "I wondered how I would ever make myself happy again. Doing something for others does it."[10]

Recent research provides tools to methodically raise your optimism and increase your happiness level. Appendix one, "Building Emotional Wisdom," provides you with a 36-day plan to embed habits into your daily routine that will increase the quality of your life for an extended period of time or even permanently.

The goal is to make you aware of what strengths you already possess so that you can use them more deliberately and effectively. These exercises also improve your self-monitoring skills as you entrain your brain with these new habits and conscious insights.

The plan has three components: me days, you days, and world days. Rotate through that sequence of days twelve times. It only takes a minute or two a day to determine your task in the morning and record it in the evening.

- Me Day: The essential ingredient in steering through chronic stress is self-efficacy—the belief that you can master your environment and effectively solve problems as they arise.[11] Recognize your strengths and make them more powerful by exercising them more often. You're drawing on a renewable resource, which continues to improve with each application. Recognizing the strengths and goodness in others is a personal strength in and of itself. Mine the gold in others and see yourself reflected in their brightness.

- You Day: Acknowledging others' strengths generates abundance by increasing its expression. Always look for the best in others. According to the Pygmalion principle, when we treat other people in ways that are consistent with the image we hold of them, they tend to behave and become like that image. We attract who we are. If we want positive people in our lives, we must commit to showing compassion, energy, tolerance, and forgiveness to all we meet. Do this for people you casually meet and watch them glow (e.g., To the clerk at the grocery store: "Your smile makes my dull shopping a little brighter. Thank you.").

  Altruistic people tend to be happy, and good deeds are the direct cause of this increase in well-being. It gives people a strong sense that they're doing something that matters. Kindness helps everyone thrive. You raise your own level of happiness when you show kindness to those who can appreciate it—a win-win situation.

- World Day: The daily news inundates us with gloom about impending global disaster, energy gluttony in the developed nations, and political unrest. Looking after the planet and its occupants of all species helps us feel like we are making the world, our home, a better place. It gives us a feeling of self-efficacy. Self-efficacy is the heart of self-esteem.

Building emotional wellness produces lasting effects that may even be permanent. William Glasser, author of *Positive Addiction*[12] shows how to make good habits a positive addiction.

ADDICTED TO EMOTIONAL WISDOM

Glasser's groundbreaking classic guides us in turning positive actions into addictions. He claims that those who develop positive addictions actually forge new neural connections. His anecdotal research shows us how these positive addictions generally live with more confidence, more creativity, more happiness, and maintain better health.

To build a positive addiction you must practice the activity (jogging, meditation, yoga, etc.) daily for at least six months. Practicing the activity on your own, for the sheer joy of doing it, produces the strongest effect.

Appendix two contains a list of 150 common strengths. Highlight those you currently have or want to acquire. Write one strength on each day of a calendar for the next six months. If you highlight thirty-five strengths, rotate through them until the six-month calendar is full. At the beginning of your day, look at your calendar, plan to exhibit your strength, and then check it off. The addiction you build is twofold: (1) to exercise your strengths habitually, and (2) to regularly note your impressive character. By building emotional wisdom, you become a powerful magnet for positive people. You not only increase your own level of happiness and optimism, you generate it in others too.

Sudden Influence provides a sound scientific foundation for the application of positive suggestions. It provides the tools and a methodical plan for creating more adapted, positive, and successful approaches to living functionally in a challenging world.

The insidious nature of soaring suggestibility and spontaneous influence warrants an ever-present vigilance. Stimulating moments are easy to recognize and control because they stand out, but some less dramatic moments can produce surprisingly remarkable effects. Learn to watch for those implicit suggestions (presuppositions) that can sneak by our conscious screening undetected. Accept those that liberate and energize while disputing those that diminish or drain you. Beware also of nonverbal messages; they too may prove tricky to detect making them difficult to assess as healthy or wounding (e.g., smiles of approval or scowls of scorn).

Spontaneous Influence Events (SIEs) are double edged; they can defeat or invigorate. They are already present in our lives to a far greater extent than we may care to admit. We need to be more deliberate and educated about interventions. If you know where someone wants to go in life, an encouraging suggestion that recruits a personal resource in that journey speeds the process, lightens the load, and may iron out some bumps along the way. If you deliver the invigorating suggestion during an Elevated Suggestibility State (ESS), you magnify the result exponentially. Squeeze some grease into someone else's axle whenever you can. Making their wheels run smoothly helps you in your journey too.

I began this book with two goals. First, I pledged to illustrate how common and natural spontaneous influence is in our lives. Until only recently, spontaneous influence remained a mysterious process, serendipitous by nature. Now unmasked, its neurological processes appear reasonable and even manageable. Second, I assured you that I would introduce tools of knowledge and practice that you could enlist to manage and even create SIEs. You now have a conceptual and practical grip on a previously intuitive but puzzling experience.

While we still can't predict which events will make indelible marks in our psyches, we now know definitively that the key lies in the receptiveness of the recipient, *not* in the persuasiveness of the event or the message. We know when we are most receptive: during emotional eruptions. And finally, we also know with whom we are most receptive: authority figures or those who speak genuinely.

While reading these pages and relating to the anecdotes herein, you've no doubt recalled many personal events in your life when you experienced or witnessed spontaneous change. That's no easy task as most influence events occur outside our conscious control and often even outside our conscious awareness. Hopefully you've enjoyed a journey of significant self-discovery. More importantly, you've discovered tools to help sculpt who you want to become. These are the same tools you use to help others maximize their growth and potential.

Your ability to use these tools creatively and regularly makes you a constructive force.

Readers who wish to contact me or submit a SIE of your own can visit my website at www.suddeninfluence.com.

Building Emotional Wisdom

Wisdom: A wise outlook, plan, or course of action.

This activity requires a time commitment of five minutes a day.

We frequently neglect opportunities to pat ourselves on our backs. I designed this exercise to help you identify your current strengths and provide an impetus to build new ones. Completing this simple three-week program helps you recognize your strengths and boosts your overall level of optimism. I divided your tasks into three categories. Rotate these themes over the next five weeks.

Me Day: Record one or more activities you did that illustrated or emphasized one of your strengths (e.g., kindness, creativity, industry, thoughtfulness, humor, intelligence, encouragement, culinary skills, athletic ability, moral values, conflict resolution skills, patience, assertiveness, nutritional awareness, etc.). See the example on page two.

You Day: Record one or more activities you did that illustrated or emphasized your efforts to improve someone else's moment/day/life (e.g., kindness, encouragement, support, aid, smiling, helping with a small/large task, pointing out someone else's strengths or abilities, patting someone on the back, lightening a moment with humor, staying out of an argument, beating a deadline, etc.). See the example on page two.

World Day: Record one or more activities you did that illustrated or emphasized your efforts to improve the conditions of our planet, its occupants, and/or its atmosphere (e.g., picking up trash, using recyclables, walking, taking mass transit, riding your bicycle, political activism, supporting those in need, planting a tree, avoiding fluorocarbons, reducing carbon-monoxide emissions, composting, recycling, conserving water, conserving . . . , etc.). See the example on page two.

INSTRUCTIONS

1.   Put this form in a place where you will see it every morning and every evening (e.g., bedside table, near your toothbrush, on the seat of your car, near your vitamins, beside the bathroom sink).

2.   In the morning, look at the theme for the day and make a plan to fulfill it.

3.   In the evening, record your activity(s) and reflections on the sheets provided.

4.   Do only one theme on each day.

5.   Do several activities if you would like, but only one is necessary. It's perfectly fine to include the same activity on several days (e.g., on World Day, you may have listed "picking up someone else's refuse" for Days 3, 6, 9, and 15).

6.   Keep your recorded responses brief.

7.   Do the activities on consecutive days, but if you miss a day, start where you left off.

8.   NOT doing or NOT saying something can be positive (e.g., NOT sneering at a clerk who treated you rudely. Of course it would be more dramatic and positive to smile and say sincerely, "Have a nice day.").

9.   Your reflections are important. Make them thorough and accurate. Write as much as you like. Use more paper if necessary. Reflections come in three forms: regular (throughout the thirty-six days), upon completion, and two weeks after completion.

EXAMPLES

Me Day   Date _____

Went jogging: keeping fit; took some time to read a good novel: relaxation and balance; acknowledged my ability to stay focused at work: hard worker; wrote to a friend: considerate

You Day   Date _____

Smiled at a clerk: considerate; said "Hi" to someone I normally don't acknowledge: kindness; told a friend that she brightens my day: encouraging; helped a colleague who didn't ask: thoughtful

World Day   Date _____

Picked up some garbage: good citizen; took a shorter shower to conserve water: conservation; took the bus to reduce greenhouse emissions: conservation; used a roll-on deodorant: avoided fluorocarbons

REFLECTIONS

You may wish to consider the following suggestions in your reflections. Be creative if you like. Use the following for a guideline but comment on whatever aspects appeal to you.

- Has this activity affected your day-to-day awareness? How?
- Has this activity affected your ongoing or long-term awareness? How?
- Are there parts of this activity you found easier than others?
- Are there parts of this activity that were more meaningful to you?
- Did this activity change the quality of your life, that of others, that of the planet's?
- Did you add any new activities to your regular repertoire of activities or did you already do most of them?

Exercising Your Strengths

Appendix 2 contains a list of 150 common strengths. Highlight those you currently have or want to acquire. Write one strength on each day of a calendar for the next six months. If you highlight thirty-five strengths, rotate through them until the six-month calendar is full. At the beginning of your day, look at your calendar, plan to exhibit your strength, and then check it off.

academic	cheerful	eager
active	clear-thinking	easygoing
adaptable	clever	efficient
adventurous	competent	emotional
affectionate	competitive	energetic
alert	composed	fair-minded
ambitious	confident	far-sighted
analytical	conscientious	firm
appreciative	conservative	flexible
artistic	considerate	forgiving
assertive	consistent	formal
attractive	cool	frank
bold	cooperative	friendly
broadminded	courageous	fun
businesslike	curious	generous
calm	daring	gentle
capable	deliberate	good-natured
careful	detailed	happy
caring	determined	healthy
cautious	dignified	helpful
charming	discreet	honest

(continued)

Continued

humble	optimistic	self-controlled
humorous	organized	sensible
imaginative	original	sensitive
independent	outgoing	serious
industrious	patient	sharp-witted
informal	peaceful	sincere
intelligent	persistent	sociable
intense	pleasant	spontaneous
introspective	poised	spunky
inventive	polite	stable
joyful	positive	supportive
kind	practical	tactful
leisurely	precise	tenacious
light-hearted	progressive	thorough
likable	prudent	thoughtful
logical	purposeful	tolerant
loving	quiet	tough
loyal	rational	trusting
mature	realistic	trustworthy
methodical	reflective	unassuming
meticulous	relaxed	understanding
mild	reliable	uninhibited
moderate	reserved	unique
modest	resolute	verbal
motivated	resourceful	versatile
natural	responsible	warm
obliging	retiring	wholesome
open-minded	robust	wise
opportunistic	self-confident	witty

Notes

PREFACE

1. *Shallow Hal*, *Twentieth Century-Fox Film Corporation*, 2001.

INTRODUCTION

1. Marlo Thomas and Friends, *The Right Words at the Right Times* (New York: Atria Books, 2002), 118–123. This story was recounted by Rudolph Giuliani. Thomas, the editor, collected stories from Luminaries and celebrities who each tell a story of a crucial turning point in their lives brought about by the right words at the right time.

2. Jack Canfield and Mark Victor Hansen, *Chicken Soup for the Soul* (Deerfield Beach, Florida: Health Communications, Inc., 1993). This series started in 1993 and has grown to more than 110 current titles.

3. The Oprah Winfrey show regularly celebrates people who influenced someone's life dramatically for the better. A public charity, formed in 1998, Oprah's Angel Network was established to encourage people around the world to make a difference in the lives of others. Oprah's vision is to inspire individuals to create opportunities that help underserved people rise to their own potential. Oprah's Angel Network supports charitable projects and provides grants to nonprofit organizations across the globe that share in this vision.

4. Jack Canfield, Mark Victor Hansen, Jennifer Read Hawthorne, Macri Shimoff, eds., *Chicken Soup for the Woman's Soul* (Deerfield Beach, Florida: Health Communications, Inc., 1996), 65–66.

5. Jack Canfield, Mark Victor Hansen, Jennifer Read Hawthorne, Macri Shimoff, eds., *Chicken Soup for the Woman's Soul* (Deerfield Beach, Florida: Health Communications, Inc., 1996), 87–91.

6. Daniel Gilbert, *Stumbling on Happiness* (New York: Alfred A. Knopf, 2006), 58. See also Cordelia Fine, *A Mind of its Own: How Your Brain Distorts and Deceives* (New York: W. W. Norton & Company, 2006), 38–39, 98.

7. Ashley Conway and Petruska Clarkson, "Everyday Hypnotic Injunctions," *Transactional Analysis Journal*, Vol. 17, No. 2 (April, 1987): 17–23.

8. This is a personal anecdote from a graduate student. When I taught at the University of Oregon and Southern Oregon State, I asked students to write stories that illustrated their own SIEs. Some of these stories are sprinkled throughout this book.

9. Most researchers have long given up the debate about which is more definitive: genes or the environment. During a presentation on the adolescent brain, prolific brain researcher, professor emeritus from the University of Oregon, Dr. Robert Sylwester stated, "Trying to determine whether nature or nurture is more important in development is like trying to determine if length or width is more important when computing area."

10. Steven Pinker, *The Blank State: The Modern Denial of Human Nature* (New York: Viking Penguin, 2002), 396–397.

11. Marlo Thomas and Friends, *The Right Words at the Right Times* (New York: Atria Books, 2002), 361–365. This story was recounted by Wendy Wasserstein.

12. Judith Rich Harris, "The Gift of Solitude," in *Curious Minds: How a Child Becomes a Scientist*, ed. John Brockman (New York: Pantheon Books, 2004), 229.

13. Daniel Gilbert, *Stumbling on Happiness* (New York: Alfred A. Knopf, 2006), 41.

CHAPTER 1. IGNITION: HOW CHARGED EVENTS MAGNIFY INFLUENCE

1. Daniel S. Janik, *Unlock the Genius Within: Neurobiological Trauma, Teaching, and Transformative Language* (Landham, Maryland: Rowman and Littlefield Education, 2005), 89–105, 142, 152.

2. A personal anecdote from a graduate student.

3. Voodoo, spell-casting, and the like, work precisely through the mechanisms of spontaneous influence and elevated suggestibility. Imagine a primitive tribe member getting caught hunting in sacred burial grounds. The witchdoctor punishes him by casting a spell of fever onto the perpetrator. Horrified (an elevated suggestibility state), he begins to feel stomach pains and goes into a delirious fever. Such stories abound in anthropological literature.

4. Lloyd Flaro, *Mending Broken Spirits: Promoting Self Esteem in Children* (Edmonton: Learning Strategies Group, 1989).

5. A personal anecdote from a graduate student.

6. Jack Canfield and Mark Hansen, eds., *A 2nd Helping of Chicken Soup for the Soul* (Deerfield Beach, Florida: Health Communications Inc, 1995), 84–86.

7. Jack Canfield and Mark Hansen, eds., 208–210.

8. Jack Canfield and Mark Hansen, eds., 212–215.

9. A personal anecdote from a graduate student.

10. Marlo Thomas and Friends, *The Right Words at the Right Times* (New York: Atria Books, 2002), 75–78. This story was recounted by Billy Crystal.

11. Extremely vivid recall goes by several terms: flashbulb memories, eidetic memories, and hypermnesia.

CHAPTER 2. WINDOWS OF INFLUENCE

1. Marlo Thomas and Friends, *The Right Words at the Right Times* (New York: Atria Books, 2002), 310–313. This story was recounted by Martin Sheen.

2. Joseph LeDoux, *The Emotional Brain: The Mysterious Underpinnings of Emotional Life* (A Touchstone Book, Simon & Shuster, New York, 1996), 267. "The picture of emotion I've painted so far is largely one of automaticity. I've shown how our brains are programmed by evolution to respond in certain ways to significant situations. Significance can be signaled by information built into the brain by evolution or by memories established through past experiences. In either case, though, the initial responses elicited by significant stimuli are automatic and require neither conscious awareness of the stimulus nor conscious control of the responses."

3. Daniel S. Janik, *Unlock the Genius Within: Neurobiological Trauma, Teaching, and Transformative Language* (Landham, Maryland: Rowman and Littlefield Education, 2005), 30.

4. Steven Pinker, *How the Mind Works* (New York: W.W. Norton & Company, 1997), 448–449.

5. Bob's vacant staring, blank facial features, and apparent "tuning out" are indications of being absorbed in some kind of mental imagery, what the Webster dictionary refers to as a trance state.

6. A personal anecdote from a graduate student.

7. Jack Canfield and Mark Hansen, eds., *A 3rd Serving of Chicken Soup for the Soul* (Deerfield Beach, Florida: Health Communications Inc., 1995), 117–119.

8. This anecdote was taken from my case notes for a student I was seeing in private counseling. I changed the name to protect his identity.

9. Carol and Sarah were children who came to me for counseling at different times. Both students produced nearly identical intellectual scores.

10. Cordelia Fine, *A Mind of its Own: How Your Brain Distorts and Deceives* (New York: W. W. Norton & Company, 2006), 81–89. Fine describes how beliefs, once accepted, become hard to refute.

11. Sora Song, "Mind Over Medicine: Hypnosis as an alternative to sedation is making a comeback in the operating room. Here's how it works," *Time Magazine*, Sunday, March 19, 2006. http://www.time.com/time/magazine/printout/0,8816,1174707,00.html.

12. Michael A. Rousell, "Hypnotic Conditions: Are They Present in the Classroom?" (doctoral dissertation, University of Oregon, 1990).

CHAPTER 3. THE FOUNDATIONS OF REALITY

1. John Ratey, *A User's Guide to the Brain: Perception, Attention, and the Four Theaters of the Brain* (New York: Pantheon Books, 2001). See chapter one "Development" and chapter two "Perception." 14–109.

2. I supervised student-teachers for several years at the University of Oregon and Southern Oregon University between 1989 and 1992.

3. The teacher planned to introduce the concept of air resistance in the next lesson. The time allotted for that lesson expired and the students prepared themselves for lunch.

4. Karen Reivich and Andrew Shatte, *The Resilience Factor: 7 Keys to Finding Your Inner Strength and Overcoming Life's Hurdles* (New York: Broadway Books, 2002), 102. Try the brief exercise on page 102 that demonstrates our innate preference for evidence that confirms our theories of the world.

5. Leonre Terr, *Too Scared to Cry: How Trauma Affects Children and Ultimately Us All* (New York: Basic Books, 1992). Terr won the Blanche Ittleson award for her research on childhood trauma.

6. Daniel Gilbert, *Stumbling on Happiness* (New York: Alfred A. Knopf, 2006), 79. Gilbert describes the process whereby false memories are constructed.

7. Joseph LeDoux, *The Emotional Brain: The Mysterious Underpinnings of Emotional Life* (A Touchstone Book, New York: Simon & Shuster, 1996): 244.

8. Joseph LeDoux, *The Emotional Brain: The Mysterious Underpinnings of Emotional Life* (A Touchstone Book, New York: Simon & Shuster, 1996). See chapter 7, "Remembrance of Emotions Past," 179–224. See also Tom Stafford & Matt Webb, *Mind Hacks: Tips & Tools for Using Your Brain* (Sebastopol, California: O'Reilly, 2005), 329.

9. Cordelia Fine, *A Mind of its Own: How Your Brain Distorts and Deceives* (New York: W. W. Norton & Company, 2006). Fine's book illustrates the brain's tendency toward self-delusion.

10. Case study from a family I was seeing that was experiencing communication difficulties and general family strife.

11. Daniel Gilbert, *Stumbling on Happiness* (New York: Alfred A. Knopf, 2006), 108.

12. Deepak Chopra, *Ageless Mind, Timeless Body: The Quantum Alternatives to Growing Old* (New York: Random House, 1994), 34.

13. Robert Rosenthal and Leonore Jacobson, *Pygmalion In the Classroom: Teachers Expectations and Student Intellectual Development* (New York: Crown Publishing, 2003). Originally published by Irvington in 1968.

14. Martin Seligman, *Learned Optimism: How to Change Your Mind and Your Life* (New York: Vintage Books, 1990). This best-seller was published again in 1998 and 2006.

15. John Ratey, *A User's Guide to the Brain: Perception, Attention, and the Four Theaters of the Brain* (New York: Pantheon Books, 2001). See chapter three "Attention and Consciousness," 110–146.

16. Steven Pinker, *The Blank Slate: The Modern Denial of Human Nature* (New York: Viking, 2002), 281. "Some debates are so entwined with people's moral identity that one might despair that they can ever be resolved by reason and evidence. Social psychologists have found that with divisive moral issues, especially those on which liberals and conservatives disagree, all combatants are intuitively certain they are correct and their opponents have ugly ulterior motives. They argue out of respect for the social convention that one should always provide reasons for one's opinions, but when an argument is refuted, they don't change their minds but work harder to find a replacement argument."

17. Jeff Hawkins, *On Intelligence: How a New Understanding of the Brain Will Lead to the Creation of Truly Intelligent Machines* (New York: Time Books, 2004), 158. "Thinking of going to the next pattern in a sequence causes a cascading prediction of what you should experience next. As the cascading prediction unfolds, it generates the motor commands necessary to fulfill the prediction. Thinking, predicting, and doing are all part of the same unfolding of sequences moving down the cortical hierarchy."

18. Steven Quartz and Terrence Sejnowski, *Liars, Lovers, and Heros: What the New Brain Science Reveals about How We become Who We Are* (New York: Quill, 2002). See chapter 7, "Friend, Lover, Citizen: The Mystery of Life Together," 148–188.

19. Steven Pinker, *The Blank Slate: The Modern Denial of Human Nature* (New York: Viking, 2002), 396.

CHAPTER 4. MORE THAN HYPNOSIS

1. Sora Song, "Mind Over Medicine: Hypnosis as an alternative to sedation is making a comeback in the operating room. Here's how it works," *Time Magazine*

(Sunday, March 19, 2006). http://www.time.com/time/magazine/printout/ 0,8816,1174707,00.html.

2. The use of the term hypnosis is rather unfortunate. "Hypno" comes from the Greek term for sleep. Physicians in Western civilization traditionally use a relaxation induction to bring about increased suggestibility and the subject usually looks like someone who has fallen asleep. Brain wave analysis reveals that hypnosis does not resemble sleep at all, nor is the traditional relaxation method typically used by Westerners the only way to achieve this state.

3. I use the term "gut reaction" very broadly here. Chapter 5 describes the neurological mechanism that we colloquially refer to as "going with our gut."

4. Richard Phillips Feynman, *Surely You're Joking, Mr. Feynman: Adventures of a Curious Character* (New York: Bantam Books, 1988).

5. I often get my graduate students to describe a time of extreme emotional arousal. This is one such episode.

6. V.S. Ramachandran, *Mirror Neurons and Imitation Learning as the Driving Force Behind 'the Great Leap Forward' in Human Evolution*, http://www.edge.org/ 3rd_culture/ramachandran/ramachandran_p1.html. See also Daniel Goleman, *Social Intelligence: The New Science of Human Relationships* (New York: Random House, 2006), 68–69. Goleman describes how mirror neurons allow us to participate in observed actions as if we were executing that action. Although this is no doubt how humans learn vicariously, mirror neurons were first discovered in monkeys. See also Lee Winerman, "The Mind's Mirror," *APA Monitor on Psychology*, Vol. 36, No. 9 (October 2005): 48–51. Also on-line: http://www.apa. org/monitor/oct05/mirror.html. Scientists using electronic sensors attached to facial muscles found that people viewing a smiling face reflect the same mood and mimic slight facial changes not visible to the naked eye. See also Tom Stafford & Matt Webb, *Mind Hacks: Tips & Tools for Using Your Brain* (Sebastopol, California: O'Reilly, 2005), 336–337.

7. Herbert Benson, *The Relaxation Response* (New York: Avon Books, 1976). The relaxation response is a simple practice that once learned takes 10 to 20 minutes a day and can relieve the stress and tension that stands between you and a richer and healthier life. The technique was developed by Herbert Benson, M.D. at Harvard Medical School.

8. Suggestopedia is a teaching method that is based on a modern understanding of how the human brain works and how we learn most effectively. It was developed by the Bulgarian doctor and psychotherapist Georgi Lozanov. The term "Suggestopedia," derived from suggestion and pedagogy, is often used loosely to refer to similar accelerated learning approaches.

9. We actually do have defenses against spontaneous influence, but that is what this book is about. Only those who understand how it operates are prepared to defend against it.

10. Written by a graduate student from my advanced Educational Psychology class at Southern Oregon University.

11. Jack Canfield and Mark Hansen, eds., *A 2nd Helping of Chicken Soup for the Soul* (Deerfield Beach, Florida: Health Communications Inc, 1995): 198–199.

12. Michael S. Gazzaniga, *The Mind's Past* (Berkeley: University of California Press, 1998). See also Daniel Gilbert, *Stumbling on Happiness* (New York: Alfred A. Knopf, 2006), 173. Gilbert shows that people are typically unaware of the reasons for their behaviors, but when asked, readily supply one.

CHAPTER 5. EMOTION IS THE RULE: RATIONALITY IS THE TOOL

1. Steven Johnson, *Mind Wide Open: Your Brain and the Neuroscience of Everyday Life* (New York: Scribner, 2004), 52. The French psychologist Edouard Claparede was a pioneer in studying memory systems a hundred years ago. His clever experiment showed that cognitive memories and emotional memories are separate. He worked with a brain injury patient who was unable to form new memories that lasted more than a few minutes. She would always greet Claparede warmly with a handshake whenever he entered the room and go through extended introductions as if they were meeting for the first time, even if after only 15 minutes. On one occasion he concealed a thumbtack in his hand and gave the patient a gentle pinprick when they shook hands. When he arrived the next day, his patient greeted him with the usual blank welcome—no memory of yesterday's pinprick, no memory of yesterday at all, until Claparede extended his hand. Without being able to explain why, Claparede's patient refused to shake hands with her doctor. The woman incapable of forming new memories had nevertheless generated a sense of danger, the trace memory of past trauma. She failed utterly to recognize the face and the voice she'd encountered every day for months. But she remembered the fear.

2. Malcolm Gladwell, *Blink: The Power of Thinking Without Thinking* (New York: Little, Brown & Company, 2005).

3. Timothy Wilson, *Strangers to Ourselves: Discovering the Adaptive Unconscious* (Cambridge: Harvard University Press, 2002).

4. Ron Brandt, "On Teaching Brains to Think: A Conversation with Robert Sylwester," *Educational Leadership* (Vol. 57, No. 7, April 2000): 70–75.

5. Antonio Damasio, *Descartes' Error: Emotion, Reason, and the Human Brain* (New York: Avon Books, 1994).

6. John Ratey, *A User's Guide to the Brain: Perception, Attention, and the Four Theaters of the Mind* (New York: Pantheon Books, 2001), 168–187. Ratey shows how mood determines perception and cognitive consideration. He uses the following illustration to emphasize this thesis. An employee receives a compliment from a colleague regarding fine work moments before receiving feedback from the boss. The boss goes over the previous work in detail asking the employee to elaborate on certain points. The employee perceives the boss's interaction as the boss's personal confidence in the employee, seeing the employee's effectiveness, and giving the employee more responsibility/greater challenge; thereby, enhancing the current state of confidence. The same interaction by the boss immediately after a criticism by a colleague is perceived as a criticism by the boss, enhancing the current state of uncertainty.

7. Daniel Goleman, *Emotional Intelligence: Why it can Matter More Than IQ* (New York: Bantam, 1997). Goleman collected extensive neurological evidence of how the thinking brain evolved from the emotional system. As the limbic system (crudely referred to as the emotional brain) evolved, it refined the two powerful cognitive tools of learning and memory.

8. Candice Pert, *Molecules of Emotion: Why You Feel the Way You Feel* (New York: Touchstone, 1999). Pert shows how emotional states or moods are produced by the various neuropeptide ligands, and what we experience as an emotion or a feeling is also a mechanism for activating a particular neuronal circuit—simultaneously throughout the brain and body—which generates a behavior involving the whole creature, with all the necessary physiological changes that behavior requires. In short, emotions don't just prompt you to act; they actually start the process.

9. Joseph LeDoux, *The Emotional Brain: The Mysterious Underpinnings of Emotional Life* (New York: Touchstone, 1996), 265–266. The imbalance of connections gives the amygdala a greater influence on the cortex than the cortex on the amygdala, allowing emotional arousal to dominate and control thinking. LeDoux suggests that these asymmetrical connections between the cortex and amygdala may explain why psychoanalysis is such a prolonged process.

10. Leslie Brothers, *Friday's Footprint: How Society Shapes the Human Mind* (New York: Oxford University Press, 1997), pp. 187.

11. Joseph LeDoux, *The Emotional Brain: The Mysterious Underpinnings of Emotional Life* (New York: Touchstone, 1996), 61–62. LeDoux refers to experiments by social psychologist J.A. Bargh. In one dramatic example, Bargh had students participate in an apparent language test. They were given work cards and asked to make sentences. Some students were given sentences about elderly people, whereas other students received sentences about other subjects. Upon completion, subjects simply left the room to go to a designated area. Subjects were secretly timed as they walked to the waiting area. Students unscrambling sentences about seniors took significantly longer to cover the distance. See many more of Bargh's examples in Bargh, J.A. (1992), "Being unaware of the stimulus vs. unaware of its interpretation: Why subliminality per se does matter to social psychology," *Perception Without Awareness*, R. Bornstein and T. Pittman, eds. (New York: Guilford).

12. Antonio Damasio, *The Feeling of What Happens: Body and Emotion in the Making of Consciousness* (New York: Harcourt Brace & Company, 1999), 301–302. Damasio sets up the following game in his lab to illustrate how unconscious emotional prodding precedes cognitive awareness and planning. The task involves a game of cards, in which, unbeknownst to the player, some decks are good and some decks are bad. The knowledge as to which decks are good and which are bad is acquired gradually, as the player removes card after card from varied decks. In his words, "By the time players begin choosing the good decks consistently and avoiding the bad decks, they have no conscious depiction of the situation they are facing and have not formulated a conscious strategy for how to deal with the situation. At that point, however, the brains of these players are already producing systematic skin-conductance responses immediately prior to selecting a card from the bad decks. No such responses ever appear prior to selecting cards from the good decks. These responses are indicative of a non-conscious bias, obviously connected with the relative badness and goodness of the decks."

13. L.A. Real, "Animal choice behavior and the evolution of cognitive architecture," *Science*, 253 (1991): 980–986.

14. Joseph LeDoux, *The Synaptic Self: How Our Brains Become Who We Are* (New York: Viking, 2002), 312–314. See also John Ratey, *A User's Guide to the Brain: Perception, Attention, and the Four Theaters of the Mind* (New York: Pantheon Books, 2001), 224–246. See also Daniel Gilbert, *Stumbling on Happiness* (New York: Alfred A. Knopf, 2006), 58. See also Cordelia Fine, *A Mind of its Own: How Your Brain Distorts and Deceives* (New York: W. W. Norton & Company, 2006), 38–39, 98.

15. Leslie Brothers, *Friday's Footprint: How Society Shapes the Human Mind* (New York: Oxford University Press, 1997), 187. Brothers uses the term "response dispositions" as tendencies to act. According to her, "Such tendencies might be fleeting and weak; or they might be fully coordinated, overt actions. Response dispositions arise by virtue of the connectivity of brain regions such as the amygdala and orbital frontal cortex to motor, endocrine, and autonomic brain regions, regions that set a blueprint for bodily states."

See also Antonio Damasio, *The Feeling of What Happens: Body and Emotion in the Making of Consciousness* (New York: Harcourt Brace & Company, 1999). His work demonstrates that we never know the contents of dispositions directly. He shows that the contents of dispositions are always nonconscious and exist in a dormant form; yet dispositions can produce a large variety of actions—the release of a hormone into the bloodstream; the contraction of muscles in viscera, or of muscles in a limb, or in the vocal apparatus. He argues that dispositions hold records of an image that was actually perceived on some previous occasion, and then attempts to reconstruct a similar image. According to Damasio, "we are never aware of the knowledge necessary to perform any of these tasks, nor are we ever aware of the intermediate steps that are taken. We are only aware of results, for example, a state of well-being; the racing of the heart; the movement of a hand; the fragment of a recalled sound; the edited version of the ongoing perception of a landscape.

All of our memory, inherited from evolution and available at birth, or acquired through learning thereafter, in short, all our memory of things, or properties of things, of persons and places, of events and relationships, of skills, of biological regulations, you name it, exists in dispositional form (a synonym for implicit, covert, non-conscious), waiting to become an explicit image or action." In Antonio Damasio, *Descartes' Error: Emotion, Reason, and the Human Brain* (New York: Avon Books, 1994), Damasio describes these dispositions as "potential patterns of neuron activity in small ensembles . . . ." These dispositions sit in a dormant firing potential.

16. John Ratey, *A User's Guide to the Brain: Perception, Attention, and the Four Theaters of the Mind* (New York: Pantheon Books, 2001), 121. Ratey describes the process whereby the limbic system influences attention by assigning emotional significance to incoming information. "Even before a sensory perception has reached the frontal lobes, where it enters conscious awareness and undergoes fine categorization, the amygdala has already branded it with a raw emotional valence somewhere along a continuum from mildly interesting to 'oh my God!' It activates the body and the rest of the brain in response to how significant it deems the stimulus to be to survival. If the stimulus seems threatening, it activates the alert centers of the brain and notifies the hormone system and brain stem to get ready to rock and roll." According to Ratey, the amygdala provides a preconscious bias of intensity to every stimulus you come into contact with, even before you pay attention to it.

17. Antonio Damasio, *Descartes' Error: Emotion, Reason, and the Human Brain* (New York: Avon Books, 1994), 184–191. Damasio states that somatic markers (what Ratey calls "emotional tags") have two avenues of action: conscious and unconscious. Somatic markers do not need to be perceived as feelings. He acknowledges that while many important choices involve feelings, a good number of our daily decisions proceed without them. Damasio shows how a body state may be activated but not be made the focus of attention. Without attention, the somatic marker will not be part of consciousness, "although it can still be part of a covert action on the mechanisms that govern, without willful control, our appetitive (approach) or aversive (withdrawal) attitudes toward the world. While the hidden machinery underneath has been activated, our consciousness will never know it." This is how neurotransmitters from an emotional response can proceed in a covert manner to influence reasoning and decision making.

18. Antonio Damasio, *Looking for Spinoza: Joy, Sorrow, and the Feeling Brain* (New York: Harcourt Books, 2003), 146–150. Damasio shows how the revival of

the emotional signal accomplishes a number of important tasks. It does this using conscious or nonconscious channels by focusing attention on certain aspects of the problem that in turn enhances the quality of reasoning over it. When the signal is conscious we sense automated alarm signals relative to options of action that are likely to lead to negative outcomes. "A gut feeling can suggest that you refrain from a choice that, in the past, has led to negative consequences, and it can do so ahead of your own regular reasoning telling you precisely the same 'Do not'." The emotional signal can also produce an enticement pointer, and urge the rapid endorsement of a certain option because it was previously associated with a positive outcome. "In brief, the signal marks options and outcomes with a positive or negative signal that narrows the decision-making space and increases the probability that the action will conform to past experience. Because the signals are, in one way or another, body-related, I began referring to this set of ideas as the 'somatic-marker hypothesis'."

19. Malcolm Gladwell, *Blink: The Power of Thinking Without Thinking* (New York: Little, Brown & Company, 2005). Caldwell coins the term "Thin-slicing" to refer to the innate ability of our unconscious to make sound decisions, quickly, on fragments of information. His book shows how our unconscious does an excellent job of sizing up the world, prompting action in a sophisticated and efficient manner. Blink shows how decisions made very quickly are often as good as decisions made cautiously and deliberately.

Bruno Maddox, "What Were You Thinking?" *Discover Magazine* (May 2006): 32–33. Maddow describes how Dutch researchers assembled a group of shoppers and divided them into two groups. Their task was to choose between four cars. One group was given elaborate descriptions with quiet time to think. The other group, given considerably less information, was distracted with anagram puzzles during their allotted decision time. "Conscious thinkers were better able to make the best choice among simple products, whereas the unconscious thinkers were better able to make the best choice among complex products." He concludes that most of involved decision making actually takes place unconsciously. These experiments and conclusions support the somatic-marker hypothesis, showing how emotional tags prompt quick and efficient judgments.

20. Antonio Damasio, *Descartes' Error: Emotion, Reason, and the Human Brain* (New York: Avon Books, 1994), 170–173. Find illustrations of how patients with prefrontal cortical damage are unable to make value laden decisions like the ones we make instinctively and rapidly.

21. Ron Brandt, "On Teaching Brains to Think: A Conversation with Robert Sylwester," *Educational Leadership* (Vol. 57, No. 7, April 2000): 70–75.

22. Antonio Damasio, *Looking for Spinoza: Joy, Sorrow, and the Feeling Brain* (New York: Harcourt Books, 2003), 58.

CHAPTER 6. ELEMENTS OF SPONTANEOUS INFLUENCE

1. "This man will always achieve more than simple appearances indicate." Does this mean money, accolades, degrees, ambitions, goals, something else, or all of these? I don't know and it doesn't matter. That weekend workshop changed how I experienced myself and my world. Have I achieved much more than appearances would indicate? For me, yes. I have far exceeded what I thought I would achieve in life so far.

2. The reason I think Dr. Lynn was unaware of the separate elements of spontaneous influence is because he never identified them. As a healing practitioner in the field of education, why would he keep that a secret? He described his methods as artful and inventive, born of experience and wisdom. Think of Wayne Gretzky, the best hockey player of all time. He dominates the record books like he dominated the game. However, he never had the hardest shot, strongest physique, nor did he ever dominate one specific measurable skill. When asked to describe the factors of his greatness, like many outstanding athletes, he simply couldn't, nor can hockey analysts.

3. Marlo Thomas and Friends, *The Right Words at the Right Times* (New York: Atria Books, 2002), 357–360. This story was recounted by Vera Wang.

4. While I paint a picture of transference figures as kind, nurturing, and benevolent, we can also project our "baggage" onto a transference recipient. For example, if our parents were kind one moment, but hurtful the next, punishing us arbitrarily, we might see transference figures as unpredictable and dangerous.

5. Teachers, particularly in the early grades, frequently refer to their students as "my children." Teachers actually spend considerably more time with students than most parents spend with their own children.

6. Bernie Siegel, *Peace, Love, and Healing: Beyond Communication & the Path to Self Healing and Exploration* (New York: Harper & Row, 1989). Siegel collected these anecdotes from a Bernard Lown introduction to Norman Cousins' book *The Healing Heart* (New York: Avon Books, 1984).

7. The teacher, a graduate student in education at the time, wrote this story as part of an assignment.

8. Daniel Goleman, *Social Intelligence: The New Science of Human Relationships* (New York: Random House, 2006), 44–61. The chapter, "A Recipe for Rapport," describes the important role rapport plays in influence. It also illustrates mirror strategies. Mirroring strategies are simply efforts to match the client's movements, posture, tone of voice, mood, breathing patterns, and the like to build a bond that puts the client at ease so that they feel a connection to the therapist.

9. Henry Ford, the father of mass production automobiles, was one of the great visionaries of his day.

10. Richard Bach, *Jonathan Livingston Seagull* (New York: Avon Books, 1976). Bach's popular classic of self-discovery continues to sell millions worldwide.

11. Given to me by a graduate student in education from the University of Oregon.

12. I've done the unicorn exercise with many students. Some get an image of a unicorn that starts to fade away or disintegrate, some see the unicorn and then it runs away, and one student saw a unicorn that was x-ed out like a no-smoking sign.

13. Other kinds of dependence exist too. Some of us may become financially dependent, or physically dependent, but I restrict my attention to the kind of dependence that brings momentary psychological discomfort.

14. Marlo Thomas and Friends, *The Right Words at the Right Times* (New York: Atria Books, 2002), 29–32. This story was recounted by Tom Brokaw.

CHAPTER 7. ASPECTS OF AUTHORITY

1. Robert Wright, *The Moral Animal: Why We Are the Way We Are: The New Science of Evolutionary Psychology* (New York: Vintage Books, 1994), 289.

2. A graduate student of mine gave me this story as one of her class reflections.

3. If she were in a hypnotist's show, we would say she produced three hypnotic trance phenomena: age regression, dysphasia (inability to speak), and aphasia (inability to understand language).

4. Cordelia Fine, *A Mind of its Own: How Your Brain Distorts and Deceives* (New York: W. W. Norton & Company, 2006), 116–117.

5. Angeline was a doctoral student in educational psychology when she wrote this story as part of an assignment.

6. Ken is now a neuro-psychologist.

7. Robert Rosenthal and Leonore Jacobson, *Pygmalion In the Classroom: Teachers Expectations and Student Intellectual Development* (New York: Irvington, 1968). An updated and expanded version is now in print (New York: Crown House Publishing, 2003).

8. Neil Postman and Charles Weingartner, *Teaching As a Subversive Activity* (New York: Delta, 1971). Postman and Weingartner discuss how most schools in the United States have classes organized into groups of "dumb" students, and even when they don't, both teachers and students both know who they are. These students suffer the opposite results, negative, of those from the famous Pygmalion study.

9. The Pygmalion effect also works with animals and even non-vertebrates. Twelve participants in a laboratory course in experimental psychology were falsely led to believe that the experimental rats were divided into two groups: intelligent and inferior intelligence. Six student trainers received thirty rats of "superior" intelligence while a separate six student trainers worked with thirty rats labeled with "inferior" intelligence. Instructors secretly assigned a batch of equally intelligent rats to these groups randomly. All sixty rats came from the same breeding stock. The rats whose trainers believed them to be especially intelligent not only performed better from the outset, but raised their achievements far above that of the "unintelligent" rats. Trainers for the "superior" rats mentioned that they petted, played with, and generally touched the rats more often.

A separate experiment dismissed the handling as a confounding variable. In this other case, experimenters did a parallel design but used earthworms rather than rats in an attempt to extinguish any attachment. In this experiment too, objectively discernable and statistically significant results favored the "intelligent" earthworms.

10. Bernie Siegel, *Peace, Love, & Healing: Bodymind Communication & the Path to Self-Healing: An Exploration* (New York: Harper & Row Publishers, New 1989), 27.

11. Howard Brody, "Tapping the Power of the Placebo," *Newsweek* (August 14, 2000): 66. Brody, M.D. Ph.D., teaches at Michigan State University Medical School.

12. Viktor Frankl, *Man's Search for Meaning* (New York: Pocket Books, 1997). First published in 1946 in Austria.

13. From the Discovery Channel Medical Stories Weekend, in "Placebo: Cracking the Code," http://www.discoverychannel.co.uk/medicalstories/feature2.shtml, 2005.

14. The term "double-blind, placebo-controlled" refers to experimental conditions whereby neither the physician nor the patient know which is the placebo pill/treatment and which is the real pill/treatment. The term single-blind refers to experimental conditions whereby the physician knows which is the placebo and which is the pill, but the patient doesn't.

15. Ann Harrington, ed., *Placebo Effect: An Interdisciplinary Exploration* (Cambridge: Harvard University Press, 1997), 3.

16. Ann Harrington, ed., *Placebo Effect: An Interdisciplinary Exploration* (Cambridge: Harvard University Press, 1997), 3. This response is from a dialog that Harrington carried on with Howard Fields, Professor of Neurobiology and Physiology at the University of California, San Francisco.

17. Herbert Benson, *Timeless Healing: The Power of Biology and Belief* (New York: Scribner, 1996), 17.

18. Dylan Evans, *Placebo: Mind Over Matter in Modern Medicine* (London: HarperCollins, 2003), 34. As an interesting side note, in one of these studies the dentists went on to give the patients a dose of naloxone, a known antidote for morphine. Both the pain and swelling returned. The researchers concluded that the power of the placebos to reduce swelling is based on the same mechanism as that which underlies their power to reduce pain—the release of endorphins.

19. Herbert Benson, *Timeless Healing: The Power of Biology and Belief* (New York: Scribner, 1996), 59.

20. Jessica Ruvinsky, "Placebo VS. Placebo," *Discover Magazine* (April 2006): 16.

21. Irving Kirsch, "Specifying Nonspecifics: Psychological Mechanisms of Placebo Effects," in *Placebo Effect: An Interdisciplinary Exploration*, ed. Ann Harrington (Cambridge: Harvard University Press, 1997), 166–186.

22. Dylan Evans, *Placebo: Mind Over Matter in Modern Medicine* (London: Harper Collins, 2003), 66.

23. Herbert Benson, *Timeless Healing: The Power of Biology and Belief* (New York: Scribner, 1996), 42.

24. Jessica Ruvinsky, "Placebo VS. Placebo," *Discover Magazine* (April 2006): 16.

25. Bernie Siegel, *Peace, Love, & Healing: Bodymind Communication & the Path to Self-Healing: An Exploration* (New York: Harper & Row Publishers, New 1989), 19–20.

26. Candice Pert, *Molecules of Emotion: Why You Feel the Way You Feel* (New York: Touchstone, 1999), 190–191. Pert discusses some of her peers' research.

27. Bernie Siegel, *Peace, Love, & Healing: Bodymind Communication & the Path to Self-Healing: An Exploration* (New York: Harper & Row Publishers, New 1989), 111–113.

28. When a drug is shown to be more effective than a placebo in a clinical trial, it is important to remember that this result applies to a particular kind of placebo. To be more precise, we should say that such drugs have been shown to be more effective than placebos that are identical in shape, size and so on. A different placebo procedure or pill (e.g., twice the size of the real medicine) might have a stronger effect.

29. Herbert Benson, *Timeless Healing: The Power of Biology and Belief* (New York: Scribner, 1996), 30.

30. Donald D. Price and Howard L. Fields, "The Contribution of Desire and Expectation to Placebo Analgesia: Implications for New Research Strategies," in *Placebo Effect: An Interdisciplinary Exploration*, ed. Ann Harrington (Cambridge: Harvard University Press, 1997), 93–116.

31. Jessica Ruvinsky, "Placebo VS. Placebo," *Discover Magazine* (April 2006): 16.

32. Ted Kaptchuk, David Eisenberg, and Anthony Komaroff, "Pondering the Placebo Effect" *Newsweek* (12, 2, 2002): 71.

33. Ann Harrington, ed., *Placebo Effect: An Interdisciplinary Exploration* (Cambridge: Harvard University Press, 1997), 5–6. Placebos used in pain relief typically trigger the release of endogenous morphine (endorphins). Even though

researchers can scientifically demonstrate the process whereby endorphins are released, they still don't understand how a person's belief in a sham treatment could send a message to the pituitary gland to release its own pharmaceutics.

34. Arthur K. Shapiro and Elaine Shapiro, "The Placebo: Is It Much Ado About Nothing?" in *Placebo Effect: An Interdisciplinary Exploration*, ed. Ann Harrington (Cambridge: Harvard University Press, 1997).

35. Dylan Evans, *Placebo: Mind Over Matter in Modern Medicine* (London: Harper Collins, 2003), 157–161.

CHAPTER 8. CREATING A WORLD OF POSSIBILITIES

1. Joseph LeDoux, *The Synaptic Self: How Our Brains Become Who We Are* (New York: Viking, 2002), 312–314. See also John Ratey, *A User's Guide to the Brain: Perception, Attention, and the Four Theaters of the Mind* (New York: Pantheon Books, 2001), 224–246. The information content provided by arousal systems is weak. Arousal systems simply say that something important is going on. When arousal occurs, for whatever reason, the environment is scanned for cognitive assessment. Weak content means that someone present at the time, or shortly thereafter, can put a positive spin on dramatic events, shaping subsequent values.

2. Martin Seligman, *Learned Optimism: How to Change Your Mind and Your Life* (New York: First Vintage Books Edition, 2006), 1–92. In the first section of his book, "The Quest," Seligman describes in detail how experiencing your setbacks as permanent, pervasive, and personal exemplify pessimism that leads to helplessness and depression.

3. Ashley Montagu, *Touching* (New York: HarperCollins, 1978).

4. Jack Canfield and Mark Hansen, eds., *Chicken Soup for the Soul* (Deerfield Beach, Florida: Health Communications Inc, 1993), 3–4.

5. Michael Gazzaniga, *The Mind's Past* (Berkeley & Los Angeles: University of California Press, 1998), 34. Gazzaniga describes how our mind-set can render almost any information either critical or meaningless.

6. Marlo Thomas and Friends, *The Right Words at the Right Time* (New York: Atria Books, 2002), 191–194. This story was recounted by John Lequizamo.

CHAPTER 9. TOOLS OF INFLUENCE

1. When I hold workshops for therapists, teachers, or parents, I always have them construct a few statements for each of their patients, students, or children. Participants find it an easy and energizing assignment. Planning positive interventions invigorates us.

2. Jack Canfield and Mark Hansen, eds., *Chicken Soup for the Soul* (Deerfield Beach, Florida: Health Communications Inc, 1993), 43–45.

3. Lenore Terr, *Too Scared to Cry: How Trauma Affects Children and Ultimately Us All* (New York: Basic Books, 1990), 24–26.

4. Jack Canfield and Mark Hansen, eds., *Chicken Soup for the Soul: A 4th.Course* (Deerfield Beach, Florida: Health Communications Inc, 1993), 39–42.

5. Daniel S. Janik, *Unlock the Genius Within: Neurobiological Trauma, Teaching, and Transformative Language* (Landham, Maryland: Rowman and Littlefield Education, 2005), 22–26, 60.

6. Daniel S. Janik, From personal correspondence in Janary 2007. "In fact my own work suggests to me that once the sympathetic 'flight or fight' process is tripped, the memory of the event is encoded traumatically first, and is saved for cognitive and metacognitive processing till later."

7. John J. Ratey, *A User's Guide to the Brain: Perception, Attention, and the Four Theaters of the Brain* (New York: Pantheon Books, 2001), 222–251. See chapter six, "Emotion," for more information on how the brain deals with trauma.

8. Barbara Strauch, *The Primal Teen: What the New Discoveries about the Teenage Brain Tell Us about Our Kids* (New York: Anchor Books, 2003), 157–172. See chapter eleven, "Wake Up! It's Noon" for a more elaborate explanation of how dreams consolidate memories.

9. Francine Shapiro and Margot Silk Forrest, *EMDR: The Breakthrough Therapy for Overcoming Anxiety, Stress, and Trauma* (New York: Basic Books, 1997), 228–229.

10. If you see a bear, talk to the bear. Make sure he sees you. Hold your arms high above your head. This will make you look like a much bigger animal to him. Continue to talk and slowly back away. Look submissive by not making eye contact. If you run he will chase you. If the bear comes for you, drop to a fetal position. Cover your head and neck with your hands. Keep on your backpack to protect your back. Even if the bear bites you, continue to play dead. Once he realizes that you are not a threat he may leave, "*How to Survive a Bear Attack*," http://www.arcticwebsite.com/BearSurvival.html.

11. Robert Sylwester, "Unconscious Emotions, Conscious Feelings," *Educational Leadership* (November 2000): 20–24.

12. Daniel S. Janik, *Unlock the Genius Within: Neurobiological Trauma, Teaching, and Transformative Language* (Landham, Maryland: Rowman and Littlefield Education, 2005), 144.

CHAPTER 10. BECOMING YOUR OWN EMOTIONAL GUIDE

1. Daniel Goleman, *Emotional Intelligence: Why it can Matter More Than IQ* (New York: Bantam, 1997), 132.

2. Howard Gardner ed., *Multiple Intelligences: New Horizons in Theory and Practice* (New York: Basic Books, 2006). Read about Gardner's respected theory of multiple intelligences and discover your own special talents.

3. Elkhonon Goldberg, *The Executive Brain: Frontal Lobes and the Civilized Mind* (New York: Oxford University Press, 2001), 124.

4. Take the Learned Optimism Test, adapted from Martin Seligman's best-selling book, *Learned Optimism*, http://www.stanford.edu/class/msande271/onlinetools/LearnedOpt.html

5. Martin E. P. Seligman, *Learned Optimism: How to Change Your Mind and Your Life* (New York, Vintage Books, 1990). Seligman's extensive and distinguished research influenced a generation of researchers to focus on positive psychology in general and optimism and happiness in specific. Most notable work in this field bears his fingerprint directly, or indirectly.

6. Karen Reivich and Andrew Shatte, *The Resilience Factor: 7 Keys to Finding Your Inner Strengths and Overcoming Life's Hurdles* (New York: Broadway Books, 2002).

7. Tim McGraw, *Live Like You Were Dying* (Curb Records, 8, 24, 2004)

8. Wisdom, Dictionary.com. *The American Heritage® Dictionary of the English Language, Fourth Edition* (Boston, Massachusetts: Houghton Mifflin Company, 2004). http://dictionary. reference.com/search?q=wisdom&x=36&y=8.

9. Martin E.P. Seligman, *Authentic Happiness: Using the New Positive Psychology to Realize Your Potential for Lasting Fulfillment* (New York: Simon and Schuster, 2003). For a critique of the research on building happiness see Elizabeth Svoboda, *Pay It Forward*, in *Psychology Today* (August 2006), 51–52. In this article Svoboda also cites research by Stanford professor Sonja Lyubomirsky. Lyubomirsky believes that 40 percent of our happiness quotient is under immediate and voluntary control.

10. For information, go to http://www.tuesdayschildren.org/index.php.

11. Karen Reivich and Andrew Shatte, *The Resilience Factor: 7 Keys to Finding Your Inner Strengths and Overcoming Life's Hurdles* (New York: Broadway Books, 2002), 19.

12. William Glasser, *Positive Addiction* (New York: Harper Collins, 1985). Glasser coined the phrase to describe addictive activities that give a person strength and improve his/her quality of life by increasing self-confidence, energy, and tolerance of frustration (e.g., jogging, meditating).

Index

ABOUT THE AUTHOR

MICHAEL A. ROUSELL is a Counseling Psychologist and also holds a doctorate in philosophy. He has spent 15 years studying spontaneous influence events. His work has included adolescent counseling, family and marriage therapy, addictions, and forensics. He has also taught across the spectrum from elementary, junior high, and high school to college undergraduate and graduate programs.